Wisdom of the Elders

Dear Robert.
Perhaps it is time to
seek some new
direction

Vivia.
07. 93.

Wisdom of the Elders

* * * * * * * *

HONORING SACRED NATIVE VISIONS OF NATURE

* * * * * * *

David Suzuki and

Peter Knudtson

* * *

Bantam Books
New York · Toronto
London · Sydney · Auckland

Wisdom of the Elders

A Bantam Book / August 1992

Book design and jacket ornamentation by
Charles B. Hames

Endpaper map by GDS/Jeffrey L. Ward

PRINTED ON RECYCLED PAPER

LIBRARY OF CONGRESS
CATALOGING-IN-PUBLICATION DATA

Suzuki, David T., 1936–
Wisdom of the elders : honoring sacred
native visions of nature / David Suzuki
and Peter Knudtson.
p.   cm.
Includes index.
ISBN 0-553-08862-9
1. Human ecology—Religious aspects.
2. Nature worship.
3. Indians—Religion and mythology.
4. Indians—Philosophy.
5. Indigenous peoples.   I. Knudtson,
Peter.   II. Title.
GF80.S88   1992   92-67
304.2—dc20   CIP

Bantam Books are published by Bantam Books, a
division of Bantam Doubleday Dell Publishing Group,
Inc. Its trademark, consisting of the words "Bantam
Books" and the portrayal of a rooster, is Regis-
tered in U.S. Patent and Trademark Office and in
other countries. Marca Registrada. Bantam Books,
666 Fifth Avenue, New York, New York 10103.

PRINTED IN THE UNITED STATES OF AMERICA
BVG   0 9 8 7 6 5 4 3 2 1

P.K.: *For my sisters Kris and Robin, and my brothers Kevin, Eric, and Tom. And for Flora Jones, who sees the world through Wintu eyes.*

D.S.: *To the new generation of spiritual and political leaders willing to share their vision for their people with all others who are receptive: Bernard, David, Diane, Don, Gary, Guujaaw, Jeanette, Matthew, Miles, Mutang, Norma, Paiakan, Pauline, Ron, Simon, Sophie, Wedlidi, and many others.*

Heart of Sky, Heart of Earth,
give us our sign, our word,
as long as there is day, as long as there is light.
When it comes to the sowing, the dawning,
will it be a greening road, a greening path?
     —*Popol Vuh,* sacred Mayan text

Contents

Acknowledgments

We would like to thank Åke Hultkrantz, Andrés Lopez, Alfonso Ortiz, and Robin Ridington for their expert review and constructive criticisms of all or part of earlier versions of this manuscript. Each of them also candidly discussed aspects of the book's themes or offered valuable suggestions concerning possible sources, as did Pam Colorado, Harvey Feit, Joan Halifax, Richard Lee, Claude Lévi-Strauss, Nicolas Peterson, Darryl Posey, Deborah Bird Rose, and Alejandro Ruiz, among others. However, we alone assume responsibility for the words we have written.

We gratefully acknowledge the authors, scholars, and informants—Native and non-Native—whose cited interpretations of indigenous thought constitute the heart of this book. Our thanks also to Thomas Banyacya and Deborah Bird Rose for their generosity in providing us valuable unpublished materials. Finally, we express our gratitude to Leslie Meredith, our editor at Bantam in New York, to Claudine Murphy, her assistant, and to Viola Thomas, our Native cultural consultant in Vancouver, for their steadfast commitment to the spirit of this project and their expert attention to the style, accuracy, and accessibility of our writings.

Authors' Note

The organization of *Wisdom of the Elders,* we freely confess, was inspired by novelist Eduardo Galeano's monumental trilogy, *Memories of Fire,* in which he ambitiously presents the whole history of the New World through a mosaic of brief, essaylike, well-documented scenes, or vignettes. Faced with a topic of comparable scope, we have followed a similar strategy.

The vignettes in each chapter cluster around a central ecological, biological, or evolutionary theme. Each chapter attempts to convey a sense of the cultural diversity, as well as the underlying unity, of an international selection of Native peoples' intellectual and experiential insights into the workings of nature and into proper human relationships with the natural world. This organization reflects our commitment to acknowledging each Native group's perspective on nature as culturally valid and worthy of respect in its own right.

Except for chapter 1 and chapter 10, each chapter is arranged as follows. First, a short introductory section provides a thumbnail sketch of modern scientific perspectives relevant to the chapter's theme. This scene-setting scientific perspective is designed to serve as a Western backdrop against which the ensuing Native vignettes are juxtaposed. These vignettes largely stand on their own, to suggest rather than to "prove" the vibrancy and validity of their moral and ecological insights. Scattered through each chapter are brief quotations from selected Western "elders" of science to provide a continuous juxtaposition of Western and Native thought, and to help stitch the culturally diverse vignettes into a quiltlike whole.

Each vignette presents a brief glimpse of one Native group's views on nature. They consist of actual Native stories and statements, as well as secondary discussions of their possible ecological meanings, anchored in direct commentaries of respected authorities. Each narrative is self-contained, fully capable of standing on its own without reference to the other vignettes. The published sources for each vignette are meticulously documented at the back of the book. Italicized words or passages denote direct quotations from those sources or scholarly interpretations of them. In the original reports, Native words are encoded in a variety of specialized linguistic systems; here, for the sake of uniformity and readability, they have been simplified to their approximate English phonetic equivalents.

As readers will no doubt note, many of the vignettes could reasonably have been placed, on the basis of their multiple ecological insights, under the umbrella of more than one broad chapter theme. This is partly a natural consequence of the innate capacity of many elements of holistic bodies of knowledge to illuminate the whole, just as a single grain of sand can, to the poet's eye, reveal a whole universe.

We have gone to considerable lengths to make sure that these glimpses into Native thought are based on the most respected and culturally sensitive resource materials available. While collectively they cover a wide array of topics, this book is not intended to be seen as encyclopedic.

Nonetheless, the sources that we have relied upon are certain to be flawed in one way or another, and we are not so naive as to believe that any of them necessarily offers a crystalline vision of "traditional" (however one chooses to define that term) Native worldviews and environmental values. Inevitably, our choices will be challenged. In some cases, academics and scholars may question the authenticity of particular texts, as well as the motives, biases, values, and credentials of their authors. They may dispute the translations and interpretations we have selected of crucial Native terminology, as well as the accuracy of observations made in culturally loaded political and historical contexts.

Nonetheless, we are dedicated in this book to honoring Native views and Native wisdom to the extent that they have been recorded. We would like to express our deep gratitude and indebtedness to the scholars and thinkers—Native and non-Native—whose ideas permeate the published works we have cited. We want to make clear that simply by citing or quoting from these publications, we do not intend to suggest that the authors, or their Native informants, would necessarily agree with the interpretations that we draw from them. Nor would we deny that innumerable other "nonecological" interpretations—dealing, for example, with internal psychological or spiritual dimensions of life rather than external ones—might as easily have been drawn from many of the same myths, stories, and symbols.

Our reliance upon these important works means only that we, as authors and biologists, have found them insightful and inspirational. And we trust that our attempts to weave elements of their ideas into a larger tapestry will be seen not as unduly derivative but rather as our sincere attempt to reach a wider public with indisputable evidence of the depth, irreplaceability, and contemporary relevance of traditional Native knowledge.

As authors, we are acutely aware of the difficulty of determining how much even some of the most widely respected published accounts of Native ecological perspectives are faithful to the enduring traditional themes of Native worldviews. To illustrate the pressing reality of such concerns, we would like to describe briefly two personal encounters with these issues that we had while researching and writing this book.

The Case of Chief Seattle

The first encounter concerns a passage from a famous speech that was purportedly delivered by a nineteenth-century Duwamish leader named Chief Seattle in 1854 in Washington territory. We had originally intended to use it to open the first chapter of *Wisdom of the Elders*. It reads, in part:

The air is precious to the red man.* For all things share the same breath—the beast, the trees, the man, they all share the same breath. . . . What is man without the beasts? If all the beasts were gone, men would die from a great loneliness of spirit. For whatever happens to the beasts, soon happens to man. All things are connected. . . . Whatever befalls the earth befalls the sons of the earth.[1]

Chief Seattle's complete testimony has long been viewed, by Natives and non-Natives alike, as perhaps the quintessential expression of the potential richness of the ecological themes shared by Native and scientific visions of the natural world. Over the last century it has emerged as the single most eloquent, succinct, and publicly accessible distillation of Na-

---

* Here, as elsewhere in the book, we have followed the convention of retaining a cited texts' assignment of gender to various elements—from celestial bodies and culture heroes to human populations—of a particular Native cosmos. This, of course, does not rule out the possibility, however historically uncertain, that some of them may have originally been either gender neutral or opposite in gender sometime in the precontact past.

tive American nature wisdom ever published. In fact, one respected Native advocacy group based in Europe has described it as "the most-quoted single statement by any native American." So we apologize in advance to any who may feel a measure of betrayal and dismay upon learning the extent to which the chief's original words have apparently been altered by outsiders.

Shortly after researching and writing the first draft of this chapter, which highlighted Seattle's famous "All Things Are Connected" speech, Knudtson chanced upon an obscure article that offered a compelling challenge to its validity. In a paper presented to the European Association for American Studies in Rome in 1984, a German scholar named Rudolf Kaiser reported that the famous Chief Seattle speech appears to be largely apocryphal. Those who listen rapturously to it, he cautioned, have every right to admire it "as an impressive ecological text in its own right." But they should also realize that Seattle's original words have been drastically altered and embroidered by a succession of non-Native writers. "This text," concluded Kaiser, "does not represent the mind of the old Chief, but the mind of a sensitive Euro-American, worried about our ecological situation and the general dualism in our culture."[2]

"Chief Seattle" was in fact a genuine historical figure of the nineteenth-century American Pacific Northwest, Kaiser reported. He was a chief of the Suquamish and Duwamish Indians, was born in 1786 and died in 1866. But his real name was not Seattle: It was Seeathl. He probably did deliver a speech of some sort between 1853 and 1855 somewhere in Washington territory—most likely in Lushotseed, his Native language. It was then translated directly by interpreters into the more widely familiar Chinook trading jargon, and, possibly, finally into English.

The speech was apparently witnessed by a physician by the name of Dr. Henry Smith, who apparently took copious notes on it. Eventually, based on his notes and personal recollections, Smith published the first version of Seattle's speech

some thirty years later in 1887 in the Seattle *Sunday Star.*
Despite its subsequent reprints, Smith's account apparently
stirred little public response for decades.

In 1931 the speech reappeared in an article published in the
Washington Historical Quarterly—this time with the addition of
a few phrases that appeared nowhere in Smith's published
reconstruction. It too was later reprinted, with a few minor
alterations, again without undue public response.

Beginning in the late 1960s and early 1970s, however, as
North American interest in environmental issues heightened,
the speech became popular and came to symbolize, in many
minds, the very essence of the environmental movement. Yet
during these years, it underwent drastic revisions. The first of
these, a minor revision that involved mostly stylistic changes,
was carried out by an American writer named William Arrow-
smith and published under the title "Speech of Chief Seattle" in
1969.

A subsequent revision, however, written by an American
university instructor and screenwriter named Ted Perry during
the winter of 1970, made significant changes in the text. This
version surfaced in the form of a script for a documentary film
on pollution that had been underwritten by a Southern Baptist
organization in Texas. It became the basic template for a
number of the popular versions of the speech (including the
one quoted above) that are currently in circulation in North
America, Europe, and elsewhere.

Perry openly acknowledges, reported Kaiser, that his version of Seattle's narrative was "fictional," and that he had
never intended that it be formally and historically attributed to
the deceased Duwamish chief. According to Perry, the film's
producers failed to credit his creative efforts properly after the
film was released, despite his repeated protests. Subsequent
published versions of the fictional speech continued to imply
that its evocative passages on Native environmental values
were Seattle's own words. "I certainly would never have
allowed anyone to believe," Perry is quoted as saying, "that it
was anything but an imaginary item written by me."

What can we learn from this sudden—and to many, unsettling—erosion of credibility of such a widely revered Native statement on the underlying interconnectedness of all life, with all its wonderful resonances with some central truths of modern genetics, evolutionary biology, and ecology? First, in the context of our own research efforts, we have come to the conclusion that it is probably impossible to be absolutely certain that any given Native narrative represents an "authentic" Native voice without first documenting the text's entire convoluted history.

Second, in broader terms, challenges to the authenticity of one or two Native texts need not be taken as serious challenges to the value and validity of traditional Native knowledge about nature, which is amply confirmed in countless other ways. In fact, these challenges can even be viewed positively, for they can serve as a reminder to non-Natives that it is time to look beyond the comfortable shallows of poetic, greeting-card-like formulations of Native ecological knowledge—to look *beyond* the clichés of Chief Seattle—into deeper, more intellectually and spiritually challenging waters.

As we have repeatedly discovered in our own research, anthropological literature contains an astonishing wealth of detailed, well-documented, and ecologically insightful accounts of Native views of the natural world. The loss of a single Native narrative, no matter how cherished, need not stand as an obstacle to an enriched cross-cultural dialogue.

The Case of the Chewong People of Malaysia

The second incident in our research that increased our sensitivity to issues involving the authenticity of Native sources took place deep in the tropical rain forests of peninsular Malaysia. Knudtson, who served as principal researcher and writer on this project, had a brief but poignant conversation with a respected aboriginal Chewong elder during a whirlwind three-month journey that he undertook in spring 1990 through North America, Europe, southern Asia, and Australia to interview academic scholars and Native elders.

At one point, Knudtson visited a stark, desperately poor, roadside Chewong community of stilted stick huts, small swidden fields of crops, and huddles of silent, malnourished children located several hours east of the capital city, Kuala Lumpur. He traveled there to confirm, among other things, the reliability of a recent book about Chewong ecological beliefs, *Society and Cosmos,* written by anthropologist Signe Howell.

Knudtson talked to a shy, elfin Chewong elder named Beng. He showed Beng a copy of Howell's book and, with the help of a government interpreter, asked him to comment on the accuracy of its different depictions of the traditional Chewong cosmos. Beng's reply was quick and unequivocal. Yes, he assured us, the book was indeed a trustworthy account of Chewong beliefs about the natural world.

How did he know? Because, he said with a toothless grin, he himself had been one of Howell's principal informants during her prolonged stay with the Chewong. (He was also, it turned out, an informant for Rodney Needham, an Oxford anthropologist, as well as other researchers decades earlier.)

In fact, he added with a smile, he happened to have his own personal copy of the book, which he kept near his handcrafted blowgun and poison-tipped darts in his nearby hut. Signe, as he called her affectionately, had been like a daughter to him. She had a solid grasp of Chewong views about the natural world. We were welcome to use her descriptions of their beliefs in the preparation of our own book.

We laughed, shook hands, and later exchanged small gifts— in total, it was hardly an extraordinary encounter. But for non-Native authors aware of the growing concern among many Native communities about the distortion or appropriation of their cultural heritage by outsiders, it was very special. It provided us with a rare opportunity to confirm personally the authority of a scholarly work and, in virtually the same breath, to secure the permission of a respected elder from the Native community that was its subject to discuss publicly aspects of his people's precious spiritual knowledge.

Given the daunting geographical, linguistic, and temporal scope of this ambitious project, any notion of trying to confirm quickly and efficiently the accuracy of every source we selected with its Native subjects or formally requesting their permission to present elements of their traditional nature wisdom quickly proved unrealistic. Nonetheless, Knudtson's conversation with Beng in the rain forests of Malaysia represented, in our own minds, a small step in that direction, and Beng's generous response seemed to suggest that, in our ongoing search for the most sensitive and keenly observed references, we were at least on the right track.

A Personal Foreword:
The Value of Native Ecologies

by David Suzuki

Before entering the ecological worldviews of indigenous people, let me explain how I came to believe that therein resides
something powerful, very relevant, and profound for members of the dominant society. I came to this belief by surprise,
heavily inclined to resist it by my education in Western culture
and scientific training.

My grandparents were born and raised in Japan. They were
driven out of their homeland by poverty and a rigid caste
system so profound that they could only escape by emigra-
tion. They were pulled to North America by the irresistible
attraction of potential wealth.

Like all the other immigrants who have poured into the
New World since Christopher Columbus, my ancestors ar-
rived in Canada with faith that they would be rewarded for
diligence and hard work. Japan was the home to which their
hearts belonged, but their children—my parents—were Cana-
dians. So they stayed, but to my grandparents, as to all new-
comers, the strange new place represented *opportunity*. Land to
them was a *commodity*, a *resource* to be bought, exploited,
developed, and sold. It was only temporarily occupied until
circumstances or accumulated wealth allowed them to move
along. My grandparents had no sense of the sacredness of the
land, as they might have had in Japan. They were too busy

making a living. Today, those perceptions and values passed down to me through my parents are part of the accepted ethos of the dominant society, all of us descendants of immigrants since Columbus.

The Scientific Paradigm Challenged

I grew up believing that schooling and honest effort would pay off in material benefits. As a good student—especially in math, chemistry, and physics—I gravitated naturally to a career in the sciences. In graduate school, I was indoctrinated into the worldview set in motion by Descartes and Newton. I embraced reductionism—the belief that by stripping Nature to its most elementary components, we can gain insights that can be fitted together like pieces in an immense jigsaw puzzle to reveal the deepest secrets of the universe.

I entered graduate school at the University of Chicago a year after Sputnik was launched, a time when the United States of America was pouring money and effort into science and universities. In my chosen field of genetics, startling discoveries and new insights into DNA seemed to promise a complete understanding of life itself. The potential benefits and vast range of science seemed limitless, and I joined my peers in exuberantly extolling the endless potential of research and development.

The power and utility of scientific reductionism had been demonstrated in physics, where energy locked in all matter was released by splitting or fusing atoms. Yet physicists themselves were finding that the Newtonian paradigm was seriously flawed. Werner Heisenberg discovered that we can never really know what Nature is like because in order to observe it, we have to pin it down and thus change it; Niels Bohr found that the properties of subatomic particles can be described only by probability, never with absolute certainty. Parts of Nature and other systems were shown to interact *synergistically* so that the actions and properties of a system as a whole cannot be predicted on the basis of what is known about its individual components. Thus, while science yields powerful insights into isolated fragments of the world, their sum total is a disconnected, inadequate description of the whole. Ironically, scientists today are faced with the devastating possibility that the whole *is* greater than the sum of its parts.

As a practicing scientist I began to realize about fifteen years ago that if Western science really could deliver the promised benefits for humankind, then the quality of human life should have vastly improved during the 1960s and 1970s, as science grew explosively. Yet we know that in spite of impressive developments in space travel, nuclear power, telecommunications, genetic engineering, and computers, life has improved significantly only for a small—and diminishing—proportion of the world's population. Even among this privileged minority—the 20 percent of humankind who live in the industrialized nations—immense problems of economic disparity, malnutrition, prejudice, alienation, violence, poverty, and drug abuse have increased rather than diminished.

But the rapid and catastrophic degradation of the planetary biosphere has been the main catalyst for a radical reassessment of the power and limits of scientific insight and application. The warnings are everywhere: in the acid-induced mortality of deciduous forests in Germany, Quebec, and the American Midwest; in the sudden and mysterious death of thousands of seals in the North Sea; and in the carcasses of beluga whales in the St. Lawrence River, which are so full of chemicals that they must be treated as toxic waste. Even weather and climate appear to be changing while water tables are plummeting, deserts are expanding, forests are disappearing, and 25 billion tons of agricultural topsoil are blowing away annually. Once-abundant stocks of cod, herring, and salmon are vanishing with frightening speed. These signs should be taken as global analogues of the canaries that coal miners once took into the pits with them to warn of poisoned air, except now, they indicate trouble on the entire planet.

Too often, most of us assume that "they"—the scientists

and engineers—will do something to pull us through. But we are waking to the dangers of clinging to a faith that science and technology can forever resolve the problems they created in the first place. The power of scientific insight is undeniable, but its consequences are wider than we ever foresee.

Consider pesticides. Powerful chemicals such as DDT are relatively selective in that insects are more sensitive than other animals. And while geneticists could have predicted that over time any pesticide would be rendered less effective by selection of mutations to resistance, target pests such as malaria-carrying mosquitoes were dramatically destroyed at first. Yet no one predicted before the extensive use of DDT that pesticides are *biomagnified* up the food chain to concentrations at hundreds of thousands of times their original levels. The reason is that biomagnification was only discovered when a high incidence of sterility in birds was traced back to pesticides. We know so little about the biological and physical properties of the planet that we cannot predict the long-term impact of our technology.

Our world is being radically transformed by our muscular technologies. But if we cannot predict the global ecological effects of our activities, how can we control or manage them? We can't, and increasingly, some of the leading scientific thinkers who are trying to find solutions to the ecocrisis are using terms hitherto considered inappropriate in science. Thus, Stanford University ecologist Paul Ehrlich believes that the answer to the global difficulties will be "quasi-religious." He suggests that our main dilemma is not a lack of information or technological capability. Rather, our problem is inherent in the way we perceive our relationship with the rest of Nature and our role in the grand scheme of things. Harvard biologist E. O. Wilson proposes that we foster *biophilia,* a love of life. He once told me, "We must rediscover our *kin,* the other animals and plants with whom we share this planet. We are related to them through our DNA and evolution. To know our kin is to come to love and cherish them." Both of these eminent scientists are suggesting that science alone is not enough to solve the planetary environmental crisis and that we must re-create for ourselves a sense of place within the biosphere that is steeped in humility and reverence for all other life.

Sacred Connections to the Land

But in a world increasingly dominated by the growth imperative of global economics, the infatuation with technology, and the ever expanding demands of an exploding human population, we cling to assumptions founded on the inadequate Cartesian and Newtonian worldview. Are there other perspectives from which to make our judgments and assessments, other ways of perceiving our place in the cosmos? I began to realize that other profoundly different notions of our relationship with Nature do indeed exist when I became involved in the early 1980s in the battle to save the forests in the southern part of the Queen Charlotte Islands. This was the first in a series of experiences I had with different aboriginal peoples that opened me up to new possibilities and different, richer perspectives for understanding the world.

Native Identity and the Land: Haida, Nisga'a and Nlaka'pamux

Canada's westernmost archipelago, off the tip of the Alaska panhandle, is the home of the Haida people, who know the islands as Haida Gwaii. As a journalist, I interviewed a young Haida carver who is now called Guujaaw. I asked him what difference it made to him whether the trees of Gwaii Haanas, the contentious area, were logged. After all, I suggested, he would still have his work, his home, and an income. "Sure," he replied, "we'll still be alive. But then we'll be *like everybody else.*" With that simple statement, he summed up a radically different relationship with nature.

Haida Gwaii has been home to its aboriginal inhabitants since the beginning of time. The land and all the creatures that inhabit it represent their history, their culture, their meaning, their very identity. Without them, the Haida are no longer

Haida. The Haida refer to whales and ravens as their "brothers" and "sisters" and to fish and trees as the finned and tree *people*. Isn't this just a different way of expressing E. O. Wilson's sense of the kinship with all other life-forms that results from our common evolutionary history?

At a meeting with the non-Haida citizens of Sandspit, the forest industry town in Haida Gwaii, loggers insisted on their legitimate right to jobs and to their way of life on the islands. Finally, a Haida elder rose and said, "Most of you have lived here for only five or ten years. Our people have been here for thousands of years. How many graves of your people are there in Sandspit?" After a stunned silence, the answer came back: "None." The elder continued, "There are Haida graves throughout the islands, and that makes the land sacred to us. This is where we belong." The Haida opened up a new world for me. Their sensitivity to human interconnection with all life on their homeland, I believe, can give us an alternative to Western culture's narcissism coupled with an ecologically destructive worldview.

Years after I first encountered the Haida, I was at the airport at Sandspit talking to Miles Richardson, the charismatic president of the Council of the Haida Nation. Turning to a map of Haida Gwaii—which resembles a long triangle standing on its apex—Miles pointed out that with the preservation of Gwaii Haanas, the southern third of his land was now saved. The northeastern corner is Naikoon Provincial Park, while the northwestern corner was unilaterally designated by the Haida as Duu Guusd Tribal Park. With these three areas secure, much of the islands will be protected from logging and development. "We want to declare the water around all of Haida Gwaii a marine park," he continued, "so the ocean resources can be managed according to Haida tradition."

Because the Haida were never conquered and never signed treaties with Canada, they believe they remain a separate, sovereign nation. Within a few years after contact with Europeans, more than 90 percent of the Haida died of smallpox. The survivors abandoned the dozens of villages spotted around the islands and now occupy only two—Massett and Skidegate. The present island population of two thousand Haida has been augmented by four thousand non-Haida new-comers. The Haida believe that a common sustainable future based on Haida respect for the land and its plants and animals is possible for all people. They want to cut back on logging and have already imposed their own fish management program, which has been accepted by commercial fishermen and most of the sport fishing lodges. Richardson told me that "ecological carrying capacity" of the islands must govern the way re-sources are harvested. If the Haida succeed, they could provide a model to the world of how people can live sustainably and in balance with Nature.

I re-encountered the perspective similar to the Haidas' years later when I met James Gosnell, the great chief of the Nisga'a, the people on the mainland east of Haida Gwaii. James once told me of his first encounter with clear-cut logging on his land. He had been walking through the forest, and he sud-denly came to a vast cleared area. "I couldn't breathe," he told me. "It was as if the land had been skinned of life. I couldn't believe that anyone would deliberately do that to the Earth."

I attended the Settlement Feast after James's death, where tribal leaders recounted the extent of the land that James had ruled that would be passed on to his successor. I was as-tounded to hear a recitation handed down orally from long ago that described in vivid detail the mountains, valleys, for-ests, and waters that made up the Gosnell territory. Nisga'a culture and history remain alive in that territory and pro-foundly linked to the past and the future.

I joined the fight to save the Stein Valley, the last un-touched watershed in the populous southwestern corner of British Columbia that belongs to the Nlaka'pamux Nation. Once again, this sense of place, of the sacredness of land, and the Native identification with it were made plain. At one of the rallies for the Stein, Chief Ruby Dunstan of the Lytton Band declared, "If a logging road is pushed into the Stein and the trees cut down, you may as well line my people up and shoot them." Like Guujaaw, she was expressing that sense that her people's identity was based on the land, the trees, and the whole of the life within it. A young Lytton Indian described the Stein Valley as his "cathedral," a spiritual place where he could go and feel the pressures of modern life fall away as he regained a sense of peace and oneness with Nature and a reconnection with the past. These are not romantic ideas of an extinct past that have no relevance to modern urban dwellers. They endure and hold the key to *our* sanity and survival. I have no rose-tinted illusions about the "noble savage," but those who deny that living remnants of an ancient aboriginal world-view still persist, speak in ignorance.

The Potlatch: Possessions and Sharing

In the dominant culture of the West, we regard property, ownership, possessions, and wealth as natural goals and rights of all citizens. But I encountered a very different attitude at a potlatch of the Heiltsuk people in Bella Bella. There it was obvious why Europeans were horrified by this ritual. Prestige and honor among British Columbia's coastal Indians come not from accumulation of wealth but from giving it away, from sharing with the community. During the nightlong potlatch celebration, guests shared food, dance, song, and speeches and were given gifts for participating in and witnessing the event. To a British Columbian coastal Native, the right to give a potlatch is a privilege that must be earned; it brings recognition that is never forgotten. To those for whom possessions and wealth are the very definition of status and importance, the potlatch would be incomprehensible. At James Gosnell's Settlement Feast, members of the very poor community gave over seventy thousand dollars to honor James and to settle obligations. Then, within an hour, the entire amount was redistributed within the community!

Native customs are evidence of an astute understanding of the psychology of human interactions. Yet aboriginal peoples around the world are in the final stages of an assault by conquerors who are intent on exploiting their land and resource base. Of course, the history of our species is one of conquest and takeovers of territories. But like the current spasm of species extinction, the destruction of indigenous people is now occurring with frightening speed. Once these people have disappeared, their body of priceless thought and knowledge, painstakingly acquired over thousands of years, will disappear forever. And like a species that has lost its habitat and survives only in zoos, indigenous people who have lost their land and eke out a living in tiny reserves or urban slums lose their uniqueness and identity.

Native Knowledge and Preservation of Nature: Innu

In government and business, departments and ministries of forests, fisheries, oceans, and atmosphere are driven by *human* priorities, not by concern for trees, animals, water, air, or soil. No representatives speak on behalf of the animate and inanimate parts of our environment. Many environmentalists are reluctant to allow indigenous people, whose cultures are built around the use of animals and plants, to exploit the land that has always belonged to them. Aboriginal peoples' relationship with other life-forms comes from a deep respect that is ultimately self-interested. Yet they do speak on behalf of the environment. Simon Lucas, a chief of the Nuu Cha Nulth people on the west coast of Vancouver Island, speaks of other animals with the same respect he has for humans. He has fought against logging in his traditional territory by arguing, "Those animals have a right to those forests too. They belong there—it is as much theirs as it is ours." Simon once told me, "If the water can no longer support the salmon, if the land can't support the deer and bear, then why do we think it will support us?"

From this attitude of respect, gratitude, and humility, aboriginal people have acquired an understanding of their "relatives" that is far more extensive than the uni-dimensional kind of information that is gleaned by scientists. In Labrador, the Innu—nomadic hunter-gatherers who depend on caribou for their way of life—are now threatened by NATO jets practicing low-level training flights over the landscape. I can attest from personal experience that the sonic booms shock the system; my heartbeat skyrocketed, and I trembled for several minutes after experiencing them. The Innu find the flights profoundly upsetting and say animals are affected adversely as well. Furthermore, chemical emissions from the afterburners are building up in the soil and water. The Innu have lived in this unforgiving land for thousands of years and have accumulated a vast lore about the animals and plants upon which they depend not only for food but for medicines and raw materials for clothing and shelter. They know the land intimately.

A handful of government scientists and assistants also study the caribou. They spend a few months every year monitoring hundreds of thousands of the animals through field observations and a few radio-collared animals. When I talked to the caribou "expert" in Labrador, I found that his technical knowledge was limited and fragmented. I was reminded of a visit I made to the World Wildlife Fund research station near Manaus in the Amazon rain forest. Three scientists, frog experts, were there at the time, and their knowledge of their subject was impressive. One of them took us on a night hike and in pitch dark, could find frogs that were barely half an inch long. But when I asked about a bird we scared up and a strange plant on a tree, he shrugged his shoulders. "Don't ask me, I'm a herpetologist," he said. Yet whenever I asked Kayapó Indians on the Xingú River in Brazil about an insect, plant, or bird, they always knew it by name and could relate an anecdote about it. Scientific expertise is so narrowly focused and specialized that it can barely comprehend the dimensions and the interconnectedness of life.

To return to the Innu, in speaking to the elders, I was impressed by the breadth and scale of their knowledge. They are the repositories of generations of observations and insights essential for their survival. The elders told me that each animal that is killed is carefully inspected as it is being butchered. The Innu check the organs, examine the fur, and look at the bones and marrow; they can detect negative changes in the quality of the animals. Today they observe abnormal behavior and an increase in miscarriages in the caribou herds. They also describe changes in the color and medicinal power of certain plants. Their knowledge is vast, yet in formal assessments of the impact of the NATO jets, Innu observations are discounted as anecdotal and folkloric, less credible than those of the "experts."

While I was staying at an Innu winter camp, I was told about the "shaking tent"—their traditional way of communicating. In the middle of winter, in a frozen skin tent, they will strip naked, fast, and chant. They are insensitive to the cold, and after several hours, they enter a state where they can "see" over long distances. I was told that a man once "flew" over a long distance and "saw" friends at a winter camp struggling for help. So the person in the shaking tent sent for help and saved them. I am not in a position to pass judgment on such stories, but as a scientist, I know that Nature possesses inexplicable mysteries. We have no theories with which to make sense of many of the phenomena that indigenous people describe. We should remember how Western scientific and medical communities dismissed acupuncture as superstitious folklore until U.S. President Richard Nixon visited mainland China. Only with the discovery of brain hormones like endorphins have we even had a theory for how acupuncture works. The phenomenon of shaking tents should arouse interest and curiosity rather than dismissive snorts of skepticism.

I cannot support the popular concept of preagrarian life as dull, short, and brutish from my experiences with indigenous peoples. While filming for the television series *A Planet for the Taking,* I went to the Kalahari Desert in Botswana. There I camped with some of the last hunter-gatherers on earth, the !Kung people. I was amazed at their ability to "read" game trails. They could see clues that were completely invisible to me and could estimate the freshness of a trail and identify the species, sex, and size of the animal that left it. Their pharmacological knowledge was also remarkable. Somehow they had discovered and understood the toxic chemicals in an insect larva, which they collect and use on the tips of their arrows. They showed me how to find water in the middle of the desert and where to dig for truffles. They were superbly adapted to survive in an environment that would have finished me off in days and they did it with a lot of time left for rest and recreation.

Small flat stones are rare on the desert, so when the !Kung find them, they keep them and carry them wherever they go. The reason became clear when I was taken to a mongongo tree, whose nuts are highly nutritious and much prized by the Natives. They built a fire, roasted the nuts, and cracked them with the rocks. It looked like fun and seemed easy to do, so I asked for a turn. To my surprise, what they did effortlessly, I couldn't do at all. I hammered away, and invariably the nut would go flying off unscathed. The !Kung watched and laughed till tears ran down their faces. Little did they know that I had a Ph.D., let alone what the degree means. All they knew was that I was totally inept at even the most fundamental of survival skills. I never did crack a mongongo nut. On that distant desert, I also experienced another universal trait of aboriginal people: a wonderful sense of humor, an ability to laugh and appreciate the simplest of things.

Enlightened Land Use: Cree and Kayapó

Rootedness in the land shapes the outlook and values of aboriginal peoples and forces us to confront our own economic value system, so out of sync with ecological principles. This is particularly true of the Cree of northern Quebec, who are resisting the blandishments of tens of millions of dollars in return for flooding their land. Robert Bourassa, the premier of the province, has referred to Cree territory as a "wasteland," empty of people. Bourassa sees immense economic opportunity: "Quebec is a vast hydroelectric plant in the bud and every day, millions of potential kilowatt-hours flow downhill and out to sea. What a waste!" The James Bay hydroelectric project is the largest development in the history of North America and has already cost more than $20 billion. Flooding more than six thousand square miles of land, it has already been an ecological disaster, yet now Bourassa is pressing to begin the second phase, which could cost $60 billion more. Phase II will dam every major river system flowing into the James and southern Hudson bays and completely alter the landscape of the area.

The Cree know from firsthand experience the consequences of massive flooding. Flooding allows bacteria to convert the minute quantities of metallic mercury that occur naturally in soil and vegetation into methylmercury, a highly toxic compound. It takes decades for methylmercury levels to peak and begin to decline after a dam is built. In the meantime, the compound accumulates up the food chain and is concentrated through biomagnification. Fish in the Cree territory have built up such high levels of methylmercury that they cannot be eaten. Unlike humans, fish-eating mammals and birds are unaware of the contamination and have been poisoned by it. Mercury has forced the Cree, to whom fish are an important part of life, to change their diet and so the fishing skills and knowledge of the elders have become irrelevant to the lives of the young. As well, flooding of traplines and alterations in the food and nesting sites of migratory waterfowl have eliminated much of the opportunity for traditional life. The social fabric of traditional Cree society has been drastically disrupted. After Phase I of the James Bay project, roads, shopping malls, and sportsmen from the south made a devastating impact on their land and culture, which the southern Cree know will worsen and be repeated in the northern villages if Phase II begins.

To Quebecois of the dominant culture, the northern part of the province seems empty. But the Cree and Inuit showed me maps of their territories crisscrossed by traplines, trails, campsites, and sacred burial sites—a land fully occupied and developed! Cree territory is divided into family areas for traplines, with 150 square miles of land composing one trapping territory. The Cree ensure that the animals aren't hunted to extinction by rotating their traplines every year in a four-year cycle. A designated "tallyman" in each family keeps track of the catch to prevent overtrapping. These practices of good conservation and sustainable harvesting are at the heart of their traditions. Once vast tracts of land are flooded, however, canoe routes, seasonal campsites, and sacred burial grounds will be lost, along with the indigenous and migratory birds and fur-bearing animals. That is why the Cree are rejecting all offers of money and compensation and are prepared to fight any further development on their lands. The resolution of their battle with Hydro Quebec will inform us whether we can change our priorities and values.

The aboriginal person most influential in my realization of alternative methods of enlightened land use lives in one of the remotest areas on earth. In 1988, while I was filming for a program on the Amazon rain forest, I met Paiakan, a Kayapó Indian whose home is on the Xingú River. Paiakan spent the first fourteen years of his life as a traditional nomadic hunter-gatherer. But he realized that the *brancos,* the Brazilian whites, were pressing in on Kayapó land and that the Kayapó would have to resist them. So he spent three years with a missionary to become fluent in Portuguese. When I met him, Paiakan was thirty-four and a renowned leader who was using all of the tools of "civilized society"—airplanes, radios, television—to defend his territory.

Paiakan once lived in Gorotire, a village that had been linked to the outside by a road. In 1985, disgusted with the materialism, alcohol, and logging that resulted from Western culture's encroachments, Paiakan led a group of his people deep into the forest to establish a traditional village called Aucre. He took me into Aucre in 1988, and I returned again with my family in 1989. Aucre was like paradise, where people live as they have lived since the beginning of human societies. Paiakan taught me much through his simple wisdom.

I invited Paiakan to British Columbia when his life was threatened in Brazil. His entire family came and stayed with us as he met with other indigenous people and raised money to support his struggle. During his travels around British Columbia, Paiakan was shocked to see the clear-cut logging and slash burning and once turned to me and remarked, "Just like Brazil." In one discussion he said philosophically, "People destroy the forest in Brazil because they are poor and they are ignorant." Then he added pointedly, "What is Canada's excuse?" And, we might add, what's the excuse of American Pacific Northwesterners, Californians, and Alaskans?

In the tropical forests where the Kayapó live, the temperature and seasons don't change as they do in northern countries. Nevertheless, regular successions of plants grow and decline during the year. Paiakan told me how his people watch for the specific sequence of different plant species to inform them about the right time to clear land, plant, and harvest. He once remarked to me: "The river is like our refrigerator that keeps fresh meat. The forest is like our drug store that has our medicines. It is like a supermarket with all of the food and things we need. Why would we poison our water or clear the forest?"

The Kayapó, like all indigenous peoples who are in contact with technological societies, enjoy some of the benefits of those societies. In Aucre, although there is no electricity or plumbing, people wear wristwatches (ornamental) and rubber thongs and use transistor tape recorders and flashlights. Paiakan has been instrumental in trying to establish links with organizations like The Body Shop and organic food stores to sell renewable forest products. "Extractive reserves" pioneered by rubber tapper Chico Mendes appeal to Indians too because they would allow Native people to sustain the forest and obtain the cash they need to buy manufactured goods.

I suggested to Paiakan that the trinkets of industrial society were limitless and irresistible. I worried that once the Kayapó were plugged into a monied economy, they would feel strong pressure to harvest more than the forests could sustain in order to increase the cash flow for all these goodies. Paiakan's answer was full of insight and wisdom. "David," he began, "I have three daughters. I don't know whether they will all reach maturity and have families. Perhaps one or two will, or I may be fortunate and all three will. I have no control over it." He went on, "I can plant fifty mahogany seeds, and they will sprout and grow. Chances are, only a few will survive to become trees. I have no power to affect that. Nature does. The forest is controlled by Nature, and we would never be so greedy or stupid as to take too much." With these few words, Paiakan expressed more understanding and foresight than the "experts" in industrialized countries who are determined to "liquidate" the forest for immediate cash and who speak so confidently of being able to regrow forests after massive clearcuts.

Paiakan has had a great deal of experience with *brancos*, both in Brazil and abroad. He found that many politicians and business people would make grand promises in private, only to deny them in public. So he learned how to use a videocassette recorder and now will have discussions only with the camera going to have a permanent record of the proceedings. He once remarked to me, "You white people *talk* a lot and think you've done things. We Kayapó *do* what we say we will." It was another version of the child's taunt, "All talk and no action." Too often today, we—especially politicians—make grand speeches, use fine words, and make promises with little intention of making good on them.

As my understanding of indigenous peoples' deep attachment to place has grown, I am impelled to support many groups seeking allies to protect their land. If biodiversity and ecosystem integrity are critical to salvaging some of the skin of life on earth, then every successful fight to protect the land of indigenous peoples is a victory for all of humanity and other living things. More and more people from dominant Western cultures are recognizing this and forming alliances with indigenous peoples. One of them is a remarkable Swiss shepherd named Bruno Manser, who sought out the nomadic Penan of

Sarawak in Malaysia and lived with them for seven years. Manser has described their gentle ways and their deep pleasures in daily life. The Penan live totally on the productive capacity of the forest and express a profound understanding of the plants and animals. I met Manser after he had left Sarawak to raise world concern and support for the Penan.

I watched Bruno's reaction to the press in Los Angeles. Like a Penan who suddenly emerges from the forest shadows into the bright light of a clear-cut, Bruno seemed to shrink and to prepare to bolt. But he stayed because the Penan are being pushed to the brink of extinction by the relentless pressure of logging, which is cutting into the heart of their territory. After years of protests, blockades, and prison, most Penan have been forced to live in squalid slums; only some sixty families remain completely nomadic. In 1991 two of the nomadic Penan were brought out of Malaysia at great personal sacrifice and risk. They came to the industrialized countries because we are the cause of their crisis. Their plea was simple and eloquent—the forest is their home, it has nurtured and protected them since the beginning of time. They do not come into *our* homes and demand to be fed and clothed, so why do we take theirs? And they expressed concern about the pain that our destructive ways are inflicting on the earth. Their words expose our economic and materialistic imperatives for what they are—illusions that have effectively alienated us from the very things that sustain us.

The ecological impact of industrial civilization and the sheer weight of human numbers is now global and is changing the biosphere with frightening speed. It is clear that major problems such as global warming, ozone depletion, species extinction, and worldwide toxic pollution will not be solved in the long run by perpetuating the current worldview and applying Band-Aids such as tax levies, greater efficiency, and recycling. Knowledge gained through science is unique and profound, yet also extremely limited. Not only does the Newtonian worldview fail to comprehend the complexity of life on earth, we have barely begun to understand its dimensions.

We need a radically different way of relating ourselves to
the support systems of the planet. My experiences with aboriginal peoples have convinced me, both as a scientist and as
an environmentalist, of the power and relevance of their
knowledge and worldview in a time of imminent global eco-
catastrophe. This is how the germ of *Wisdom of the Elders*
formed in my mind. The book became possible when Peter
Knudtson expressed similar concerns and hopes. Knudtson
had also been trained in science and later encountered Native
people in Alaska and California who shaped his appreciation
of the power of their knowledge and attitudes. Our shared
perceptions and fundamental belief in the validity and power
of aboriginal notions of the sacredness of Nature have produced this book.

1

Visions of the Natural World

Shaman and Scientist*

I see no reason why mankind should have waited until recent times to produce minds of the caliber of a Plato or an Einstein. Already over two or three hundred thousand years ago, there were probably men of similar capacity, who were of course not applying their intelligence to the solution of the same problems as these more recent thinkers.

—Claude Lévi-Strauss, anthropologist[1]

* According to the great historian of religion Mircea Eliade, the term *shaman*, strictly speaking, refers to "the great master of ecstasy," who characteristically "specializes in a trance during which his soul is believed to leave his body and ascend to the sky or descend to the underworld." Here we use the term more broadly to symbolize and personify a host of other traditional bearers of Native wisdom and knowledge, from healers and medicinal experts to holy people and other elders as well.

Today, Navajo Indians in the deserts of the American Southwest still speak lovingly in their ancient stories of Changing Woman, one of the Holy People from the primordial era of world creation, who fashioned the first Navajo people from a mixture of cornmeal and shreds of her own epidermis. She is the very embodiment of life's orchestrated diversity and nature's awesome cyclic powers of rebirth and regeneration. In some sense, she is also a reflection of the wondrous, endlessly self-renewing, maternal earth itself, whose form traditional Navajo envision as a woman. Mountains and mesas are the contours of this feminine earth's body, the geological expression of her *heart, skull, breast, and internal organs*. Fertile soil is her living flesh. Vegetation is her dress. The spinning of the seasons is a visible manifestation of her dynamic beauty, ecological balance, and vitality.[2]

Living Seminole elders in the Southeastern U.S. still recall tales of a primordial time of world creation, when the antics of ancestral beings formed the contours of the land. After the Creator shaped the earth, they say, He first dispatched a woodpecker to survey what He had done. As the woodpecker flew over the virgin landscape, its rapidly beating wings *hit the ground and that was how mountains were created.* Then the Creator dispatched a gliding buzzard. *Where his wings hit the ground, that was where we had the flatland and the valleys.* Finally, the Creator instructed all the animals not to trample on the moist surface of the youthful earth until it had fully hardened. *But the raccoon didn't listen. He started digging in the soft land for crayfish. That was how the swamps were created.* Chastized by the angry Creator, the foolish raccoon wept, wiping the tears from his eyes with his muddy hands. *That was how the raccoon got his black eyes.*[3]

3

In the Guatemalan highlands of Central America, an elderly Maya Indian occasionally still pauses to murmur a heartfelt prayer to Pokohil, guardian of the forest, after helping to slay a pair of deer at the edge of his *milpa,* or maize field. His words express an achingly heartfelt concern for the finite capacities of nature, as well as the fearsome power of Pokohil to retaliate against those who abuse the animals whose well-being he oversees:

> *O Pokohil, today you have shown favour,*
> *And have given some of your beasts, some of your deer.*
> *Thank you Pokohil.*
> *See, I bring you flowers for your deer.*
> *Perhaps you have counted them,*
> *Two of them are missing;*
> *They are the ones the Old One [the hunter] caught,*
> *You gave them to him.*[4]

By thanking this spiritual protector of the animals for the "favor" of killing two of his deer, the hunter in some sense is attempting to fill with his gratitude and his grief the two "holes" he has temporarily made in the fabric of the universe. With the gift of a handful of blossoms, his gesture to Pokohil is complete.

Oceans away, deep in the tropical rain forests of peninsular Malaysia, Chewong storytellers, displaced now from their sacred traditional lands, sometimes still speak darkly of impending world's end, the result of unbridled human greed, pollution, and excessive killing of animals. In time, they say, such human irresponsibility may render the world *too dirty, too hot.* Then Tohan, who sculpted the first Chewong from soil and breathed life into them, will simply *not want this earth to continue any longer.* He will turn it upside down, unleashing a deluge, then patiently etch new rivers and valleys in the earth's naked underside, just as he did *a long time ago.*[5]

Such tales are mere droplets in the vast global reservoir of traditional indigenous knowledge about the natural world.

However fragmentary, they reveal a profound understanding, often ingeniously encoded in symbolic systems, of the underlying interconnectedness of the universe—a perspective, increasingly echoed by modern science, that is exceedingly relevant to our times. They remind us, however metaphorically, of the shared origins of all forms of life, the ecological integrity of natural systems, and the ancient bonds of kinship between human beings and other species. They underscore the fundamental relationship between life and land. They illuminate the cyclic temporal processes of nature, the role of ordinary human beings in maintaining its precarious balances, and the prospect of sinister, long-term consequences in the wake of human greed, hubris, and neglect.

In mainstream Western society it has long been relatively easy to embrace elements of traditional Native knowledge about nature, as long as they are suitably couched in sentimental, romantic, or culturally subordinate terms. Most of us, for example, have grown quite accustomed to glowing Native ecological aphorisms like "All things are connected" and to evocative allusions to "sacred" landscapes, "circles" of life, and Mother Earth on commercial paraphernalia from posters and greeting cards to trendy T-shirts. But the instant that Native visions of the natural world—and the intellectual capacities of the generations of Native minds that helped shape them—are presented on a par with vaunted Western ideas, presumed by many to have long since culturally superceded and displaced them, our cultural and racial biases often become more apparent.

Wisdom of the Elders is an exploration of the often striking parallels between traditional Native ecological perspectives and Western scientific ones, particularly in modern biology. As biologists, one specializing in animal behavior and the other in genetics, we have found ourselves increasingly intrigued in recent years by the shared truths, as well as the undeniable differences, in these two distinct, yet often strikingly complementary ways of knowing about the natural world.

One of these ways of knowing might be called the world of the shaman—the ancient, ecstatic healer and holy person of many traditional indigenous societies who serves as a primary repository of Native nature-wisdom. The other might be called the world of the scientist—particularly, for our purposes, as interpreted by some of the most articulate, compassionate, and wise "elder statesmen" of science, whom we see as science's true "elders." We refer to these shared ecological truths collectively, as the book's title suggests, as the nature "wisdom of the elders."

We believe that it is time, at long last, for modern, science-driven industrial societies to begin to grant traditional Native nature-wisdom and the long-suffering First Peoples* of the world who are its guardians and rightful heirs the respect they have always deserved. Judging by recently renewed public interest in the imperiled status of indigenous cultures around the world, we are not alone. This reawakening of intellect and conscience could hardly take place at a more appropriate decade. Spain and a number of other nations on both sides of the Atlantic Ocean proudly proclaimed 1992 a year of international celebration, commemorating Christopher Columbus's momentous encounter with the "savage" New World on October 12, 1492, setting into motion a proud Age of European "Discovery" and global expansion. Today, indigenous peoples around the world tend to look upon this very same

---

* For the purposes of our discussion, the term *First Peoples* applies broadly to a vast multitude of traditional, often tribal, nature-based societies around the world—each of course with its own distinctive identity, values, history, and contemporary plight—that seem to possess not only the oldest but also, in many ways, the most intimate relationship with a local landscape and its distinctive flora and fauna.

This general and imperfect term will be used, almost interchangeably with several others, despite their sometimes subtly different and overlapping connotations. Among them: *aboriginal* (which emphasizes particularly the connection between the "original," or precolonial, inhabitants of a place and their surroundings); *primary* (in the sense of, again, originality, or possessing an ancient relationship to particular places or ideas); *indigenous* (referring to the "natural" occurrence, or innateness, of a people to a region), and *Native* (capitalized to grant it greater cultural and racial focus and referring, like the others, to the "original" inhabitants of a place—that is, the people who have "always lived there").

five-hundred-year period of history as nothing less than Five Centuries of Suffering and Resistance.

But beyond the boundaries of a number of bold Native communities, who will publicly bear witness to the more tragic dimensions of this collision of Old World and "New" that was heralded by Columbus's first voyage? Who will pay appropriate respect to Native memories of the past several centuries of oppression—the murderous violence, rapes, and military assaults; the catastrophic epidemics of deadly introduced diseases; the epochs of brutal slavery and forced labor; the fierce religious persecution; the state-sanctioned erosion of sacred traditional landholdings; and the relentless political and economic exploitation at the hands of a succession of foreigners? And who will pause to pay tribute to the impressive precontact intellectual, spiritual, and social achievements of First Peoples in the Americas and elsewhere and openly acknowledge that some of the recent arrivals have attempted to raze this precious legacy from the face of the earth?

On the eve of Columbus's "discovery," the New World was hardly "an empty continent," as historian Alexis de Tocqueville wrote in 1835. It was a verdant and kaleidoscopic landscape and seascape, teeming with plant and animal life. It also supported a population of between 9 and 120 million human beings—50 million is widely viewed as a reasonable estimate—who had successfully inhabited the hemisphere for tens of thousands of years before Columbus or any other earlier European adventurer drifted in upon the scene. They lived in groups ranging from small seminomadic communities of subsistence hunters and gatherers to great, literate, agricultural-based urban civilizations like those of the Inca, Aztec, and Maya, whose insights into agriculture, architecture, astronomy, and mathematics often rivaled or surpassed state-of-the-art fifteenth-century European knowledge in these fields. And despite the often venomous racial, religious, and cultural preconceptions held by the many European soldiers, settlers, and clergy who first flooded into the Americas, the original inhabitants of this New World (mistakenly christened "Indians" by a geographically disoriented Columbus) were not somehow "bedeviled" or "less than human," contrary to the then prevailing view. Each one of them was, of course, as exquisitely endowed with intelligence, love of family and friends, and the capacity to feel joy and pain, to experience awe in the face of surpassing natural beauty, as were any of their more militarily sophisticated Old World brethren.

The tragic story of the relationships between Native and non-Native peoples over the past five hundred years—not just in the Western Hemisphere but all around the world—is a poignant and unfinished story. In this century alone, for example, approximately 90 of Brazil's 270 Indian tribes, along with their precious legacies of languages and traditional knowledge, have been utterly erased from the face of the earth. Many others have endured but have lost much of their distinctiveness through loss of their lands or the cultural assimilation of their children. Among those tribes in Brazil that have managed to survive, fully two-thirds now number fewer than one thousand souls. Such stories, endlessly repeated around the globe, are not likely to impel a thoughtful person to uninhibited patriotic fervor over a triumphant colonial "Age of Discovery" inaugurated by Christopher Columbus. Nor, for that matter, are they our primary focus here.

Nonetheless, it is crucial to understand that the recent political and cultural domination of Native communities around the world by foreign influences has contributed to an exaggerated devaluation of Native thought, including traditional Native ecological insights. As a result, Native views of nature have too often been unjustly denigrated as somehow inherently "simple," "primitive," or "naive"; reflective of an earlier and therefore inferior "stage" in human cultural "progress"; and beyond this, however poetic or endearing, as completely irrelevant to our sophisticated modern needs and times.

We must reevaluate the relevance of indigenous knowledge to our spiritually and environmentally turbulent modern lives, and, in recognizing its intrinsic value, take immediate actions to honor and protect Native cultures around the world. Here we invite readers to take a very different kind of voyage, one we believe stands in stark cultural counterpoint to the one Columbus took five centuries ago. It is a challenging cross-cultural journey through a virtually uncharted archipelago of spiritually and linguistically distinct—yet often uncannily similar—Native visions of the natural world and of the proper place of human beings within it. And unlike Columbus, we embark on this uncertain voyage in a spirit of respect for aboriginal worldviews and gratitude for the compassion and the contemplations of generations of Native peoples who have long lived intimately immersed in nature.

We begin at the beginning: by identifying First Peoples; then by probing the conceptual roots of their sacred visions of the patterns of nature, their sacred ecologies; and, finally by pointing out possible parallels between Native and scientific knowledge.

Who Are the First Peoples of the World?

On this voyage, we will encounter a variegated global tapestry of Native cultures and populations that can be called First Peoples. Indigenous peoples themselves generally know very well who they are, even if time and disruptive political policies have sometimes blurred traditional group names, linguistic divisions, and geographic boundaries. In fact, this sense of self-identification is perhaps the single most crucial element of any working definition of indigenous, aboriginal, or First Peoples.

Indigenous peoples are generally viewed as the descendants of the original inhabitants of a given geographic territory that may have been subsequently taken over—militarily, politically, or simply through settlement—by outsiders. Consequently, they are usually seen as historically, politically, and culturally dominated—although not necessarily conquered—peoples. (Some aboriginal populations have survived by simply sidestepping, in some fashion, destructive foreign impacts.)

In many areas of the world, where wave after wave of foreign intrusion has inundated certain regions, the issue of geographical primacy is dauntingly complex. In much of the Indian subcontinent, for example, as well as in other areas of Asia, time has clouded a particular tribal group's clear claims to antecedence as a First People. In Africa, North America, Latin America, and elsewhere, massive domination by European colonial powers has not only imposed arbitrary political boundaries upon traditional aboriginal territories but has drastically altered the composition of precontact aboriginal populations.

Finally, indigenous peoples are generally considered to possess distinctive cultures—in which, at least traditionally, they have a profound and deeply rooted sense of place and relationship with the entirety of the natural world. No neat laundry list of cultural criteria has emerged to determine quickly and unequivocally a group's status as indigenous. But there is broad consensus that the vast array of aboriginal communities scattered across the earth's surface, despite their incredible cultural diversity, is bound together in part by an assortment of shared primary ecological perspectives and themes.

Where does this meandering definition of indigenous peoples leave us? Even with its occasionally uncertain boundaries, it circumscribes a fairly large number of people—now estimated to be four percent or more of the entire world population. A report on the status of aboriginal populations entitled *Indigenous Peoples: A Global Quest for Justice* (published by the Independent Commission on International Humanitarian Issues in 1987) cites an estimate of more than 200 million indigenous people worldwide (in 1991, the United Nations estimated more than 300 million), including:

❖ an estimated 150 million in Asia—including more than 67 million in China, 50 million in India, and 6.5 million in the Philippines;

❖ an estimated 30 to 80 million in Latin America (the smaller represents government figures, the larger those of indigenous leaders);

❖ an estimated 3 to 13 million in North America (depending on whether Chicanos and Métis are included);

✦ an estimated several million in Africa; as well as perhaps 250,000 Australian Aborigines, 300,000 New Zealand Maoris, 60,000 Scandinavian Sami (or Lapps), and 100,000 circumpolar Inuit (or Eskimos), among others.

Native and Scientific Ways of Knowing about Nature

Before we embark on our journey to aboriginal visions of the natural world, we should discuss some of the most important differences between Native and scientific ecological perspectives, between the kinds of questions each "asks" of nature and the kinds of "answers" each is, in turn, likely to receive.

Few Westerners have written more lucidly on this subject than French anthropologist Claude Lévi-Strauss. In his book *The Savage Mind,* his classic study of this topic, Lévi-Strauss completely sidesteps Western society's long-standing tendency to prejudge the Native Mind,* and shamanism or magic, as little more than a spiritually stunted cultural antecedent to the nobler, more clear-eyed vision of modern science. Rather, Lévi-Strauss refers to the worlds of the shaman and the scientist as *two parallel modes of acquiring knowledge about the universe* that have managed to give birth independently to *two distinct though equally positive sciences.* In these two fundamentally different modes of thought, *one [is] roughly adapted to that of perception and the imagination: the other at a remove from it.*[6]

The Native Mind and the Scientific Mind are embodied in

---

* In the context of his writings, Lévi-Strauss's use of the French term *sauvage* was quite devoid of the pejorative connotations that English translations of his work introduced with the term *savage.* The English word *savage* might suggest an inferior, or even subhuman, state of rudeness, fierceness, or lack of civilization. Lévi-Strauss seems to have used the word *sauvage* to subtly suggest an often admirable and more elusive quality of "wildness" in terms of a society's outlook upon the world.

To avoid misunderstanding, we will use the more neutral term "Native Mind" interchangeably with Lévi-Strauss's term "Savage Mind." Throughout the book, this and other related terms such as *primary, aboriginal,* and *Native* are intended to refer *nonjudgmentally* to the distillation of a global diversity of traditional, pantheistic, nature-centered, aboriginal worldviews—contemporary and extinct.

the traditional ecstatic healer, or shaman, and scientist, respectively. The first of these two vital traditions of thought is virtually as old as humankind itself—its taproot descends deep down in the rich Pleistocene soil of an ancient hunting-gathering way of life, and its tender leaves still unfurl to this day. This Native Mind, this aboriginal vision of the natural world, in its various incarnations and with constant modification, helped Homo sapiens navigate through countless crucial cultural transitions—ranging from the domestication of animals and early agriculture to the margins of modern industrialization. The Scientific Mind is, in comparison, a relative upstart. Its roots are for the most part in the much shallower soils of seventeenth-century European Christianity and natural philosophy, although some of its ideas descend into the deeper tilth of ancient Judeo-Christian and Greek thought.

Despite the profound differences in the sensibilities and separate historical lineages of these two modes of thinking, argues Lévi-Strauss, both are alive and neither is inherently "superior" or "inferior" to the other. Each tradition is endowed with an originality, an internal coherence, and an intellectual integrity that renders it independently beautiful, adaptive, and worthy of respect in its own right. Each aims also to discover some sense of order within the physical universe and conjures up visions of nature that, when seen side by side, can seem strikingly *complementary*.

The critical difference between these two traditional ways of knowing (there are of course others) arises from the opposite ways in which each asks questions about the universe. Their different perspectives—not simply the historical timing of their emergence—fundamentally determine the kind of knowledge about the natural world that each has accumulated over the centuries. Writes Lévi-Strauss:

Certainly the properties to which the savage [or Native] mind has access are not the same as those which have commanded the attention of scientists. The physical world is approached from opposite ends in the two cases: one is supremely concrete, the other supremely abstract; one proceeds from the angle of sensible qualities and the other from that of formal properties.[7]

The predicament of the traditional shaman and the modern scientist might be compared to that of the proverbial troupe of blind men who, after each has been permitted to touch a different area of the same elephant's anatomy, proceed to pontificate—"ethnocentrically," strictly on the basis of each man's circumscribed experience—on the underlying "truth" of elephant-ness.

The savage mind, says Lévi-Strauss, *totalizes.* In other words, the Native Mind's perspective tends to be holistic, multisensory, and boundless in scope. Shamans (along with an assortment of medicine people, healers, artists, and other traditional figures of authority who have long served as precious repositories of aboriginal knowledge) reach out to embrace the *entire* cosmos—not just the most tangible or accessible part of it. Shamanic images of the natural world are largely rooted in the rich soil of generations of revelatory personal encounters with the concrete, sensible aspects of the cosmos. The Native Mind yearns to envelop the *totality* of the world and brings a *totality* of mental capacities, beyond cool reason, to the task.

In a parallel quest, scientists set out to confront the awesome mysteries of the cosmos with sensibilities that are in some sense *one step removed,* to borrow Lévi-Strauss's phrase, from the primary, experiential, holistic perceptions of the Native Mind. Rather than becoming active participants in nature—rather than ecstatically immersing themselves in the immediacy of its sensory juices—they observe nature as an object—as an inanimate "other"—and consequently "from afar." They view nature as a distant abstraction: a composite of the clever, fragmentary insights they have painstakingly gleaned from the measurable aspects of nature.

The individual scientist's ultimate goal, seen as part of a multigenerational enterprise of scientific inquiry, is in some ways far grander than that of the ecstatic, world-embracing shaman. The scientist seeks nothing less than eventually to comprehend the workings of the whole universe—to "explain" it rationally by somehow reducing all of its seemingly unfathomable mysteries to a finite set of natural laws that grant order to the cosmos. In this audacious quest, the scientist relies upon an extraordinary intellectual and technological tool-kit that greatly amplifies certain perceptions and powers. He possesses precision instruments, for example, ranging from microscopes and telescopes to supercomputers, and clever sleights-of-hand such as mathematical equations and shared rules of logic and evidence—the legacy of centuries of scientific thought.

Paradoxically, as these tools and strategies have inched scientists ever closer to the subjects of their intense scrutiny, they have also tended to insulate scientists from the potentially psychologically overwhelming impact of nature's totality—familiar territory to the shaman. By dissecting nature, by rationally reducing it to bits and pieces, the scientist remains aloof from that swirling vortex of ecstatic joys, terrors, and mysteries captured with breathtaking clarity by novelist George Eliot in *Middlemarch*:

If we had a keen vision and feeling of all ordinary human life, it would be like hearing the grass grow and the squirrel's heart beat, and we should die of that roar which lies on the other side of silence.

Science's vaunted "objectivity" does not render it in every way supreme, however. What might the Native Mind glimpse that the scientist's more myopic gaze cannot? What creative images of the cosmos might holistic minds that are equally gifted intellectually conjure up if they were granted limitless access not just to the mind's reason but also to its capacity for feeling, compassion, visceral experience, and soaring imagination as it struggles to convey its personal vision of nature's boundlessness?

Traditional Native knowledge about the natural world is

often extremely sophisticated and of considerable practical value. Prescientific aboriginal systems for identifying, naming, and classifying soils, plants, insects, and other elements of local environments and deriving medical and economic benefit from them are perhaps the most powerful illustration of this. In the rain forests of the Philippines, for instance, the Hanunoo people know how to distinguish sixteen hundred different plant species. Preliminary studies suggest that the Kayapó Indians of the Amazon jungles of Brazil rely upon more than 250 different species of plants for their fruits alone, and hundreds more for their roots, nuts, and other edible parts. Traditional Bolivian healers use some six hundred different medicinal herbs, and their counterparts in Southeast Asia may use up to 6,500 kinds of plants for their medical concoctions. In addition, more than seventy-five percent of the 121 prescription drugs used around the world that are derived from plants are said to have been discovered on the basis of initial clues found in traditional indigenous medical practices.

Many aspects of ancient Native nature lore and preevolutionary "taxonomy" are grounded in supremely thorough field observation. Native schemes of names and classification, seen in the context of the cosmos that shaped them, are intelligent and coherent. While Native thinkers, writes Lévi-Strauss, searched for the elemental basis for nature's orderly designs

without perfected instruments which would have permitted them to place it where it most often is—namely, at the microscopic level—they already discerned "as through a glass darkly" principles of interpretation whose . . . accordance with reality have been revealed to us only through very recent inventions.[8]

Native and Scientific Knowledge about Nature

If shamans and scientists for centuries have asked very different kinds of questions of the cosmos, how different are the "answers" each has elicited? One way to distill the differences between Native and scientific knowledge about nature is simply to list some of the fundamental qualities of Native ecological perspectives and contrast them with conventional scientific ones. By listing them, we do not mean to imply that all these characteristics will necessarily be found in *every* indigenous belief system. Nor are we implying that *no* scientist subscribes in any way to any of the Native viewpoints and values that we are suggesting. Nor do we believe our list to be exhaustive.

First, traditional Native knowledge about the natural world tends to view all—or at least vast regions—of nature, often including the earth itself, as inherently holy rather than profane, savage, wild, or wasteland. The landscape itself, or certain regions of it, is seen as sacred and quivering with life. It is inscribed with meaning regarding the origins and unity of all life, rather than seen as mere property to be partitioned legally into commercial real estate holdings.

The Native Mind is imbued with a deep sense of reverence for nature. It does not operate from an impulse to exercise human dominion over it.

Native wisdom sees spirit, however one defines that term, as dispersed throughout the cosmos or embodied in an inclusive, cosmos-sanctifying divine being. Spirit is not concentrated in a single monotheistic Supreme Being.

Native wisdom tends to assign human beings enormous responsibility for sustaining harmonious relations within the whole natural world rather than granting them unbridled license to follow personal or economic whim.

It regards the human obligation to maintain the balance and health of the natural world as a solemn spiritual duty that an individual must perform daily—not simply as admirable, abstract ethical imperatives that can be ignored as one chooses. The Native Mind emphasizes the need for reciprocity—for humans to express gratitude and make sacrifices routinely—to the natural world in return for the benefits they derive from it—rather than to extract whatever they desire unilaterally. Nature's bounty is considered to be precious gifts that remain intimately and inextricably embedded in its living web rather than as "natural resources"* passively awaiting human exploitation.

Human beings are to honor nature routinely (through daily spiritual practice, for example, or personal prayer) rather than only intermittently when it happens to be convenient (on Earth Day, for example, or following a particularly moving speech or television documentary, or in the throes of personal despair over a pressing local environmental crisis). And human violations of the natural world have serious immediate (as well as long-term) consequences rather than comfortingly vague, ever "scientifically uncertain," long-term ones.

The Native Mind tends to view wisdom and environmental ethics as discernible in the very structure and organization of the natural world rather than as the lofty product of human reason far removed from nature.

The Native Mind tends to view the universe as the dynamic interplay of elusive and ever-changing natural forces, not as a vast array of static physical objects.

It tends to see the entire natural world as somehow alive and animated by a single, unifying life force, whatever its local Native name. It does not reduce the universe to progressively smaller conceptual bits and pieces.

It tends to view time as circular (or as a coillike fusion of circle and line), as characterized by natural cycles that sustain all life, and as facing humankind with recurrent moral crises—rather than as an unwavering linear escalator of "human progress."

It tends to accept without undue anxiety the probability that nature will always possess unfathomable mysteries. It

* One group of British Columbia Natives has translated the word in their language that most closely corresponds to the Western concept of "natural resource" with the luminous English phrase "Grasping the Handle of All Life." For an aboriginal society—past or present—with the ethos and vocabulary of a viscerally felt bond with the natural world, efforts to economically develop sacred tribal landholdings might well be a far more excruciating and soul-searching process than it has historically been for the West.

does not presume that the cosmos is completely decipherable to the rational human mind.

It tends to view human thought, feelings, and communication as inextricably intertwined with events and processes in the universe rather than as apart from them. Indeed, words themselves are considered spiritually potent, generative, and somehow engaged in the continuum of the cosmos, not neutral and disengaged from it. The vocabulary of Native knowledge is inherently gentle and accommodating toward nature rather than aggressive and manipulative.

The Native Mind tends to emphasize celebration of and participation in the orderly designs of nature instead of rationally "dissecting" the world.

It tends to honor as its most esteemed elders those individuals who have experienced a profound and compassionate reconciliation of outer- and inner-directed knowledge, rather than virtually anyone who has made material achievement or simply survived to chronological old age.

It tends to reveal a profound sense of empathy and kinship with other forms of life, rather than a sense of separateness from them or superiority over them. Each species is seen as richly endowed with its own singular array of gifts and powers, rather than as somehow pathetically limited compared with human beings.

Finally, it tends to view the proper human relationship with nature as a continuous dialogue (that is, a two-way, horizontal communication between Homo sapiens and other elements of the cosmos) rather than as a monologue (a one-way, vertical imperative).

This unfinished litany of Native ecological themes suggests that there is a fundamental division between Native and Western ecological perspectives. Within Native worldviews, the parts and processes of the universe are, to varying degrees, holy; to science, they can only be secular. Thus, this ancient, culturally diverse aboriginal consensus on the ecological order and the integrity of nature might justifiably be described as a "sacred ecology" in the most expansive, rather than in the scientifically restrictive, sense of the word "ecology." For it looks upon the totality of patterns and relationships at play in the universe as utterly precious, irreplaceable, and worthy of the most profound human veneration. To indigenous peoples around the world, the sacred is, and always has been, waiting to be witnessed everywhere—diffusely scattered to the four directions of the winds—and "everywhen" (a term coined by Australian Aboriginal scholar W.E.H. Stanner)—continuously, throughout all time.

The eminent Swedish historian of religion Åke Hultkrantz suggests that the narrow Western term *nature* seems incapable of enfolding Native notions of a vast, spiritually charged cosmic continuum, in which human society, biosphere, and the whole universe are seamlessly rolled into one. *The Western religious dichotomy between a world of spiritual plentitude and a world of material imperfection, a dualism pertaining to Christian and Gnostic doctrines,* he states, *has no counterpart in American Indian thinking. Indians value highly life on earth, and their religion supports their existence in the world. The whole spirit of their religion is one of harmony, vitality, and appreciation of the world around them.*[9]

According to Alfonso Ortiz, a Tewa Indian and well-known anthropologist: *Indian tribes put nothing above nature. Their gods are a part of nature, on the level of nature, not supra-anything. Conversely, there's nothing that is religious, versus something else that is secular. Native American religion pervades, informs all life.*[10]

At the same time, it is important to emphasize that this inherent spiritual dimension does not mean that Native nature-wisdom is somehow naively romantic, ethereal, or disconnected from ordinary life. Native knowledge about nature is firmly rooted in reality, in keen personal observation, interaction, and thought, sharpened by the daily rigors of uncertain survival. Its validity rests largely upon the authority of hard-won personal experience—upon concrete encounters with game animals and arduous treks across the actual physical contours of local landscapes, enriched by night dreams, contemplations, and waking visions. The junction between knowledge and experience is tight, continuous, and dynamic, giving rise to "truths" that are likely to be correspondingly intelligent, fluid, and vibrantly "alive."

This experiential basis of knowledge, explains Canadian anthropologist Robin Ridington, who has spent years studying British Columbia's subarctic Beaver Indians, or Dunne-za, *allows for a "science" that is negotiated in the same way that people negotiate social relations with one another.* This does not mean that aboriginal people are *colorful and spiritual but somehow not really connected to the real world in which we now live,* he continues. *They are real. They are translators. They remember. We forget or ignore what they know at our peril.*

To be sure, Native attitudes toward the natural world are not without certain tensions. After all, nature is not only sacred and beloved—it must daily be exploited, to some extent, in order to survive. Native knowledge embodies an ethos for mitigating this universal conflict, but it cannot be expected always to do so in perfect harmony. Historians suggest that Native peoples too have, on occasion, committed environmental "sins"—through wasteful hunting and trapping practices, for example, or the gradual depletion of agricultural soils. But the worst of these excesses were generally of relatively recent vintage and occurred under the influence of powerful, imposed, non-Native economic incentives and value systems. The earlier, precontact ecological infractions that took place certainly were done without the terrible technological leverage of modern Western infractions.

Modern science looks out upon the same universe through a very different lens. Through an often laborious process of debate and discussion, the *community* of scientists itself agrees for a time upon an interpretation of some aspect of the world—a new, more intellectually satisfying paradigm, or model, of reality, the latest in a long, lurching succession of ever-provisional scientific "truths."

Native and Scientific Thought as Mutually Enriching

Despite this gulf between Native and scientific ways of know-ing about nature, each tradition has much to learn from the other. A cross-cultural resonance can be felt in the ringing public statements issued by some of our wisest and most re-spected elder statesmen of science. They speak knowingly of the genetic and evolutionary kinship of all species and of our fundamental dependency upon the systems of nature. They describe the intricate, lifelike homeostatic processes that regu-late the chemical balance of the earth's oceans, soils, and atmo-sphere. And they plead for a new global environmental ethos based on this scientifically documented unity—one that might grant all forms of life an inherent value and right to exist and burden human beings with a greater sense of responsibility for maintaining long-term ecological balances in the biosphere.

Shaman and Scientist

Despite their different perspectives on the natural world, shaman and wise scientist seem to be issuing strikingly similar messages about the underlying interconnectedness of all life and warnings about the deteriorating state of natural systems. *Wisdom of the Elders* is an exploration of a few of these shared ecological themes. It represents a search for points of intellec-tual, emotional, and poetic resonance between some of the most profound truths of modern life sciences—particularly evolutionary biology, genetics, and ecology—and those of the time-tested nature—wisdom of First Peoples around the world—ranging from American, Andean, and Amazonian Indians of the New World to indigenous peoples of Africa, Southeast Asia, Australia, and beyond.

A landmark 1987 report by the World Commission on Envi-ronment and Development, popularly known as the Brundt-land report, boldly addresses the value of indigenous ecological perspectives to many global efforts to deal with ongoing environmental crises. It pleads for the prompt resto-ration of traditional land and resource rights to the world's remaining indigenous and tribal peoples, and it calls for a renewed respect for their ecological wisdom.

Their very survival has depended upon their ecological awareness
and adaptation. . . . These communities are the repositories of vast
accumulations of traditional knowledge and experience that links
humanity with its ancient origins. Their disappearance is a loss for
the larger society, which could learn a great deal from their traditional skills in sustainably managing very complex ecological systems. It is a terrible irony that as formal development reaches more
deeply into rain forests, deserts, and other isolated environments, it
tends to destroy the only cultures that have proved able to thrive in
these environments.[11]

We wholeheartedly concur with the Brundtland report's
stand on the urgency of protecting Native rights, lands, and
knowledge. Native spiritual and ecological knowledge has intrinsic value and worth, regardless of its resonances with or
"confirmation" by modern Western scientific values. As most
Native authorities would be quick to point out, it is quite
capable of existing on its own merits and adapting itself over
time to meet modern needs. For it is, after all, a proud, perceptive, and extraordinarily adaptive spiritual tradition, every bit
as precious, irreplaceable, and worthy of respect as Christianity, Judaism, Islam, Buddhism, and other great spiritual
traditions. In our view, respect for Native spirituality and the
nature-wisdom embedded within it is inseparable from respect for the dignity, human rights, and legitimate land claims
of all Native peoples. (See U.N. Draft Universal Declaration on
the Rights of Indigenous Peoples, p. 251.)

Seen in this light, Native knowledge and spiritual values are
not simply "natural resources" (in this case, intellectual ones)
for non-Natives to mine, manipulate, or plunder. They are,
and will always be, the precious life-sustaining property of
First Peoples: sacred symbols encoding the hidden design of
their respective universes; mirrors to their individual and collective identities; and ancient and irreplaceable maps suggesting possible paths to inner as well as ecological equilibrium
with the wider, ever-changing world.

✺

2

Distant Times

Recognizing the
Kinship of All Life

Even the most atheistic scientist doesn't know how the world got started, nor does anyone know what was there before the Big Bang. Just look at the incredible quality of our molecules: nucleic acid molecules that replicate so beautifully; phosphates that transfer energy; proteins, enzymes, that facilitate all sorts of metabolic processes . . . There is much that the scientist cannot explain.

—Ernst May, evolutionary biologist[1]

The essence of the living state is found in [even] very small organisms [and] evolutionary thinking further affects our thinking by suggesting the same basic principles of life exist in all living forms.

—James D. Watson, molecular biologist, et. al.[2]

Our universe was born, some astrophysicists say, out of a searing hot, amorphous mix of matter and radiation more than 15 billion years ago. In this scientific creation story, the cosmic birth throes took the form of a stupendous, generative explosion—the so-called Big Bang.

The Big Bang was utterly unlike any explosion that could have been experienced on earth. It rocked the entire expanse of the universe simultaneously. It instantly propelled all the minute particles in the primal cosmic center outward in every direction, sending them careening toward the farthest reaches of space and setting in motion an expanding universe that continues to swell today, billions of years later.

During the first one-hundredth of a second after this cataclysmic event, the density of the cosmos was beyond human comprehension—perhaps four billion times the density of water. At this point, the temperature of the universe is thought to have been nearly 200,000 million degrees Fahrenheit (a torrid 100 billion degrees Centigrade)—hotter by far than the infernal cores of the hottest stars in the heavens today.

At this time the Big Bang's flying, superheated shrapnel may have been so hot that it was a fluid mix of minute bits and pieces no larger than the tiny subatomic building blocks of atoms—electrons, positrons, and other so-called elementary particles. The physical "stuff" of this chaotic primordial cosmos had not yet cooled and condensed sufficiently to form the orderly, geometric molecular structures that we routinely encounter in matter today. Throughout this cosmic drama of matter and energy in motion, the primeval fireball of the Big Bang bathed the whole universe in bright light.

As the fierce fireworks continued, flinging debris to the far corners of space, its temperature began to subside. With this gradual cooling, the structures of physical substances crystallized, and the small subatomic particles of the vast cosmic soup began to coalesce into larger, more complex clumps of matter. As they did, the latent forces freed by the fusion of particles released prodigious quantities of nuclear energy. First protons and neutrons—and then a mere few hundred thousand years later, lightweight atoms such as hydrogen and helium—began to materialize out of the hot and previously atomless primeval brew. In time, portions of the great clouds of interstellar gas and dust that were still billowing outward in all directions slowly began to coalesce under the influence of increasingly powerful gravitational forces. These freshly formed condensations of matter continued to subdivide, creating vast three-dimensional archipelagos of stars, the embryos of future galaxies.

As these galactic dust swirls became increasingly seasoned with heavier atoms such as carbon, oxygen, iron, and silicon, one of them condensed into a single central star, encircled by a cottony disk of cooling cosmic debris. From this peripheral cloud-disk, again under the gentle urging of gravitational forces, emerged nine smaller gaseous whirlpools, each of them a proto-planet, each confined to its own separate orbital path within the concentric pattern of nine star-encircling rings.

Today, we refer to that pivotal star as the "sun," and the entire celestial ensemble of sun, nine orbiting satellite planets, and associate moons, comets, and other interstellar miscellany as our "solar system." The nearly five-billion-year-old planetary body that occupies the third orbital tier from the sun is, of course, none other than our own earthly abode.

In the beginning, Earth was utterly devoid of life. Its primordial atmosphere—an oxygenless mix mostly of hydrogen, methane, ammonia, and water vapor—would have been lethally toxic to most modern forms of life. But gradually, with the dispassionate patience of geological time, the Earth's initial sterility and relative inhospitality to life gave way to a quiet biological revolution. Within its great, sun-struck primeval seas, an assortment of subtle, spontaneous chemical transformations gradually occurred over enormous spans of time, giving rise to the first populations of primitive, bacterialike, self-replicating forms of life. These pioneering single-celled organisms eagerly feasted on the flotsam of energy-laden compounds adrift on the seas. With this bounteous energy subsidy, they grew, and with the aid of the crude self-replicating hereditary molecules, they left behind reasonable chemical facsimiles of themselves.

Life's emergence on Earth, however rudimentary and tentative at first, quickly set in motion the first throbbings of the vast "engine" of biological evolution. Evolution's endless environmental siftings of heritable biological differences within populations of living organisms resulted in the staggering diversity of species that share this planet with us today. Over spans of hundreds of millions of years, wave after wave of fresh biological innovation has washed up on the evolutionary shores of the biosphere. Among them, countless cases of evolutionary failure and success, from marine mollusks and shellfish to seed-bearing plants and backbone-stiffened creatures like fish, frogs, birds, bats, and human beings. During this process of evolutionary trial and error, every imaginable ecological niche—in the sea, on the land, in the air—was exploited for a time by one form of life or another: ocean bottom and estuarine bay; river canyon; fertile tropical plain; arctic shore; cloud-piercing mountain peak.

This still-unfolding evolutionary story of life is perhaps the single most eloquent, detailed, and compelling statement that Western societies possess of their fundamental, time-mediated interconnectedness with *all* forms of life on this planet. Each living species in our company is far more than simply some savvy evolutionary survivor. Each species represents the single, vibrant tip of one of the living branches of the towering evolutionary tree. The tree's trunk corresponds to the ancient ancestral unity of all living things—to their unequivocal biological kinship and their shared record of unbroken success within their respective evolutionary lineages. The tree's deep subterranean roots, which descend into the unknown past, are a reflection of the mysteries that surround life's first stirrings upon the sterile, primeval planet, a planet built of nothing but the Big Bang debris of simmering stardust, silently circling a newly wrought sun, out in the breathtaking black boundlessness of space.

∧∧∧∧∧∧∧∧∧∧∧∧∧∧∧∧∧∧∧∧∧∧∧∧

The Power of the Sun's Yellow Light[3]

COLOMBIA (NORTHWESTERN AMAZON):
Desana

We consider naive the early Darwinian view of "nature red in tooth and claw." Now we see ourselves as the products of cellular cooperation—of cells built up from other cells. Partnerships between cells once foreign and even enemies to each other are at the very root of our being.

—Lynn Margulis, evolutionary biologist[4]

Through the dense, humid, equatorial rain forests of eastern Colombia, the turbulent Papurí River courses with spectacular rapids and thundering waterfalls, as do the nearby tributaries of the northwestern Amazon River. Along their banks live a small population of Tukano Indians, known to anthropologists as the Desana. Numbering only about a thousand souls as recently as 1962, they are highly skilled hunters, fishermen, and horticulturalists who make their homes in large, rectangular, palm-thatched, multifamily dwellings known as *malocas*. They refer to themselves as *wirá-porá*—or sons of the wind.

In the Desana cosmos, the Creator of the Universe was *pagë abé*, the Sun, and Moon was his twin brother. In one origin story, the paternal Sun created the first men by plunging his phallic stick rattle deep into the Earth until it penetrated the womblike, yellow-green paradise of the lower world called

28

ahpikondiá, or the River of Milk. (Yajé Woman, the first female human being, would appear in a different setting some time later.) Then, holding the stick vertically so that it cast no shadow, he released droplets of supernatural sperm, which cascaded down it, inseminating the maternal Earth and bringing forth men. They exited the cosmic womb by climbing up the Sun's stick rattle, emerging at the Earth's surface as fully formed Desana men.

Through this act of creation, the Sun gave shape to the world *with the power of his yellow light and gave it life and stability.** This *stability* in nature, the Desana are eager to emphasize, is not merely a static seesaw state of balance. Rather, it is a dynamic state embodying a vast and continuous multiplicity of exchanges among all the components of the Sun's wondrous creation—not unlike what a contemporary ecologist might refer to as a "biological equilibrium."

According to the Desana, this inherent *stability* of the natural world is rooted in a vast web of reciprocal relationships that have always existed between all elements in nature. A reciprocity between the earth—with its myriad mountains and forests and rivers—and the first forms of life—the animals, the plants, the Desana people—exists in harmony with all of the rest of the universe. For as traditional Desana tell it, the *Sun planned his creation very well, and it was perfect.*

In its original form, say the Desana, the Sun was something far greater than the visible solar disk that we see passing across the sky today. This familiar "sun," however vital, is merely the original Sun's earthly stand-in, or representative. Today, by acting through this mundane "sun," *the Creator Sun exercises his power, giving his Creation light, heat, protection, and above all, fertility.*

The original Creator Sun was not simply *a word or thought,*

---

* Italicized words or passages denote direct quotations from Native sources or scholarly interpretations of them. In the original sources, Native words are encoded in a variety of specialized linguistic systems; here, for the sake of uniformity and readability, they have been simplified to their approximate English equivalents.

but a state of being. It was a primal and procreative light—yellow in color—from which all Creation flowed, without fixed purpose or plan. Thus, this Sun served as the original creative principle: it was earth-molder, breath-giver, and time-keeper of the endless cycles of nature.

This first Sun also gave the Desana the precious, immutable rules that were to help them form and maintain a healthy and proper relationship with the rest of the inhabitants of the teeming tropical rain forest. So elegant and complex was the Sun's "code of conduct" that it could not be transcribed into mere words in the Desana language; it could be described only through the medium of rich, evocative visual metaphors.

Seen from the paradisal netherworld *ahpikondiá*, our own familiar earth appears to be a sun-drenched, bloodred realm inhabited by men and animals. But it also takes on a second, more stunning form: it looks like an enormous, translucent spiderweb, fresh and glistening in the searing tropical sunlight. The intricate, earth-spanning canopy of interconnected silken threads that make up this fantastic "cosmic web" is, according to living Desana, *like the rules that men should live by* in this world. For ordinary human beings, they say, *are guided by these threads, seeking to live well, and the Sun sees them.*

ᴧᴧᴧᴧᴧᴧᴧᴧᴧᴧᴧᴧᴧᴧᴧᴧᴧᴧᴧᴧᴧ

Makers and Formers [5]

AMERICAN SOUTHWEST:
Hopi

The Creator and Creation cannot be separated.
The two of necessity become intimately interfused
and evolve together in a relation of mutual inter-
dependence. Thus, what destroys, degrades or
enhances one does the same to the other.
—Roger Sperry, Nobel Prize–winning
neurobiologist[6]

Pueblo creation stories reveal the awe, reverence, and sense of dynamic change Pueblo peoples perceive in the powers of nature, for they do not assign absolute roles to the gods and goddesses inhabiting their cosmos. In some Pueblo myths, for example, the creator, or "Thinking Woman," is female; in others it is male. In some, she dwells in the underworld, thinking everything—all life on earth—into existence. In others, Thinking Woman assumes the form of a sacred spider, the only living creature in the dim underworld, who spins and sings other beings into existence. In many Hopi stories, this feminine creator is known as Spider Grandmother.

The Hopi call the beginning goddess "Hard Beings Woman." While she lives in the heavenly world, where she owns the moon and the stars, she is of the Earth, and her son is the god of crops. She gives the Earth its solidity, its shape and its inhabitants. She created the first humans, but not by giving birth to them.

In the earliest mists of time, Hard Beings Woman made her abode in a kiva located in a solitary bluff in the West. It was the only piece of solid ground in existence. There was nothing else in the world but water and a few hard substances that came from corals and shells, which Hard Beings Woman fashioned into beads to adorn her body. Sun lived far to the East. But each night he entered Hard Beings Woman's kiva in the western sea and descended through a hatch into the underworld, to rise in the East again each dawn. In time, these two deities raised dry land in the waters around them, causing the seas to recede to the East and West. These waters became the oceans of the world, linked by a labyrinth of subterranean channels connecting them to the lakes and sacred springs of the earth.

On another visit to her kiva, Sun and Hard Beings Woman decided to create the first human beings. After feeding the Sun honey and other savory items, Hard Beings Woman removed a piece of cuticle from her finger and hid it under a blanket on her bed. From it emerged first a maiden and then a male youth.

In another creation story, the unformed earth was nothing but dense fog, rising slowly like steam. The great androgynous being A'wonawil'ona created clouds and the great waters of the world from his own breath. *He-She is the blue vault of the firmament. The breath clouds of the gods are tinted with the yellow of the north, the blue-green of the west, the red of the south, and the silver of the east of A'wonawil'ona; they are himself, as he is the air itself; and when the air takes on the form of a bird it is but a part of himself. Through the light, clouds, and air he becomes the essence and creator of vegetation.*

Hopi communities tell different tales of the emergence of the first human beings from the underworld where they had already existed, although not necessarily in their familiar earthly forms. The underworld is often conceived of as a rather unpleasant environment. Because it was the place where life first took form, it had become crowded and even contaminated with being. Unfinished creatures abounded, crawling over each other in filth and darkness. Some legends emphasize the chaos of subterranean human society—the feuding of men and women, their failure to faithfully observe sacred laws and offer grateful prayers.

In an Acoma Pueblo account of the creation of humans, the first two human beings born were female. At first, living in a subterranean realm devoid of light, these twin sisters could only feel each other as they gradually grew. Grandmother Spider nursed them and taught them their language, and eventually gave them each a basket filled with seeds and small images of each kind of animal that they were to help bring forth into the world.

Trees sprouted from the seeds that the sisters planted, but they grew very slowly in the darkness of the underworld. In time, one tree punched a hole through the surface of the earth, permitting in a few rays of sunlight to enter. The sisters then created Badger, who excavated an opening big enough for them to climb through. After they had crawled into the upper world, they created Locust to seal the opening behind them. Grandmother Spider then taught them prayers and songs, instructing them to express their reverence and gratitude to the Sun. After they had done this, they created all the living inhabitants of the world and also put in place mountains marking the four cardinal directions. A steaming mist impregnated one of the sisters, who subsequently gave birth to twin sons. The other sister adopted one of the boys, who grew up to become her husband. After many years, they gave birth to the Pueblo people.

In another creation story, the forces of nature again help the Pueblo people to emerge. Twin brothers dwelling in the dark underworld wondered if there was any light up above. *First, Cottonwood went up but could not see any sunlight. Then the cedar tried, but came back down. Then the spruce tree was going to try. But Spruce saw that he would need an opening. . . . So Woodpecker Boy flew up to the top of the spruce tree and began to peck at the ceiling . . . Eagle flew up to the top of Spruce tree and built a nest for Badger . . . As Badger worked upward,* spruce grew taller so Badger could more easily carry out his task of helping the people to reach the upper world inhabited by the Sun. The people thanked Spruce and told him that his branches would forever be used in Pueblo prayers.

In one story's poignant climax to the appearance of the First People in the upper realm of sunshine and beauty, humankind gradually works its way up from the underworld over the course of four ages and through stages in which *they could see each other . . . covered with dirt and with ashes. They were stained with spit and urine and they had green slime on their heads. Their hands and feet were webbed and they had tails and no mouths or exits. . . .* After they finally emerged into the sunlight of the upper world, they wept with joy at its beauty, even as they were compelled to cry out in the pain at the Sun's bright, searing light. *Their tears ran to the ground. Everywhere they were standing the sun's flowers (sunflowers and buttercups) sprang up from the tears caused by the sun. The people said, "Is this the world where we shall live?" "Yes, this is the last world. Here you see our father Sun."*

The excruciating sensitivity of the Hopi worldview to the inherent beauty and the fragility of the natural world is eloquently expressed in such tales. Through such luminous narratives of life's origin, the fates of human beings and other forms of life are revealed as inextricably interwoven, and, with their somber warnings that the world that we now inhabit is "the last world," we are reminded once again of the terrible tenuousness of life on this planet.

∿∿∿∿∿∿∿∿∿∿∿∿∿∿∿∿∿

In Distant Times It Is Said 7

ALASKAN INTERIOR:
Koyukon

The creative principle of the universe and its organization and intelligence is not an external principle but an internal one. All of the past that we can ever know is contained in the world at this instant.

—John Platt, biophysicist[8]

All things in this world, say the Koyukon Indians of subarctic Alaska, are connected by a common ancestry. Everything that exists on Earth—whether it be human beings, animals, or plants; rocks or rivers or snowflakes—shares a spiritual kinship arising from shared origins. Each entity is the expression of a timeless story that can be traced back to a primordial era that traditional Koyukon people know as *Kk'adonts'dnee*: literally, "In Distant Time It Is Said," or, more succinctly, simply "Distant Time."

According to Richard Nelson, an Alaskan anthropologist and author of the book *Make Prayers to the Raven*—a respected and lucid account of Native ecological perspectives—the Koyukon refer to themselves in their own native Athapaskan language as *Tleeyaga Hutanin*. Today they number no more than a few thousand souls, scattered among a dozen or so remote Alaskan villages in a region straddling the Arctic Circle west of Fairbanks that lies along the great Yukon River and its tributary the Koyukuk. Within the Koyukon cosmos, Distant Time represents nature's timeless substratum. This primal, creative epoch of life on Earth is the fertile, boundless, mythic soil in which *everything—all things human and natural*—in this world is ultimately rooted.

Distant Time is a dim but potent memory, illuminated largely by traditional stories and spiritual practices; it forever lies beyond precise measure or clear human understanding. It is a sacred era, a time of heroic adventure, earthly upheaval, and transformation on an enormous scale; a time of astronomical, geological, biological, and experiential metamorphosis that underlies and lends meaning to the recurring patterns of the natural world.

Into the primal order of the Distant Time, it is said, appeared Raven—creator-trickster extraordinaire—along with a host of other Koyukon spiritual figures. Raven acts as a principal creative force and culture-bringer in the Koyukon cosmos and in some sense seems to be the living embodiment of *all* human qualities, from wisdom and ingenuity to gluttony and wanton sexual desire. Like Coyote, the Great Hare, and other paleolithic trickster figures across North America, Raven is paradox incarnate, often ingeniously so. He is wise and foolish, compassionate and cruel, chaste and lecherous, potent and petty.

On a cosmic scale, the trickster embraces the very forces of chaos and mystery that modern science finds most frustratingly intangible and elusive. Yet these forces are as much a part of the cosmic whole as are its more readily measured aspects—ranging from hereditary DNA molecules to the spectral light emitted by a distant star—and they are as vital to our understanding. In the words of comparative mythologist Joseph Campbell, the Native trickster represents *the chaos principle, the principle of disorder, the force careless of taboos and shattering bounds. But from the point of view of the deeper realms of being from which the energies of life ultimately spring, this principle is not to be despised.*

35

During Koyukon Distant Time, the trickster Raven brought the gift of sunlight to the world. To do this, Raven transformed

himself into a tiny spruce needle so he could be swallowed by a
woman in whose house the missing Sun was hidden. She gave
birth to a baby boy and raised him. When he had grown strong
enough, the boy found the sun beneath a blanket and rolled it
out the door. Then he magically metamorphosed back into
Raven and, taking flight, transported the sun up into the sky,
bathing the Earth once more in radiant, life-generating light.

Raven and his heroic Distant Time companions served as
cosmic catalysts in an epoch of explosive creativity and
change. During this time the Earth's powerful original
inhabitants—extraordinary hybrid human-animal beings—
were somehow abruptly transformed *into animal and plant
beings, the species that inhabit Koyukon country today.*

That crucial transformation, according to the accounts of
living Koyukon elders, took place within the crucible of
a great, era-ending catastrophe: a world flood. Raven placed
representatives of each of the primal life-forms on a raft.
Through these heroics, he saved the humanoid plant and animal beings. By the time the waters of the great deluge had
subsided, however, the creatures no longer possessed their
original physical, social, and linguistic attributes. They had
been physically transformed into ordinary plants and animals.
Nonetheless, their *dreamlike metamorphoses left a residue of human qualities and personality traits in the north-woods animals.*

Knowledge embedded in Koyukon tales of the *In Distant
Times* epoch breathes life into their local subarctic landscape.
That landscape is climatically harsh, and dominated by blue
northern skies, coniferous forests, and, depending on the season, crystalline or cascading waters. Their knowledge lends
meaning to the local tapestry of forest and tundra, rivers and
muskeg. It reveals the underlying choreography of the seasonal movements and activities of caribou, moose, waterfowl,
salmon, and other precious game species that provide sustenance to their people. And it reveals the ultimate sources of
the growth and fertility of local plant species ranging from the
stunted stands of black and white spruce to lush, fruit-laden
thickets of bog blueberry, cranberry, and cloudberry.

Because all things on Earth harbor a divine ember of *Distant Time,* it is virtually impossible for traditional Koyukons not to feel somehow spiritually connected to everything in their natural surroundings. From this perspective, everything in the natural world—fish, flesh, or flower; stone, star, or rain shower—continuously bear witness to a shared past in its own way.

In Richard Nelson's eloquent appraisal, traditional Koyukon people live in a natural world that *watches, in a forest of eyes,* and, as they travel across the familiar landscape, they are never truly alone. *The surroundings are aware, sensate, personified. They feel. They can be offended. And they must, at every moment, be treated with proper respect.* From their point of view, everything in the natural world is endowed with *a special kind of life, something unknown to contemporary Euro-Americans, something powerful.*

Saya, the First Hunter[9]

NORTHEASTERN BRITISH COLUMBIA:
Dunne-za (Beaver)

It is a century now since Darwin gave us the first glimpse of the origin of species. We know now what was unknown to all the preceding caravan of generations: that men are only fellow-voyagers with other creatures in the odyssey of evolution. This new knowledge should have given us, by this time, a sense of kinship with fellow-creatures; a wish to live and let live; a sense of wonder over the magnitude and duration of the biotic enterprise.

—Aldo Leopold, ecologist[10]

Charley Yahey is a modern Dreamer among the Dunne-za, an Athapaskan-speaking hunting people of the western Canadian subarctic. In the beginning, according to a creation story he relates, all that existed in the world was a vast expanse of water; there was no land. The Creator marked a spot on the surface of the primordial water and called upon the water-dwelling creatures of the world to plunge deep below to bring to the surface a clump of bottom silt. This clump was to be placed upon the designated cosmic center to become the source from which future landscapes were generated.

It soon became apparent that none of the water creatures could physically carry out this challenging task: The dark, abyssal waters were far too deep. But finally Muskrat tried, and he succeeded in retrieving a small quantity of muck from the bottom. When he surfaced, he deposited his precious cargo upon the cosmic center that the Creator had marked, saying simply, "You are going to grow." From this innocuous clod of earth, the surface world *started to grow and kept on growing every year like that.* In this way, through a series of creative acts and agents, the world can be said to have grown *from an idea in the mind of the Creator* into the bounteous physical realm that is so intimately familiar to the Dunne-za people.

In that boundless mythic time (the very same *time out of time* that the Dunne-za revisit in their youth during empowering personal encounters with wild animals of the forest during initiations, or vision quests), Muskrat's earth-diving heroics were followed by countless other acts of creation, catalyzed by a host of other creative forces, processes, and beings within the Dunne-za cosmos. Among them was the appearance of human beings, as well as a number of large and fearsome *giant animals*. Relationships between humans and animals during this period were not the same as they are today. In fact, the roles of hunter and hunted were completely reversed: the *giant animals* assumed the role of hungry hunters, and people were their prey.

Into this perilous, primordial scene stepped Saya, the Dunne-za culture hero. He would prove to be *the first person to follow the trails of animals, the first person to "know something," the first hunter.* Called Swan in his youth, he grew to be a potent and creative figure who, through the accumulation of sacred knowledge, helped shape the very order of the natural world.

Saya boldly stalked the *giant animals* that had been hunting and killing human beings. After slaying one particularly enormous beast, he scattered the remnants of its flesh in all directions. As he did this, he called out the names of the various wild animals that populate traditional Dunne-za lands to this day—among them weasels and wolverines, martens and cougars and lynx—thereby bringing them into being.

Those *giant animals* that he did not slay, he pursued, chasing them relentlessly until, in their desperation, they sought refuge from Saya under the earth's uppermost crust. There the great beasts rested. Their huge, quiescent bodies lay just beneath the surface of the earth, wrinkling it here and there like a blanket, with characteristic hills and valleys and mountains. Because of the subterranean flight of these *giant animals* from the First Hunter, *every contour of the country the Dunne-za know reveals the backs of the giant animals lying beneath the surface,* and all the curves of Dunne-za trails correspond *to the shapes of the giant animals lurking below.*

Today the earth itself—its rugged texture, the interlaced natural histories of its rich flora and fauna, its fragile clusters of human communities—continues to be the final repository of Dunne-za meaning, holding memories of the wondrous mythic time of world creation and the establishment of the enduring patterns of nature and of human experience.

The country, and people's actions in relation to it, are merely a surface that covers over mythic time. The time of myth and vision continues to be literally an underlying force of nature. Beneath the appearance of everyday reality, the stories of Saya and the giant animals he sent beneath the earth are still being enacted.

Talaiden: A Sacred Law Against Laughing at Animals[11]

MALAYSIA:
Chewong

*The evolutionary unity of humans with all other
organisms is the cardinal message of Darwin's
revolution for nature's most arrogant species.*
— Stephen Jay Gould, evolutionary
biologist[12]

The Chewong people are one of the numerous Orang Asli, or
"original peoples," who have long inhabited the now-
dwindling but biologically rich tropical rainforest ecosystems
of peninsular Malaysia. In their world, *all* species of animal
inherently deserve profound human respect. Today, the very
existence of the Chewong, like that of so many other Orang
Asli, is imperiled by the modern industrial non-Native society
that surrounds and threatens to engulf them. The beleaguered
Chewong's traditional land base is withering rapidly under the
pressures of logging and encroaching urban populations, and
their children are often malnourished. They numbered no
more than 131 in 1979. Nonetheless, the power of some of
their most cherished traditional values regarding human responsibility for the natural world remains undiminished.

Nowhere is this more evident than in the ancient Chewong
prohibition against ridiculing animals, as embodied in the sacred laws known collectively in the Chewong language as
talaiden. One of the major tenets of *talaiden*, concerned specifi-
cally with proper human attitudes toward other animal species, mandates that *no animal whatsoever may be teased or
laughed at.*

40 If a group of young children in a Chewong village playfully
taunt a captive bird or snake—or even if they are behaving too

boisterously in the vicinity of animal flesh that is being prepared, cooked, or eaten—an adult member of the community
is likely to step forward, scold them sternly, and insist that
they stop it at once. *"Talaiden!"* the scolder might hiss to the
careless Chewong children. *"The snake will gobble you up!"*

The ravenous snake's authority is invoked as a possible
source of severe punishment for unthinking acts offensive to
the spirits of wild animals, captive or slain. But it is no ordinary
reptile—it is none other than Talòden asal, the Original Snake,
as every traditional Chewong child learns early in his or her
life. Talòden asal, a huge, coiled, primordial serpent, lives in
the dim watery depths of the underworld beneath the familiar
hot, humid, and sun-drenched terrestrial realm of everyday
forest life known to the Chewong simply as Earth Seven.

The Original Snake has a dual manifestation, according to
the Chewong: It embodies both a reptilian and a feminine
principle. Talòden asal is a supernatural woman in snake form,
of a strength and size so breathtaking that, with no more than
the idle twitch of her muscular body, she can unleash catastrophic, life-threatening natural disasters. These she metes
out as punishment to human beings whom, in her silent omni-
science, she senses have violated the sanctity of any of the all-
encompassing diversity of animal species under her care.

The wrathful Talòden asal might retaliate by releasing vol-
leys of deafening thunder, white-hot lightning, and shrieking
wind as part of a fierce tropical rainstorm. She thereby makes
the towering but shallow-rooted trees near an offending
Chewong community tremble and bow until they crash to the
rain-drenched forest floor with the impact of a small explosion. Or she might cause inky waters from the vast reservoirs
in the underworld to seep ominously upward and threaten a
world flood, should impudent human infractions against the
well-being of rainforest fauna persist.

In spite of her awesome destructive powers, however, Talòden asal is *not* viewed by the traditional Chewong as an
embodiment of evil or a malevolent force of nature. They

seem to look upon her, rather, as a reflection of the complexity, multidimensionality, and mystery that characterize the natural world itself.

Like Tanko, her masculine counterpart and husband who dwells high in the cloud-flecked skies over Earth Seven, Talòden asal is steeped in the same powers and paradoxes that the Chewong encounter in nature. In fact, Tanko's behavior, like hers, sometimes suggests an unapologetic alloy of comedy and tragedy, hilarity and grief. In myth, he occasionally displays mirth at the endless personal foibles and predicaments of the mortal human beings who act out their petty lives in Earth Seven; along with his stinging lightning bolts, he issues raucous thunderclaps of laughter.

In the words of Signe Howell, the only Western anthropologist who has lived long and intimately in recent years with the Chewong, both Talòden asal and Tanko can be seen among other things as *abstract symbols of nature,* in all its stupendous, creative, and ultimately utterly indescribable complexity.

Openly laughing at or teasing an animal may be the most blatant human violation of the Chewong's *talaiden.* But more subtle transgressions against animals are also forbidden, including using ridiculous or demeaning images of animals for human entertainment, as most Western societies so routinely do. If the Chewong traveled abroad, they might well see worrisome breaches of *talaiden* in Hollywood's long legacy of buffoonish cartoon creatures, ranging from a perpetually adolescent song-and-dance mouse named Mickey to strange, semiliterate, karate-kicking, masked Ninja turtles born of subterranean urban toxic waste dumps. They might justifiably invoke *talaiden* rules upon seeing Ringling Brothers circus bears astride bicycles or wide-eyed monkeys dressed up in clownish human attire; stylishly coiffed pet poodles or overcoddled Siamese cats draped with sparkling rhinestone collars and destined to be buried in monumental cemeteries. To Chewong sensibilities, each of these would seem to represent a bonafide case, however unconscious, of direct human affront to the inherent dignity of a fellow animal.

Another of the ancient Chewong *talaiden* says that a human being diminishes another species by treating it as if it were a mere toy. A Chewong legend recorded by Howell reveals the precise nature and consequences of such transgressions.

A Chewong man and his fiancée happened to catch a live squirrel while they were walking in the tropical rain forest. Perhaps because they were young and still childless, they unthinkingly decided to bring the captive animal home to their village, where they would keep it as a cherished household pet.

Momentarily forgetting their fundamental obligation to honor any animal they might encounter in the forest, the young couple eagerly placed the squirrel in a string hammock, woven to cradle a human infant, that hung expectantly from the ceiling of their thatched hut. Then—treating the terrified creature almost as if it were the unborn human baby of their shared dreams—they playfully rocked it back and forth, murmuring all the while the same soothing Chewong words that they intended to sing someday soon for their offspring.

Simply by *pretending* that their helpless captive was human, they had committed a grievous offense against the squirrel and its multitudinous kind. They had, in effect, denied the animal its fundamental right to its own natural identity and its place in the cosmos. However gently, they had broken one of the rules of *talaiden*.

The guardian of all animals was quick to respond. Talòden asal, the all-knowing Original Snake, was fully aware of their flagrant breach of *talaiden* the very instant it occurred. She awakened with a start from her eternal subterranean slumber and went into a fury at the plight of the single, tiny squirrel. Twisting her long, multihued body into a silent, simmering coil of rage, she unleashed a terrible storm, like a spear, into the Chewong village above her. Relentless winds, torrential downpours, and a rising tide of groundwater converged on the young couple's hut, sweeping it from the face of the earth as if it were nothing more than a speck of dust. In a final act of horror, the fearsome head of the great serpent reared up from the cavernous underworld, gripped the two offending Chewong viciously in her gaping jaws, and gobbled them up in a single predatory gulp.

But Talòden asal did not simply devour their flesh and bones, as she might some ordinary prey. She obliterated their very existence for all time. As she swallowed them, she deliberately extinguished the fragile flame of vitality that flickers in and animates every human being and, equally, *all* life-forms on Earth Seven, as it has done since the primordial times of creation, when all living beings possessed the power of speech. By so righteously snuffing out the precious *ruwai,* or souls, of the young Chewong, she ensured that they would not glow on in realms beyond Earth Seven after death—as they would have in the absence of so grave an offense against nature.

What is the message of this Chewong tale? According to Howell, its meaning may well be at once exceedingly simple and ecologically profound. The implication is, she says, that *different species of animals* [including Homo sapiens] *must be kept separate according to their characteristics. Each has its own role to play, and proper behavior on the part of humans vis-à-vis them must be observed.*

Another intriguing Chewong belief, a corollary to this maxim, has obvious potential application to the practices of modern biotechnology and genetic engineering in which genes from one species are casually swapped for those of evolutionarily distant others. Based on hundreds of generations of accumulated experience in tropical rainforest ecosystems, the contemporary Chewong believe that *any* human attempt to foster unnatural matings between distinct animal species violates *talaiden,* including the mere idea of somehow "marrying" creatures as patently distinct as a cat and a dog. In the traditional Chewong cosmos, all species—not just Homo sapiens—are imbued with uniqueness, an identity, and an inviolability that renders them equally sacred in their membership in the natural world. Human beings have a solemn duty to recognize that, in Howell's simple but poignant phrase, the very *boundaries between classes of beings must be upheld.*

Dreaming Laws[13]

NORTHERN TERRITORY, AUSTRALIA:
Yarralin Community

*God is not some kind of watchmaker, as the old
apologists mechanically wished us to suppose.
They were as deceived as all the other mecha-
nists, from not looking closely enough at the
flowers of the field. The factory that makes the
parts of a flower is inside, and is not a factory but
a development. God is more like a chromosome,
a thought, than a watchmaker.*

—John Platt, biophysicist[14]

A small Australian Aboriginal community is based at the settlement called Yarralin, located in the valley of the great Victoria River, which meanders north through the Northern Territory toward the blue waters of the Timor Sea. Elders of that
community know that the legacy and the lessons of the mythical time of the world's creation are firmly etched into the living
texture of the local landscape.

The sprawling sand-strewn deserts, the tree-pocked savannah grasslands (yellowed under a scorching tropical sun), and
the scrub woodlands that cover the Victoria River valley are no
mere landscape. This orderly mosaic is a sacred map. Within
the often startling contours of its weathered sandstone mesas,
hillocks, and basalt and limestone plains—in the serene colors
of its rust-red patches of soil, its green-sheathed gum trees,
and its electric blue skies—is a living record of the primordial
origins of the earth and all its life-forms, known simply as the
Dreaming, or Dreamtime.*

---

* We retain the terms *Dreamtime* and *Dreaming* used in the original sources
because they are widely employed in popular and anthropological literature.
Some Australian scholars argue, however, that these bear a connotation of dreamlike "remove from reality" and therefore prefer original Aboriginal words or the

According to members of the Aboriginal community at Yarralin, *the earth is female: she gave birth to all the original creative beings;* she is *the initial mother and, by virtue of being original, is now and forever the mother of everything.*

The Yarralin people (the Aboriginal residents of the settlement at Yarralin, who may speak any of several different Aboriginal languages in the area) believe that the earth's surface is an enduring physical record of this fundamental truth. As moist and pliable as clay in its Dreamtime infancy, the land today retains for them the living geological impressions of the great mythic actors and creative acts of the transformative era.

In their stories, the colossal adventures and interactions of these original figures wreaked such geologic havoc upon the young earth's crust that their spoor populated the earth's surface with artful patterns of vegetation and wildlife. In certain womblike caves, springs, and other particularly potent places, they quickened it with a lasting power to replenish these precious species. In the Dreaming—that timeless epoch of creativity that gave form to the diversity of life, set in motion nature's cycles, and left its enduring imprint upon the earth's crust—all species,including kindred humans, were subtly entwined within a transcendent web of meaning that renders eternally sacred the processes, places, and personages of the natural world.

In this way, the land in its entirety—its physical topography, its seasonal changes, its hardy flora and fauna—has been left as a *kind of logos or principle of order* governing the relationships between Aborigines and the rest of the natural world, as Australian anthropologist W. Stanner puts it. And in the words of Deborah Bird Rose, an American ethnographer who has lived intimately with Yarralin people and sensitively chronicled some of their perspectives on nature, the Dreaming itself—its boundless mythical time frame, its clever metamorphic animal heroes, its monumental acts of creation, its

more neutral term *Creation Time.* We will use the latter term interchangeably with *Dreamtime* and *Dreaming* to make clear our intention to convey a sense of this potent Aboriginal idea about the earth's origins rather than to judge it.

deeply embedded code of human conduct in nature—is an enduring *model for, and celebration of, life as it is lived in the present and the source which makes possible all maps and celebrations—life in its variety, particularity, and fecundity.*

The Dreaming's inherent ethos regarding the proper relationship between human beings and other species can be roughly distilled down to four basic Laws, suggests Rose. In her soon-to-be-published book *Dingo Makes Us Human,* based on her research, she offers her interpretation of these transcendent rules.

❖ Balance: *A system cannot be life enhancing if it is out of kilter, and each part shares in the responsibility of sustaining itself and balancing others.*
❖ Response: *Communication is reciprocal. There is here a moral obligation: to learn to understand, to pay attention, and to respond.*
❖ Symmetry: *In opposing and balancing each other, parts must be equivalent because the purpose is not to "win" or to dominate, but to block, thereby producing further balance.*
❖ Autonomy: *No species, no group, or country is "boss" for another; each adheres to its own Law. Authority and dependence are necessary within parts, but not between parts.*

Within the traditional cosmos of the Yarralin community, the ancient roots of the creative Dreaming epoch grow fresh green shoots and tendrils that intricately entwine and encounter every thought, feeling, and action in the present. Its ancient Laws remain timeless, eternally binding human beings to live in harmony with and respect for other species.

In this context, the Yarralin people view Europeans, who for more than a century have ravaged and displaced them and other Aboriginal communities in the Victoria River region, as tragically out of synchrony with Aboriginal Dreaming Laws. In their cultural detachment from the true dynamics of life's origins and the fundamental burdens and boundlessness of time, these arrogant intruders are hopelessly confused. *Not knowing what to remember and what to forget, they follow dead laws, fail to recognize living ones, and in their power and denial promote death.*

Yarralin people themselves, who have lived in accordance with their Dreaming Laws for tens of thousands of years on the Australian continent, insist that they see very clearly their own role in the universe, a universe that often strikes non-Aboriginal people as disturbingly vast, inhospitable, and even dangerous, capable of dwarfing frail human existence. Embodied in the Dreaming Laws, theirs is a role of perpetual human protection, maintenance, and renewal of the entire natural world and respectful dialogue with its kindred membership. Yarralin people firmly believe, suggests Rose, that the Dreaming fuses past and present, creation and contemporary life, thereby imposing eternal moral obligations upon them collectively. They constantly remind themselves: *All that preceded us and all that comes after depend on us. What we do matters so powerfully that to evade our responsibilities is to call down chaos.*

∧∧∧∧∧∧∧∧∧∧∧∧∧∧∧∧∧∧∧∧∧∧∧∧∧∧

Life Goes on Without End[15]

NORTH AMERICAN ARCTIC:
Barren Grounds Inuit

The past few years have made us aware as we have never been before of the depth of kinship among all living organisms. . . . So all life is akin, and our kinship is much closer than we had ever imagined.

—George Wald, Nobel Prize–winning
biologist[16]

The Inuit live upon the vast expanse of the windswept, treeless tundra of north-central Canada, nature's backdrop for the great caribou migrations upon which they traditionally have relied. Especially during the long dark months of the Arctic winter, they lift their eyes to the star-studded sky dome overhead. The heavens high above, they say, are the sacred abode of a mighty spirit. The *anatkut* (wise ones) say that it is a woman. To this place in the skies and to this potent feminine spirit, the souls of all who die are conveyed.

To these Arctic peoples, the soul embodies the very essence of each form of life. They envision the soul as a tiny being, a minute version of the creature that it animates and transforms. Appropriately, they believe that the soul is located in *a bubble of air in the groin,* the same general anatomical area to which the modern biologist assigns the gene-laden germ cells, egg and sperm, bristling with DNA-encoded instruction for assembling a new life. Thus, the soul of a human being is a tiny human being, the soul of a caribou a tiny caribou, and that of a seal is a tiny seal.

At death, the soul is not extinguished. It lives on to surface again in another organism, investing it with a sacred spark of vitality and consciousness. One story from this northern region describes the meandering path that one wandering human soul took after its mother treated it disrespectfully at birth. First it was reincarnated in a dog, then in a seal, a wolf, a caribou, a walrus, and finally, perhaps out of nostalgia, once again in a seal.

But this time the seal decided to sacrifice itself willingly to a hunter, whose wife happened to be barren. As she flayed the seal's lifeless carcass, its wandering soul passed into her body, and she became pregnant at last. In time, she gave birth to a healthy boy, who became a hunter and was very skilled, partly because of the wisdom his soul had accumulated during the course of its challenging, interspecies journey.

Following death, souls lodge temporarily in the heavenly female spirit's lofty dwelling place. Here they undergo a profound transformation: *the souls of the dead are reborn,* and are subsequently *brought down to the earth again by the moon.* The Barren Grounds Inuit know that the moon is hard at work helping to carry out this task when its luminous face disappears for a time from the night sky.

But the skyward passage of souls is not yet complete. Once

they have been thus revitalized by *the woman up there* and returned to the familiar tundra lands whence they came, they are destined to follow countless possible paths. *Some become human beings once more, others become animals, all manner of beasts.*

And so life goes on without end.

3

Mother Earth

Nature as a Living System

After the sun's energy is captured by the green plants, it flows through chains of organisms dendritically, like blood spreading from the arteries into networks of microscopic capillaries. It is in such capillaries, in the life cycles of thousands of individual species, that life's important work is done. Thus nothing in the whole system makes sense until the natural history of the constituent species becomes known. The study of every kind of organism matters, everywhere in the world.

—Howard T. Odum, systems ecologist[1]

At its heart, modern ecology is a continuation of the ancient human quest for a deeper understanding of the often invisible and mysterious web of *relationships* that connect living things to one another and to their surroundings. Today's infant science of nature's patterns and relations has scarcely begun to unveil the tangles of bonds that exist between the species, forces, and materials of the natural world. But to the extent that it has begun to illuminate them, it continues to reveal a central biological truth: The earth's fragile, enveloping film of life and life-supporting air, water, and soil is a single ecological whole, or biosphere.

While the biosphere is an integrated unit of ecological structure and function, it is also a mosaic of smaller, subtly interconnected spatial subunits of biological interdependency known as "ecosystems." Each ecosystem is a localized cluster of ecological interactions between the members of a characteristic community of animals, plants, microbes, and their surroundings.

Because ecosystems are human constructs to which nature is blind, their boundaries are often mapped rather arbitrarily; depending on a scientist-cartographer's research interests, they can be drawn to a wide range of scales. An ecosystem can be as conveniently compact as a transient, anemone-carpeted tide pool along British Columbia's rocky Pacific coast. Or it can be as visually spacious as the sprawling savannah grasslands of eastern Africa, or the seemingly endless stands of thick tropical rain forest that flourish in the fragile Amazonian heartlands of South America. Or it can be the entire biosphere itself.

Embedded within the thin curvature of the great planetary biosphere (and within each of its constituent aquatic, marine, and terrestrial ecosystems) lies an elaborate hidden circuitry, through which pass vital flows of energy and matter. This labyrinthine, invisible network gives an ecosystem its structural and functional integrity. It shapes it, fuels it, and grants it, at least for a time, a measure of continuity.

The biosphere's elusive *energy* pathways commence, of course, with the sun. Although that familiar star—a yellow dwarf—lies some 93 million miles away, it remains closer than any other to our orbiting earth. The sun's blazing interior, a nuclear furnace, emits huge quantities of heat and light energy, only a fraction of which ever reaches our distant planet. After piercing the earth's atmosphere, a tiny portion of this incoming shower of solar radiation manages to impinge on living chlorophyll-bearing cells—in rafts of marine algae, in swaying grasses, in the rustling green leaves of a tree.

Here sun rays are biologically transformed, through an ancient assembly line of linked biochemical processes collectively called photosynthesis, into minute stores of chemical energy locked within the very structure of the living green plant. When a plant is devoured by a herbivorous organism, that botanical store of converted solar energy stokes the metabolic fires of the plant-eater and enters new repositories within that animal's own bodily structures. A similar process takes place when the plant-eater is consumed by a flesh-eater, whose body in turn burns and caches, for a time, this precious quota of food energy. This process continues to the next ravenous creature in nature's long, often overlapping food lines, until eventually, the star's entire initial gift of radiant sunlight has dissipated into the environment in the form of randomly rattling atoms and molecules that we call heat. During its unidirectional cascade through the living systems of earth, this same energy ultimately fuels the vital activities of the entire community of organisms within that ecosystem. It grants an energy-expensive structural order and integrity to the ecosystem as a whole, as well as to the jewellike biochemical and structural order of the organisms that are its living parts.

In sharp contrast to the meandering linear, one-way currents of sun-generated energy in ecosystems are the often hidden *material* pathways of an ecosystem. Viewed from afar and over vast spans of time, these pathways are gracefully circular, if meandering. Along them, the chemical substances upon which living plant, animal, and microbial cells depend are continuously recycled. Great, geologically patient gyres of atoms, molecules, and minerals circulate both locally and globally within the vast arena of the biosphere. Over time, these huge planetary currents, downdrafts, and upwellings of carbon, oxygen, nitrogen, phosphorous, and countless other life-sustaining substances within the earth's atmosphere, waters, and crust endlessly resupply the seemingly insatiable material needs of ecosystems.

Both kinds of underlying circuits—energetic and material—are absolutely central to the relationships among organisms and their surroundings (living and nonliving). Collectively, the biosphere's life-driven torrents of energy and matter connect the earth's incredible diversity of life-forms to the land-, air-, and seascapes that support them—thereby forging a sprawling patchwork of populations and communities into an integrated biospheric whole. In fact, so exquisitely orchestrated is this global system of flowing energy and matter that the biosphere as a whole seems at times to have the self-perpetuating qualities that we normally associate only with intact living organisms. The entire earth, with its extraordinary capacity (within limits) to regulate and maintain its own global ecological balance, acts as if it were a single, great "superorganism" of planetary proportions.

Most scientifically trained observers insist on describing this global self-regulating ecological system strictly in the scientific vernacular of their profession, calling it simply the "biosphere," or in the Russian scientist Vladmir Vernadsky's evocative phrase, the earth's "envelope of life." And they tend to view its exquisite self-regulating tendencies as merely a manifestation of the system's many machinelike feedback mechanisms, referred to collectively as "homeostasis."

But others are increasingly more inclined to view it in a more poetic light. After years of study, some scientists, such as the British chemist James Lovelock, have opted to openly express their awe and reverence for this *complex entity involving the Earth's biosphere, atmosphere, oceans, and soil* and its *cybernetic system which seeks an optimal physical and chemical environment for life*. In his writings, Lovelock has lovingly christened this wondrous lifelike biosphere system Gaia, *this total planetary being*, in honor of the earth goddess of Greek myth.[2]

For their part, Native elders the world over continue to address the very *same* planetary ecological system—or any of the transcendent aspects or spiritual dimensions they perceive with it—with names that convey the same sort of undisguised love, respect, and awe at its workings. In fact, many openly embrace it, as their people have often seemingly done for many centuries, as their own honored bloodkin: their living, nurturing, reciprocally affectionate Mother Earth. When they pause reverently to address this spiritual and ecological totality in ceremonial prayer or song, the words of one of their familiar salutations—"All my relations!"—would not seem entirely out of place coming from the lips of an ecstatic systems ecologist strolling through an Amazonian tropical rain forest teeming with interacting species.

The Building Blocks of the Universe[3]

COLOMBIA (NORTHWESTERN AMAZON):
Desana

The statement that the earth is our mother is more than a sentimental platitude: we are shaped by the earth. The characteristics of the environment in which we develop condition our biological and mental being and the quality of our life. Even

were it only for selfish reasons, therefore, we
must maintain variety and harmony in nature.
—René Dubos, microbiologist[4]

The universe, say the Desana, is made up of four basic elements: land, water, air, and energy. These four ingredients are ordered and arrayed in an infinite number of combinations and constitute the essential ingredients of the entire cosmos and of the life-forms—including human beings—that animate it.

The earth itself is fashioned from land and water. Land—the expansive, flat, mountainless floodplain of tropical vegetation—is said to be imbued with a "masculine" or "giving" character. Water—the labyrinthine network of slow-moving, anacondalike rivers, punctuated here and there with thunderous, spiritually potent rapids, pools, and falls—tends to have a "feminine" or "receiving" character.

This is more than a superficial "sexualization" of nature. It is a reflection, in the minds of the Desana, of a profound underlying order in the world composed of *opposing but complementary elements*. Thus, a forest, intrinsically masculine, is locked in a reciprocal embrace with the river, feminine in its flows, that courses through it. The complementary exchange between these two opposing elements—forest and river—spawns countless shifting and subtle interactions, creations, and obligations within the natural world, of which humankind is an integral part.

Air, the third sacred element, is devoid of either male or female sexuality. Spiritually neuter, its primary role is to expand to fill the space that lies between *this world and the supernatural world, between the biosphere and the exosphere*. In so doing, it serves as a vital medium of communication between these realms.

Energy, the fourth and final element, represents a generous gift from the Sun to the world. It fuels the eternal continuity of life on earth by sustaining all the processes of fertility and reproduction in nature. At the same time, energy spins the seasons. It rotates the stars, stimulates seasonal surplus and scarcity in the local food resources upon which the Desana depend, and subtly shapes and influences countless other rhythmic processes within the vibrant, living Amazonian rain forest. In the end, say the ecologically sophisticated Desana, the Sun's energy *makes women conceive and give birth, makes the animals reproduce and the plants grow and causes the fruit to ripen.*

ᗯᗯᗯᗯᗯᗯᗯᗯᗯᗯᗯᗯᗯᗯ

The Path of Our Elder the Sun [5]

NEW MEXICO:
Tewa (Eastern Pueblo)

Without the decay of the Universe there could have been no Sun, and without the superabundant consumption of its energy store the Sun could never have provided the light that let us be.

—James Lovelock, chemist[6]

It is late December, and the hours of brilliant, blue-skied desert sunlight are waning. Each morning and evening the Winter Chief of San Juan Pueblo, whose sacred duty it is *to lead and care for the people during the winter,* takes note of the precise points where the path of the sun's incandescent disk intersects with the mountains to the east and west.

This is no idle activity. As soon as his practiced eye tells him that the seasonal drift of the sun's daily journey has almost reached its southernmost limit, the Winter Chief makes a most important announcement. He is a living descendant of the first generation of spiritually initiated Made People, who ascended into the world from the dim subterranean place called Sipofene, beneath Sandy Place Lake. He will proclaim that it is time once again for the Tewa to honor the winter solstice and time to make preparations for the new solar year.

The Winter Chief's message is transmitted to the people of San Juan Pueblo by designated guardians of the community known as the Towa é. The Towa é are also living descendants of the first generation of Made People. They trace their proud ancestry to the twelve brothers whom the original Corn Mothers—*the first mothers of all the Tewa*—sent up from the depths of Sipofene to *watch over the people.* Following the Winter Chief's command, the Towa é instruct the people of San Juan Pueblo to ready themselves for the final flurry of spiritual activities, the last in an annual cycle of nine spiritual *works,* known as the Days of the Sun.

For the next two days, routine activities in San Juan virtually come to a halt. Every household in the community is expected to carry out an assortment of traditional duties as its contribution to the coming celebration. They prepare feasts; sweep clean their mud-walled homes; pay debts; bathe young children—all in anticipation of the impending conclusion to the yearlong, cyclic journey of the respected figure of *our elder the Sun.*

In the Tewa worldview, which is, in essence, like all worldviews, a system of symbols designed to transform the awesome physical dimensions of the cosmos into experiential ones, the Sun is a beloved humanoid figure, *clothed in white deerskin and ornamented with many fine beads,* who dwells with his wife in a house to the east. As the sun and moon deities periodically journey from the eastern to the western horizon along *trails which run above the great waters of the sky,* these celestial bodies *see and know as do Indians here on earth.* Upon reaching the western horizon and setting, they descend through an aperture in a lake to the underworld. Then, after traveling all night toward the east, they reemerge through another lake and *start on their trails again.*

The residents of San Juan Pueblo begin the Days of the Sun with a four-day-long period of quiet reverence in honor of the ancient all-knowing Sun. For most, it is a potent time, filled with feelings of hope and foreboding. During these four days, say the Tewa, the travel-weary winter Sun sets so low in the evening horizon that it enters the primal netherworld Sipofene, far to the north beneath the sacred waters of Sandy Place Lake.

What follows is the Sun's sacred year-end rendezvous with his fellow elders—powerful supernatural figures who continue to live in moist, shadowy Sipofene, deep beneath the sacred lake. The Sun talks to the gathering in Sipofene, reminiscing about the significant events that have taken place among the Tewa over the past year. He unerringly recounts births and deaths; loves won and lost; moments of bitter tragedy and of stupendous joy. And he reminisces about other memorable things that have happened in the lives of the people of San Juan in the hard, dry, sun-splashed world high above Sipofene.

The Sun also indulges in a few dark prophecies. Even though the new year has not yet begun, the Sun already knows exactly what fate awaits each living creature in the upper world—where, even now, the Tewa are earnestly praying. In his wisdom, he foresees every death that will occur in the yearlong journey he is about to begin across the New Mexican skies. Bird or mammal, insect or human being—the death of each living being is visible to *our elder the Sun,* long before it ever takes place.

At this sacred moment, perhaps to lessen the terrible burden of his knowledge, the Sun pauses to offer the Tewa a warning of what lies ahead for them. During his four-day sojourn in Sipofene, he carefully places a distinctive marking, a sign, on each earthly creature that is destined to die. He might painlessly cut a slice out of the ears of the deer, rabbit, and other game animals whose destiny it is to be slain in the coming year. He might pluck a number of feathers from the birds doomed to be shot from local skies. In the months ahead, when Tewa hunters discover that the animal prey they have killed have slits, still crimson with freshly drawn blood, in their ears—or that slain birds are conspicuously missing a few feathers—they will feel reassured once again that all is well with the world. To the Tewa, this is vivid confirmation of the

Sun's enormous generosity toward the earth's people. It is concrete *proof that the animals were marked for their taking.*

And what of the Tewa themselves? How will they fare in the year ahead at the hands of the life-giving Sun? The Sun sometimes provides subtle signs to those people destined to perish in the year ahead, but not always as visibly as he does with animals. So the Tewa, keenly aware of their fundamental dependency upon the Sun's annual passage, devote considerable effort to honoring the human-solar relationship, thereby enhancing their prospects for long life.

During the four perilous days of solar transition, each household in San Juan Pueblo shares in a period of rest and spiritual retreat within their home as an expression of collective awe and respect for the Sun. To enhance their prospects for longevity, they carefully dab sticky resin, harvested from pine trees, on their foreheads, armpits, and on all joints. At each of these strategic anatomical sites, the natural adhesive serves as a symbol of their physical attachment and spiritual union with the ancient figure of the Sun. During this sacred time of solar devotion, villagers may briefly depart from home to go on errands. If they encounter a neighbor, they do not offer ordinary words of greeting. Rather, as they pass each other, they proclaim their sense of spiritual solidarity with the Sun. They do this metaphorically, by declaring aloud the precise part of the great solar elder's sacred attire to which they believe themselves symbolically bound by the pine resin adhesive that ritually adorns their bodies.

"I am holding on to the sash of our elder the Sun," an elderly woman might murmur, declaring her faithful *attachment to the Sun and his path.* At the same time, she reduces her likelihood of being *chosen* by the Sun *for illness or death during the coming year.*

Through this and other ritual observances during the Days of the Sun, the Tewa people pay tribute to the pivotal role of the Sun's warm, nurturing presence in their lives and in the lives of all species. They have collectively remembered to honor the generous spiritual and ecological gifts of the Sun.

In Praise of the Red Ant Ally [7]

AMAZONIA:
Kayapó

A few of the species [in the tropical forests of
Surinam] were locked together in forms of symbiosis so intricate that to pull out one would bring
others spiraling to extinction. Such is the consequence of adaptation by coevolution, the reciprocal genetic changes of species that interact with
each other through many life cycles.

—E. O. Wilson, entomologist and
evolutionary biologist[8]

The Kayapó Indians are a people who, against great political
and economic odds, continue to inhabit and lay claim to vast
tracts of tropical rain forest in the Amazonian heartlands of
Brazil. Deeply embedded within their nature-embracing
myths are timeless beliefs that pay homage to ancient reciprocal relationships among animals, plants, and human beings.

Few of the precious, orally transmitted Kayapó hymns of
praise to the primordial interconnectedness have ever been
recorded. Inevitably, many of those that have found their way
into the anthropological literature have been stripped of much
of their original oral vitality. But even lying embalmed in the
symbols, vocabulary, and cultural preconceptions of scholarly
treatises and foreign tongues, severed from their cultural content and context, some of these dissected tales nonetheless
still glow with enduring ecological meaning.

One recently recorded Kayapó story appears on the surface
to be little more than a modest mythical account of why
women in Kayapó society adorn their faces with paints partly
62 made from the crimson-colored bodies of crushed ants. Kayapó women have always accorded profound reverence to a

particular genus of tropical red ant, but if one examines the myth more closely, its message seems far more profound.

The central figure in this brief tale is *mrum-re*—the red ant— a familiar insect (probably a species within the genus *Pogomyrmex*) that frequents vegetable gardens around Kayapó communities. In these garden plots Kayapó women have long cultivated *kwyry* (manioc), *tyryti* (bananas), *katere* (squash), *môp* (yams), *bây* (corn), and numerous other domestic plants to supplement the wild animal and plant foods they glean from the surrounding tropical forests, grasslands, and rivers.

This particular version of the Kayapó red ant myth was recorded in July 1978 by Darryl Posey. Posey is a highly respected American ethnobotanist who not only has developed an exceptional rapport with contemporary Kayapó in the course of his field research but has played a crucial role in facilitating their first attempts to bring to international attention their case against the Brazilian government's proposed massive hydroelectric development within traditional Kayapó lands. The story was told to an unnamed Kayapó woman by her grandmother in the Northern Kayapó village of Gorotire, not far from a major tributary of the Amazon River called the Xingú River.

> *The trails of the fire ant* (mrum-kamrek-ti) *are long.*
> *They are ferocious* (akrê) *like men.*
>
> *But the little red ant of our fields* (mrum-re)
> *is gentle like women;*
> *They are not aggressive* (wajobôre).
> *Their trails meander like the bean vines on the maize.*
> *The little red ant is the relative/friend of the manioc.*
> *This is why women use the little red ant*
> *to mix with* urucú
> *to paint their faces in the maize festival.*
>
> *The little red ant is the guardian of our fields*
> *and is our relative/friend.*

At the beginning of this tale, the storyteller uses Kayapó gender concepts to distinguish the peaceful bent of the red ant from the more combative inclinations of one of its local relatives. The garden-variety red ant tends to be rather gentle, even feminine in its nature, compared to the markedly more aggressive and masculine fire ant known as *mrum-kamrek-ti*. As every Kayapó child learns, the little red ant is harmless; its pathways in the soil loop gracefully through garden plots. The fire ant, in sharp contrast, is armed with a venomous sting; its trails are long and linear, as if reflecting its soldierlike single-mindedness.

The storyteller proclaims a pivotal place for the little red ant within the Kayapó cosmos. The red ant, she says, is bound by deep bonds of friendship and kinship to the manioc plants in the garden, whose roots are a precious source of food for the seminomadic Kayapó. But the words of the storyteller suggest that this primordial alliance between ant and plant does not exist in isolation.

Human beings, by the very nature of their agricultural efforts as cultivators of manioc, also have a reciprocal relationship with this plant. It requires that they be grateful and dutiful in their dealings with the manioc plant. This parallel bond between human beings and manioc gives rise to a third reciprocal relationship within the natural world—the bond between human beings and the little red ant that is friend to the beloved manioc plants growing in Kayapó gardens.

Out of their shared sense of reverence and responsibility for the humble manioc, humans and red ants care for one another. The essence of their reciprocal bond seems captured by the final line of the story. That essence can be summed up, suggests Posey, in a single sentence: *mrum-re,* the red ant, *is the friend of the fields and the women, who are the cultivators of Kayapó culture.*

The myth suggests that out of their abiding affection for their tiny ant ally and kindred spirit, Kayapó women color their faces with paint mixed with the bodies of red ants. It is a gesture of respect, perhaps even a prayer, lovingly addressed to the entire kingdom of red ants. At the same time, Posey notes, Kayapó women seem to view the face-painting process as a means of assimilating the qualities of individual industry and coordinated social action that they admire in the red ants.

To skeptical Western eyes, the Kayapó red ant myth might seem little more than a quaint, perhaps childishly naive cultural expression of affection between species. But such a cynical and enthnocentric reading might be transformed and illuminated by the knowledge that the story is steeped in genuine ecological and evolutionary meaning.

In recent decades biologists have devoted considerable time and effort to studying a specialized evolutionary process in nature known as "cooperative" evolution, or coevolution. Coevolution is what might be thought of as a tandem, or "synchronous," form of evolutionary change that takes place reciprocally, over time, in two (or more) species that are intimately engaged in a reciprocal ecological relationship of some sort. (It might occur, for example, between a tropical orchid and the insect that pollinates it. Or between a species of butterfly and the botanical species of plant it prefers to feed upon.) In any case, when coevolutionary processes are at play, the two ecologically linked species undergo a series of subtle evolutionary changes that are partly due to the evolutionary influences that each exerts upon its "partner."

The domesticated manioc plant planted by the Kayapó in their vegetable gardens is a partner in just such a coevolutionary dance. Manioc both nurtures and benefits from the activities of the little red ant in a relationship that has been evolutionarily refined over countless centuries. The young manioc plant secretes a nectar that is apparently savored by the scurrying hordes of red ants in the garden. In their rush to indulge in the plant's sweet nectar, their senses aflame and their keen-edged mandibles gnashing like miniature machete blades, columns of red ants gradually clear paths that grant other red ants in their community access to the manioc. In the process, they slash through the green tangles of bean vines that were sown along with the manioc, maize, and other vegetables in the mixed garden and that have begun to grow up around the young manioc plants.

This reciprocal relationship between red ant and manioc has resulted in mutual evolutionary blessings, according to modern biologists. First, the manioc's sweet juices provide a reliable source of food to the surrounding red ant colonies. Second, during their highly coordinated food-gathering frenzies, the trail-blazing red ants free the young, vulnerable manioc plants from the green tendrils of the growing bean vines that threaten to stunt or completely engulf them. (The neatly pruned bean plant is not fatally damaged by the red ant's punitive intrusions. It simply redirects its shoots to nearby corn stalks, which it climbs to bask in the tropical sunlight without ill effect to the Kayapó garden.)

Over the millennia, Kayapó society has directly experienced the myriad interrelationships at play in living tropical rainforest ecosystems on a daily basis. During that immense span of time the Kayapó have not only painstakingly observed and pondered the meaning of such bonds between life-forms but have actually thrived on the basis of this hard-won knowledge about nature. They may have devoted little effort to monitoring and measuring ancient transformations between pairs of species in the same ways that modern biologists study coevolution. But, clearly, their culture *recognizes certain coevolutionary complexes*—and even spiritually cherishes them as manifestations of a sacred, richly interconnected natural world of which humans are an integral part. Moreover, their awareness is often meticulously *encoded for their cultural transmission in their myths.*

Modern anthropology has not always been eager to acknowledge the profound ecological insights poetically expressed in many Native myths, songs, and stories. But a growing body of evidence in the burgeoning field of ethnoecology—the study of *indigenous perceptions of "natural" divisions in the biological world and plant-animal-human relationships within each division*—reflects a partial retreat from the deep-seated cultural biases of the Western observer. Nonetheless, Posey laments that Native *myth has not seriously been studied as a transmitter of encoded ecological knowledge.*

∧∧∧∧∧∧∧∧∧∧∧∧∧∧∧∧∧∧∧∧∧∧

The Nature of Things [9]

CANADIAN SUBARCTIC:
Waswanipi Cree

The ecological model is a model of internal relations. No event first occurs and then relates to the world. The event is a synthesis of relations to other events. . . . [Thus] the elements in the cell relate to one another and to the cell as a whole more like the way the animal as a whole relates to its environment.

—Charles Birch, biologist and
John B. Cobb, Jr., theologian[10]

In the Waswanipi world, the web of relationships between the myriad beings and forces at play is not *mechanical*—as is the relationship between the whirling wheels and gnashing metal gears that "animate" a ticking alarm clock. It is not strictly *logical*—as is the cool, rational relationship between the lines of a computer program, unerringly encoded in binary digits and computer languages, that "animates" the screen of an office word processor. Nor is it primarily *abstract, intellectual,* or *theoretical*—as are the abstract, lifeless, mathematical and conceptual models constructed by population and systems ecologists as they strive to render more intelligible the wondrous complexities and unities of entire ecosystems—whole forests and seas, mountain slopes, and grassy plains.

The relationships among the countless elements of the Waswanipi cosmos—that breathe life, meaning, and sanctity into it and that grant it lasting coherence—are more fluid, more elusive, more steeped in symbolism than what any of these potent but fragmentary Western images of the natural world is capable of imparting. Traditional Waswanipi society tends to view the totality of nature through the same lens through which the Waswanipi people view themselves: the bonds of human kinship.

The diverse inhabitants, forces, and physical forms of the Waswanipi universe are believed to be alive and imbued with the same qualities of character and temperament as human beings. Human beings, animal and plant species, local land-forms, celestial bodies, winds and storms, and other natural phenomena are instantly eligible for a very different kind of relationship from those of Western science's more distant and disassociated images of nature. The diverse inhabitants of the natural world are seen as intimately bound together by virtue not only of their common mythic origins but their kindred "human" qualities, their capacity for consciousness, their inherent and unquestioned "social" worth. They are *thought of as being "like persons" in that they act intelligently and have wills and idiosyncrasies, and understand and are understood by men.* They are unabashedly embraced as kindred relations.

Viewed through the same reverent lens of human kinship through which Waswanipi people daily look upon their own beloved mothers and fathers, uncles and aunts, children and grandparents—what might seem overwhelmingly complex becomes infinitely more familiar and comprehensible. No longer disturbing, alien, or aloof, all of nature is revealed as a community in the fullest sense of the word. It is a vast, scintillating web of social memories, conversations, and relationships—each potentially replete with the same dimensions of pleasure and sorrow, misunderstandings and mysteries as are ordinary human ties of blood kinship, love, and camaraderie.

At the very heart of the differences between the traditional Waswanipi and the modern scientific perspectives on nature lie fundamentally different notions about the underlying causes of natural features and phenomena. Because Waswanipi ideas about causality are rooted in a blood- and bone-deep sense of kinship with nature's diverse forms and faces, they tend to be primarily *personal, not mechanical or [even] biological.* Just as the unfolding drama of human actions and reactions within a Waswanipi family might be partly illuminated by its past, the personal qualities of its members, and its surrounding influences, so might the wider community inhabiting the whole Waswanipi cosmos be illuminated by a grasp of the diverse personages animating the universe. Thus, when a traditional Waswanipi man or woman encounters a sudden winter snowstorm, the shimmering northern lights in the heavens, or some other vivid display of nature's extraordinary repertoire, he or she might understandably be more inclined to address the natural world by asking, *"Who did this?"* and *"Why?"* rather than *"How does that work?"*

This basic difference does not diminish the value of either worldview—Waswanipi or scientific. Canadian anthropologist Harvey Feit, in his perceptive studies of Waswanipi Cree society, suggests that modern Western ecology and traditional Waswanipi Cree thought may have much in common. Each in its own distinctive way sheds genuine light on the sense of awe-inspiring interconnectedness, the persistent resiliency, and the raw beauty that long, intimate contact with nature evokes in patient, sensitive human beings, regardless of their geographic, racial, or cultural pedigree. In fact, these two contemporary visions of the natural world are not only beautiful in their own right but are mutually enriching, each somehow supplying something that the other lacks.

Feit readily acknowledges that traditional Waswanipi concepts of cause and effect in nature are infused by vibrant images of human character and kinship bonds that are utterly foreign to the sensibilities of modern science. But many broad *patterns* and processes of the natural world captured in the Waswanipi map of the cosmos often coincide remarkably well with the broad *patterns* discerned by ecologists, as in their studies of predator-prey relationships in Waswanipi lands. Concludes Feit, *Despite the difference in world views, the Was-*

wanipi are recognizably concerned about what we would call ecological relationships, and their views incorporate recognizable ecological principles.

Among the shared *ecological principles* that, in Feit's view, represent possible common ground between Waswanipi and scientific notions is the idea that relationships between human and prey populations are made up of a diversity of dynamically interacting elements that, taken together, create a living, unified, harmonious whole. Thus, while *the causality that animates the Waswanipi ethno-ecosystem model, is very different from a scientific account, the structural relationships described are for the most part* [similar to] *those of a scientific account of the relationship of hunter animal population.*

Traditional Waswanipi nature-wisdom, rooted in and evocative of concrete experience with life and land, tends to follow the same contours of enlightened Western scientific schemes for the long-term, sustainable management of many natural resources. To the extent that Waswanipi ecological insights successfully infuse relationships between human beings and the natural world with the visceral sensibilities and onerous burdens of human kinship, they are capable of elevating this shared land ethic from a lifeless theoretical abstraction to a passionate imperative.

ᴧᴧᴧᴧᴧᴧᴧᴧᴧᴧᴧᴧᴧᴧᴧᴧᴧᴧᴧᴧᴧ

The World Energy Circuit [11]

COLOMBIA (NORTHWESTERN AMAZON):
Desana

When a person is part of a system, he cannot easily see what his role accomplishes. . . . Unless he understands the system thoroughly, he will not have any inkling of the network of controls that may or may not exist to keep the flow[s] contin-

—Howard T. Odum, systems ecologist[12]

Within the ancient traditional worldview of the Desana Indians of the Amazonian rain forest of eastern Colombia, solar energy is not only biologically potent but in some sense divine.

The power of the Sun's radiant bursts of yellow rays to quicken life is seen everywhere:

❖ A small seedling sprouts on a patch of forest soil that, by chance, has been daily splashed with nourishing sunlight. Each day it slowly tracks the movement of the Sun across the sky, as if in gratitude, by continuously turning its newly emergent green leaves sunward.

❖ After weeks of illness from the ravages of intestinal parasitic infections, a young Desana boy hobbles out of the shadows of his family's thatched shelter, or *maloca,* to bask for a moment in the warm, healing rays of the morning Sun.

❖ And high in the uppermost branches of the towering canopy of the rain forest itself, leaves and branches seem to reach longingly toward the Sun—the ultimate source of the life-giving, honey-colored solar semen that cascades down from the sky to fertilize the ripe, receptive womb of the maternal earth.

But the Sun's energy, say the Desana, does more than simply release the stores of procreative energy that are inherent in all of nature. Within the intricate pattern of its life-sustaining flows, it bears a timeless message to the Desana people about their relationships with all other inhabitants of the surrounding rainforest ecosystem. The Sun is neither fickle nor flawed in distributing its fluid, radiant, earth-inseminating light; it is orderly and systematic. The total pattern of solar energy flow in nature can best be visualized as a single *huge closed circuit in which the entire biosphere participates*. It constitutes a precious reservoir of spiritual and biological power that is capable of supporting only a finite number of organisms. In sum, it represents *a fixed quantity of energy that flows eternally between man and animal, between society and nature.*

The Desana refer to this enormous network of energy pathways as *bogá*—literally a "current," or more evocatively, a circle or flow of creative and transformative feminine power.

The ethical consequences of this ecological insight are profound. For in a world in which *all* forms of life—not just human beings—necessarily draw upon a single reservoir of solar energy for their survival, each creature's action cannot help but affect all the rest. Moreover, human life lived within this vast natural feedback loop of solar energy is fraught with responsibility. The reason is simple. The Desana believe that *the quantity of energy being fixed, man must remove what he needs only under certain conditions and must convert this particle of "borrowed" energy in a form that can be re-incorporated into the circuit.*

This vision of nature as an orderly solar-powered energy circuit elegantly parallels the modern ecologist's notion of the sun's stepwise cascade of energy down the nutritionally interlinked organisms of a food chain. When a Desana elder looks out upon the sacred circuit of sunlight that oozes slowly through the vast rain forest that engulfs him and his community, he sees inherent in this system a mandate to human beings to "borrow" no more than they absolutely require from these precious, primal flows and to give back to the great system, through prayer and practice, gifts comparable to what they have been given.

The ecologist is unable to divine a sacred ethos in this forest ecosystem that would guide human beings to sustain the continuity and diversity of the whole. But he or she is certainly keenly aware that the biological processes of the system, many of which are readily discernible to scientific sensibilities, impose unimpeachable natural restraints on human beings. Like all forms of life on earth, people draw from the finite energy flows of the sun-driven rain forest and inevitably (in obedience to the second law of thermodynamics) increase its entropy (or level of disorder) as they metabolize it and disperse it as heat. Such diversions of energy and matter from the system, the ecologist knows, cannot go on indefinitely or be accelerated without eventual ecological cost.

Thus, when a Desana hunter takes the life of a tapir, he extracts a quantity of the Sun's energy not only from that animal but from the total *bogá,* or circuitry, of the tropical rainforest ecosystem. By utilizing the tapir's body for food with respect and efficiency—without excessive pride or waste—the hunter successfully transforms the animal into human flesh and human action. These, say the Desana, are embodiments of the very same biological energy that earlier coursed through the free-living tapir. In the process of human consumption, the energy transferred from tapir to human being is returned in essence to the rain forest's total reservoir of biological energy, upon which the fate of all species depends.

Failure to hunt responsibly—whether through personal gluttony, the wanton slaughter of game, forgetting to recite a sacred preparatory prayer, or failure to properly dress and distribute a fresh kill—represents more than a simple violation of the rules of Desana society. It violates the very integrity of the *bogá* circuit, of which a single Desana community is but a minuscule part. Through reckless disregard for the vital energy flows in nature, an individual is thought to cause a potentially perilous break in the circuit. Therefore, he will be held accountable for his failure to restore dutifully to the *bogá* system the stores of energy he has temporarily "borrowed."

Within the larger scheme of things, it is hardly surprising that even in birth and in death, human beings play an integral part in helping to maintain nature's elaborate energy network. First, the death of every Desana reverberates throughout the natural world. The Master of Animals dwells in sacred places deep within the rain forest and possesses the power to replenish animals seasonally that have been taken by Desana hunters; he requires a continuous supply of souls of dead humans to carry out his vital task. The souls of most deceased Desana are destined to return to those sacred sites where, in womblike reservoirs of spiritual and biological energy, they become fuel for future generations of local animals. The message is clear: Were there no death among the Desana, there would be no births among the deer, turtle, fish, and other denizens of the tropical rain forest.

Second, the appearance of each newborn Desana baby exerts an inexorable influence on every single part of the ecosystem. Each birth—like the sexual union that preceded it— represents an incremental withdrawal of energy from nature's finite budget of spiritual and biological energy. For this reason, if through ignorance or indifference the Desana community were one day to rapidly increase its numbers, all of the local flora and fauna could be expected to suffer as a result.

Why? Because by carelessly causing human populations to soar to dangerously high levels, these rashly irresponsible generations of people would necessarily deplete the energy available to other species in the forest, whose fates are, as always, bound together within nature's great *bogá* circuit of energy.

4

Ways of Seeing Nature

Native Natural Histories

There are limitations on what kinds of questions you can scientifically approach. Asking the purpose of the universe is an unscientific question. There might be an answer, but it won't be a scientific one.

          —Alan Guth, physicist[1]

My mind seems to have become a kind of machine for grinding general laws out of large collections of facts.

          —Charles Darwin

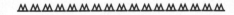

Science's basic strategy for making sense of the natural world is to break it up into conceptual fragments. Faced with the almost overwhelming complexity and size of nature, it prudently opts to engage it not all at once in its fearsome totality but in piecemeal fashion, one digestible morsel at a time. Scientists focus their bright analytical spotlights upon a single, meticulously defined scientific problem. By carefully controlling, for a time, any distracting influences of the wider world that would impinge upon the problem, they carry out an ingenious and intellectually potent deceit. By deliberately setting out to partition the fluid natural world, they in effect create an artificial theater in which they observe ongoing natural phenomena and anticipate the outcomes of future ones.

Most scientists are aware that they are probing a natural world that is no longer whole. But they prefer this form of mental myopia—this distorted "nearsightedness" that inevitably arises from peering up close at a fractured cosmos—to being "blinded" by the full force of its breathtaking size and complexity, its overwhelming sensory richness, its persistent mysteries. Science's progressive mirroring of the universe in provisional models has paid handsome intellectual, material, and economic dividends, of course, over just a few brief centuries.

Nonetheless, many scientists and nonscientists alike realize that they take profound risks if they rely too exclusively upon the verifiable "truths" of scientific knowledge when they define human relationships to the natural world. If we, as members of modern science- and technology-driven industrial societies, are seduced into embracing science's ingenious intellectual mosaic as a complete portrait of nature, we risk more than profound illusion. Science and technology can, as recent history amply confirms, lure us into behaving in life-denying and destructive ways toward nature.

In the early part of the twentieth century, physics demonstrated that the notion of scientific "certainty"—at least in the realm of subatomic phenomena—was extremely elusive. In fact, within the microcosm of a single atom, nature is *never* fully knowable. Its fleeting parts and processes are not revealed to the curious physicist's "eye" in sharp relief; rather, they appear as if glimpsed through a perpetual haze, as cottony clouds of statistical probability.

The life sciences, too, have had to face comparable limits to our vaunted scientific ways of knowing. For decades, brain researchers have debated the basis of human consciousness— free will, dreams, agony, ecstasy, and all the rest. Is the human mind nothing more than the ultimately predictable expression of its myriad biological parts? some have asked. Or is "mind" something far more elusive: a tangled, perhaps ultimately indecipherable, multidimensional web of relationships between *all* of the brain's billions of living parts and *all* of their surroundings—with new, unanticipatable "emergent" properties arising at each successive level of complexity? Can the microanatomy and codified chemical messages of DNA molecules ever possibly fully "explain" to molecular geneticists what it is to be human? And can computer software programs that model incredibly complex communities—ranging from tropical rain forests and coral reefs to abyssal ocean waters rich in commercial fish stocks—ever accurately reflect nature's infinitely subtle ecological dynamics?

Modern science's dazzling achievements in rationally dissecting the natural world may also be contributing to a sense of psychological, emotional, and spiritual detachment from the rest of the natural world. We might legitimately ask what sort of ecological values, if any, are likely to flow from such a human-centered view of the natural world. We might ask who or what will help guide us in the years ahead as we arrogantly set out to engineer the biosphere with only science's sterile blueprints of nature. We might at least explore the nature-wisdom of traditions that refuse to separate human knowledge about nature from human obligations to maintain nature's balances. By looking upon other life-forms as evolutionary and spiritual *equals,* or kin, rather than as *its,* or objects, we might glimpse the long-term consequences of human greed and irresponsibility as well as gain concrete empirical knowledge. We might even stop to wonder what as yet unimaginable qualities of the cosmos are now, and may forever remain, beyond the reach of rigidly rational scientific understanding. For all their precious and undeniable powers, human logic and mathematical proofs do not seem to cast an equally brilliant light on every corner of the cosmos.

Albert Einstein echoed a similar thought about the limits of his beloved science when he was asked one day by a friend, "Do you believe that absolutely everything can be expressed scientifically?"

"Yes, it would be possible," replied the aged, white-maned scientist serenely. "But it would make no sense. It would be description without meaning—as if you described a Beethoven symphony as a variation of wave pressure."[2]

An Observational Biology[3]

AFRICA:
San Bushmen

One cannot but be in awe when [one] contemplates the mysteries of eternity, of life, of the marvelous structure of reality. It is enough if one tries to merely comprehend a little of this mystery each day. Never lose a holy curiosity.

—Albert Einstein[4]

79

The San Bushmen of southern Africa, armed with traditional bow and poison-tipped arrow and a profound understanding of their quarry, are hunters par excellence. Yet according to Canadian anthropologist Richard Lee, their ancient, time-tested strategies for the exploitation of a broad spectrum of local food resources effectively shatters the long-standing anthropological myth that the so-called "hunting and gathering" way of life—*to date, the most successful and persistent adaptation man has ever achieved* and a way of life that was, until the dawn of agriculture some 10,000 years ago, the universal mode of human existence—was necessarily exceedingly grim and precarious, accompanied by chronic scarcity, hunger, and misery.

The !Kung Bushmen inhabit the parched lands surrounding a series of permanent waterholes near the Aha Mountains in the Dobe region of northeastern Botswana. They have refined their repertoire of hunter-gatherer skills to an art (although few, if any, of them rely solely upon hunting and gathering anymore). They have accumulated such an extraordinarily detailed understanding of the organization and rhythms of their natural surroundings that little in their food-gathering efforts is left to chance. According to Lee:

Their knowledge of the local environment, of the habits of game and of the growth phases of food plants is virtually exhaustive. The people know where the food is at each season of the year and how to get it. They do not allow themselves to get into difficult situations, and even during the time of scarcity at the end of the dry season gatherers never come home empty-handed.

This "ecological consciousness" is not, of course, purely ideological; it arises from the concrete, daily requirements of survival. Yet, despite the austerity of their landscapes, the !Kung often seem to have considerable surplus time available for leisure and spiritual activities. The adults in the community can reliably meet the basic subsistence needs of their nomad population, which includes a high proportion of dependent young and elderly members, by each devoting an estimated twelve to nineteen hours per week—about six hundred to a thousand hours per year—to the quest for food. This is a more modest work requirement than has been observed in some agricultural societies.

Nowhere is the Bushman's food-getting art more apparent than in his almost legendary skills in tracking, stalking, and killing wild animals. The !Kung Bushmen can reportedly recognize and name some five hundred species of local plants and animals within their lands. Among their quarry are not only large African mammals such as the kudu, wildebeest, and giraffe, but smaller mammals ranging from warthog and porcupine to spring hare and a variety of small antelope. Far more reliable than wild game are the more than one hundred species of edible plants local to the Dobe area. Among them are thirty species of roots and bulbs; thirty species of berries and fruits; and a variety of melons, nuts, gums, and leaves. Some staple vegetable foods, such as the mongongo nut, are tasty and exceedingly rich in protein—about 27 percent by weight— and are found in abundance far beyond normal Bushmen needs. Others—certain melons and roots, for instance—are far less nutritious or desirable, but they represent a precious reserve food supply should the need arise.

Regardless of the ultimate source of their food, the way the members of the community choose to distribute it reveals the Bushmen's basic values regarding the natural world. Here, reciprocity is the rule. Food is generally considered the property of whoever has procured it, but it is routinely shared with others upon their return to the camp. During the evening, portions of roasted roots or freshly harvested nuts might be passed casually from one family fire to the next. After a successful kill of kudu or other large game, a hunter might allocate only one-fifth of the butchered carcass directly to his own family and another one-fifth for drying but give the rest to closely related kin in the camp who, in turn, pass some of it on to others.

Bushmen traditionally seem to exhibit no pressing need to amass personal wealth or food surpluses. The natural world that surrounds and sustains them and gives their lives meaning is owned by *no one exclusively*. In essence, they see *the environment itself as their storehouse*.

The key to the Bushmen's balanced relationship with nature lies in their reservoir of countless generations of hard-won knowledge of nature's workings and of the Bushmen's place within it. The Bushmen *know everything there is to know about what their environment has to offer. This knowledge is, in effect, a form of control over nature*—albeit a gentle, deeply reverent, and ultimately sustainable one.

To outsiders, the Bushmen's extraordinary knowledge of the natural world at first seems limited strictly to their survival needs. But beyond mastering the more practical aspects of meeting daily survival needs, the Bushmen also possess, like modern scientists, what might be called an "intellectual" relationship with nature. Simply put: He (or she) shows *extensive curiosity, and lives in a world that he has studied intimately*. He (or she) is quite capable of creating thoughtful, coherent mental models of aspects of the natural world. These are often at once logical, founded on expert observation and solid empirical evidence, capable of being revised to accommodate new findings, and quite unfettered by short-term economic reward.

In this sense, the Bushman might also be called the *original scientist*. For example, many Bushmen possess a keen interest in and respectable knowledge of anatomy. The !ko Bushmen of Botswana can name with considerable precision a variety of the bones, muscles, and organs of familiar animals. In their own way they seem to fully appreciate—not unlike the savvy evolutionary zoologist—*the homology of muscles, bones or organs between different species*. However unconsciously, their naming system reflects the evolutionary truth that sometimes certain anatomical features observed in very *different* kinds of creatures deserve the *same* name, even if these structures outwardly bear little resemblance to one another.

The Bushmen are also competent students of animal physiology. Consider just a few biological aphorisms from the oral "textbook" of !ko Bushmen physiology, recorded virtually verbatim by Hans J. Heinz:

❖ On respiration: *The air we breathe is the same as that which causes the wind and it has the same name. God (Gu/e) made it, and it is as necessary to animals and plants as to man.*

❖ On perspiration: *When we run we become short of breath and perspire because the body is hot. The perspiration makes the body cold. The water comes from the muscles. The more we drink, the more we perspire.*

❖ On digestion: *In the stomach, the food becomes more broken up and watery and there is water in the stomach called* ka'a, *which is different from spit because it is sour when we vomit. . . . From the stomach the food goes to the intestines. It moves through these because they "contract" and squirt the food forwards.*

❖ On circulation: *There are different kinds of blood vessels. The thick-walled ones lie on the inside of the legs and arms, and they beat like the heart; the thin-walled ones lie on the outside of the limbs, but they do not beat.*

❖ On reproduction: *The testicles make the man's* !ghwa *(spermatic fluid). . . . The man's* !ghwa *passes into the penis through a little tube. . . . The woman has a little head (ovary) at the top of the house (uterus) where the baby starts to grow before it goes to the uterus. In the beginning the baby is a little spot of blood in the ovary and the man's* !ghwa *comes there and this makes the baby. The baby then passes to the uterus. The man's* !ghwa *and the woman's blood form a baby: this stops the monthly bleeding. It is the same with animals.*

Finally, the Bushmen seem, at times, to be somewhat less prone to bouts of hubris, or excessively bloated human pride, concerning their insights into the functioning and organization of the natural world, than the most self-congratulatory of their scientific counterparts. When the !ko Bushman is confronted by a probing question about animal anatomy or physiology that he finds himself unable to answer, he is said to express no shame in acknowledging the limits of his personal understanding of the nature of things.

After all, he is likely to say, the ultimate source of such knowledge resides not in him but in the wisest and most experienced elders of his community. It is they who have had frequent encounters with nature's pervasive spiritual potency, or *ntum,* as well as with the more pragmatic elements of the local landscape and its economically useful plant and animal inhabitants. He simply cannot be held responsible for knowledge that wiser individuals, or the world-transforming gods of nature that instruct them, have not yet chosen to communicate to him.

The quest to understand the deeper, more elusive spiritual dimensions of the natural world is largely a personal one. In traditional Bushman society, such knowledge is generally sought in frenzied rituals that take place during exhausting communal ceremonial dances. At this time, the boiling spiritual energy known as *ntum* rises up in the trance dancer who has received a spiritual calling. As it surges within him, the dancer's spirit enters a *state of half-death* and *flies along threads of spider silk to the sky,* which represent *the ways of passage of the gods and spirits of the dead between earth and heaven.* Here, fully immersed in the fearsome, fluid forces of an animate universe—facing the gods directly—the entranced Bushman is permitted to observe the wonders of the natural world from a perspective quite different from that of the ordinary earthbound hunter.

This ecstatic experience of the ancient, awesome, underlying order of nature is beyond words, though elements of such visions find their way into Bushman stories, dances, and songs. *"When people sing, I dance,"* proclaimed one trance dancer as he attempted to explain to an anthropologist his terrifying shamanic trek across the silken threads of a spider's cosmic orb. *"I enter the earth. I go in at a place like a place where people drink water. I travel a long way, very far. When I emerge, I am already climbing threads. I climb one and leave it, then I climb another one. . . . You come in small to God's place. You do what you have to do there. . . . [Then] you enter, enter the earth, and you return to enter the skin of your body. . . . Friend, this is what it does, this* ntum *that I do, here that I dance."*

∧∧∨∧∧∨∧∧∨∨∧∧∧∧∨∨∧∧∧∨∨∧∧∧

The Architecture of the Human Brain[5]

COLOMBIA (NORTHWESTERN AMAZON):
Desana

If you want, as an experiment, to hear the whole mind working, all at once, put on [Bach's] The St. Matthew Passion and turn the volume up all the way. That is the sound of the whole central nervous system of human beings, all at once.
—Lewis Thomas, physician and essayist[6]

It seems to me certain that it will always be impossible to explain the mind on the basis of neuronal [nerve cell] action within the brain.
—Wilder Penfield, brain surgeon[7]

Within the traditional nature knowledge of the Desana of the eastern Colombian rain forests, few elements of the natural world have been the subject of such intensive scrutiny and contemplation as the seat of human curiosity, the brain.

In a sense, the Desana have actually "mapped" the human brain. They have not mapped it in the same ways that modern Western brain scientists have done—by systematically placing microelectrode probes into the pale, numb rind of the brain's cortex; by injecting minute doses of chemical tracers or neurotransmitters into the scintillating circuitry of its interior; or by monitoring the faint rhythms of its electrical storms on electroencephalograms. Rather, the Desana mapped it in what to

Western eyes appears to be a more poetic, perhaps metaphorical, but in some ways no less artful, way—through the application of their keen intellect, imagination, and mythological imagery to its mysterious form and functions.

What could have initially drawn Desana attention to this extraordinary human organ, locked as it is in the bone-chambered darkness of the cranium—especially in the midst of a resplendent rain forest populated with dazzling distractions, encompassing every hue of the rainbow, ranging from bright-feathered hummingbirds and woodpeckers to glistening jaguars and boa constrictors? We cannot know the answer, but their keen interest in the brain does not come at the expense of their concern about other aspects of their natural surroundings, judging by their insights into the workings of nature.

Still, it is not difficult to speculate how such anatomical curiosity first arose. Like many groups of Amazon Indians, contemporary Desana are avid tropical agriculturalists, cultivating staples like bitter manioc in patchwork fields carved out of the jungle. But as they have done for centuries, they continue to rely heavily upon animal protein gleaned from the rain forest through hunting. By daily stalking, slaying, and butchering animal prey from tapir and peccary to monkey and deer, Desana hunters have amassed over generations an impressive body of practical knowledge about the brain anatomy and physiology of these and other animals.

Over time, in the course of patiently pursuing countless wounded prey through the forest, a keen-eyed Desana hunter notes the correlation between the precise location of an animal's head injury and its ensuing muscle spasms and convulsions (sometimes restricted to the left side of its body, sometimes to the right) during its death throes. Or as he gazes contemplatively at a freshly killed monkey carcass being roasted over a communal cooking fire, he observes that its convoluted pale brain, vividly exposed when the heat-seared skull cracks open in the flames, bears an uncanny resemblance to the human organ exposed after someone has been clubbed by an angry warrior or fallen from a towering tree.

Or perhaps a Desana shaman prepares hallucinogenic extracts from sacred plants and consumes them in various settings prescribed by traditional elders. In so doing, the shaman in effect has carried out and recorded a lifelong series of pharmaceutical "experiments" on his own brain's physiological responses to extremely subtle variations in each drug's dosage, influenced by contextual sights, smells, and sounds.

In speaking of the human brain, the Desana shaman refers to its distinctive, paired cerebral hemispheres as the *other house* or the *other dimension*. He tends to look upon these two halves as structurally symmetrical. What the modern neurobiologist calls the "right hemisphere" of the cerebrum, the Desana shaman calls *side two*. The "left hemisphere"—in the Desana worldview, the more important—is called *side one*.

A deep linear fissure, or wrinkle, in the brain's prunelike outer cortex runs along the midline from forehead to crown, like a natural border separating the two halves. To the Desana shaman, this fissure is no mere anatomical landmark. It is sacred, a meandering riverine gorge, formed, it is said, by the primordial burrowing of a mythic ancestral anaconda snake. Through this ancient cerebral groove (or, in modern medical terminology, sulcus) flows a rushing river of cosmic energy, according to the Desana. They call this potent current of life-sustaining power *bogá*.

The Desana shaman refers to the totality of the human brain as *dihpú ka'í*: literally *head-mind* or, in a slightly more evocative translation, *essence of awareness*. Echoing such pioneering brain biologists as American Nobel laureate Roger Sperry (who has called certain dimensions of the human mind that arise unexpectedly from the brain's neural circuitry "emergent properties"), the Desana shaman seems implicitly to look upon the living brain as a whole that is joyously and inexplicably somehow greater than the sum of its constituent parts.

The Desana shaman refers to each of the countless ridges of the brain's wrinkled, walnutlike exterior as *kae*. Each serpentine *kae* (or gyrus, as a modern brain scientist would call it) has a functional as well as a structural role in the Desana's mythic model of the brain. Each *kae* is viewed as the locus of a rich reservoir of distinctive sensory images, personal qualities, and colors characteristic not only of that particular site in the brain's surface but of a given individual's identity and lifetime of experiences. In this sense, the Desana shaman looks upon each *kae* as a miniature "brain" within the brain. Each *kae* acts, in essence, as a local, self-contained subunit of the brain that is fully capable of generating a stunning array of sensations, forms, and personality traits that contribute to the person's outlook and identity. At the same time, each *kae* plays a vital role within the workings of the brain as a system, in graceful harmony with other, distinctly different *kae*.

This dynamic system of linkages among *kae* is not seen as "wired" to the tangible, glistening white cords of nerve tissue, which reductionist Western brain biologists picture as fashioned from microscopic neurons engaged in chemical dialogue. The more intuitive- and holistic-thinking Desana view the brain's circuitry as far more elusive, consisting of a vast array of fine ethereal *threads* conducting luminous impulses from one region of the brain to another. This fantastic web, in turn, gives rise to the ultimate source of all human thought and action: the *ka'i,* or mind.

Faced with such compact and breathtaking beauty and complexity, the Desana shaman grasps for evocative words with which he might communicate what he has "seen" to other members of his community. In this, his dilemma resembles that of the most perceptive and imaginative modern brain biologists—from the great Spanish Nobel laureate Santiago Ramón y Cajal (whose nineteenth-century drawings of the vertebrate nervous system captured for the first time the notion of the brain as a vast archipelago of physically independent neurons), to Roger Sperry (whose classic studies in the 1960s revealed the independent roles of the left and right cerebral hemispheres in humans). Shaman and scientist alike, it seems, are impelled to try to communicate some of the most ephemeral and awe-inspiring processes and patterns of brain organization (admittedly witnessed from quite different perspectives) through imperfect models and media, from sacred stories and scientific jargon to cave paintings and electroencephalograms.

In an extraordinary 1981 report titled "Brain and Mind in Desana Shamanism," the distinguished Colombian anthropologist Gerardo Reichel-Dolmatoff recounts a traditional Desana metaphor for the human brain as an exquisite, crystalline rock—composed of countless, closely packed hexagonal prisms, each of which emits an energy of a subtly different hue. In another Desana metaphor the human brain is a great, teeming beehive, or perhaps a termite nest—meticulously organized and literally vibrating with life. This stupendous "hive," says the Desana shaman, consists of an elaborate, multilayered structure of honeycombs. Each honeycomb, in turn, consists of a labyrinth of tiny hexagon-shaped cellular subunits. And each of these cells is filled with a minute dollop of pure honey—not ordinary honey, mind you, but a most extraordinary, perhaps supernatural kind of honey that subtly varies from one hexagonal cell to the next, not only in color but in countless other qualities. It varies in flavor, odor, and texture, and in certain cells—as if in an intuitive Desana nod to the notion of a maturing neuron in the growing brain—it varies in the precise larval stage of the tiny, living, immature insect that dwells there, gorging itself on sacred honey.

Still another lucid Desana image of the brain relies strictly but no less evocatively upon light and color. Here, the brain is pictured as a dazzling, symmetrical, bilateral bouquet of distinctively colored hexagonal columns. Each constituent column of *side two*—the right hemisphere—radiates one of three possible colors: red, yellow, or blue. By contrast, the bundle of columns making up *side one*—the left hemisphere (and, according to scientific accounts, the one that tends to dominate in language, logic, and certain other crucial mental skills in most people)—emits a veritable rainbow of hues, encompassing virtually every color in the spectrum.

So riotous and richly multicolored is the collective appearance of the numerous columns making up *side one* of the brain, says the Desana shaman, that its appearance is simply beyond the powers of human description. Here, once again, the Desana shaman and the Western brain scientist seem to converge—on the basis of quite distinct paths of knowledge—upon a common, or at least *complementary,* ground. Each, overwhelmed by the breathtaking beauty of what they have witnessed in the power, elegance, and endless paradoxes of the living human brain, seems to experience what can only be called an epiphany of discovery.

Some of the most gifted of Western brain biologists, in the wake of their great paradigm-shattering discoveries, have gone on to devote much of the remainder of their lives to philosophizing, often with almost religious fervor, about the most elusive qualities and processes of brain and mind. Among their themes are the ultimate nature of human consciousness and creativity, the brain's reservoirs of memories, and its spinning of dreams—the components of ordinary human experience that seem to evaporate into thin air under the searing gaze of scientific scrutiny and analysis. *In the human head,* Sperry states succinctly, *there are forces within forces, as in no other cubic half-foot in the universe.*

We hear echoes of this same epiphany in the serenely eloquent words of a contemporary Desana shaman, spoken to Reichel-Dolmatoff. Faced with the awesome organization and spectrum of mental capacities of the brain, the shaman confided (in a rapturous statement that seems to resonate with that of the equally bedazzled Western brain scientist), the Desana can do no more than murmur softly: *"It contains colors that we don't even know the names of."*

On Nurturing Nature [8]

AMAZONIA:
Kayapó

*Familiarity with basic ecology will permanently
change your world view. You will never again
regard plants, microorganisms, and animals (including people) as isolated entities. Instead you
will see them—more accurately—as parts of a
vast complex of natural machinery—as, in the
dictionary definition, "related elements in a system that operates in a definable manner."*

—Paul Ehrlich, ecologist[9]

The Kayapó of central Brazil, like other indigenous peoples of
the Amazon region, use ingenious strategies to enhance the
availability of food and materials from the tropical rain forest.
Because their integrated array of hunting, gathering, fishing,
and agricultural practices tends to be rooted in perceptions of
the natural world that do not precisely coincide with modern
Western notions of "natural resource management," they
have not, until quite recently, been fully appreciated by Western scientists.

In the first place, when Native people gaze out upon the
vast tropical forests and rivers of Amazonia, they do not
necessarily see the same *natural divisions* that modern ecologists tend, by general consensus, to impose upon the landscape. The Northern Kayapó—a seminomadic group that
numbered approximately two thousand five hundred people
in 1978 and occupied nine villages within an Indian reserve in
the Brazilian interior covering approximately 800,000 square
miles—have a keen eye for detecting subtle changes in local
associations of life-forms and their physical surroundings.
These possess both spiritual and practical significance to
daily Kayapó survival.

The Northern Kayapó refer to the regions of tropical grassland, or savannah, within their homelands as *kapôt,* a single, all-encompassing category. Within the sprawling *kapôt* grasslands they recognize variations on the grassland theme (as well as, in some cases, further variants of each variation). They recognize a type of grassland they call *kapôt-kên*: patches of open savannah in which short-stemmed grasses predominate. They recognize *kapôt-kam-bôiprek*: patches of grassland in which longer-stemmed grasses predominate. They recognize *pykati'krãi*: patches of grassland speckled with trees. And *kapôt-kemẽpti*: patches of grassland marked by distinctive clusters of trees. Each Kayapó subdivision of *kapôt* is a visibly discernible association of plants, animals, and soils that is intimately known by Kayapó hunters, gatherers, and cultivators.

At the same time, the Northern Kayapó generally do not look upon such ecological partitions of savannah, forests, or mountain areas as absolute. The boundaries of the subdivisions are seen as diffuse. As a result, the Kayapó pay more attention to the transitional ecological areas—often unnamed—that fade into and out of named ecological areas.

In fact, so vital are these intermediate areas that the Kayapó actively seek them out as preferred sites in which to locate their communal villages. The advantage of these transitional sites is clear: Living there centers the Kayapó community at both the temporal (that is, time of harvest) and spatial (that is, distribution of potential harvest) crossroads of a rich variety of nonhuman ecological "communities" of plant and animal species utilized by the Kayapó. By so doing, the Kayapó position themselves in the very *midst of maximum species diversity, with each zone providing natural products and attracting different game species at different times of the year.*

Kayapó strategies of subtly shaping aspects of the natural world around them have also tended to be invisible to Western observers because the strategies do not readily fit into typical Western notions of what traditional aboriginal peoples do for a living. Anthropologists have often presumed that the principal food-gathering activities of primal peoples can be neatly divided into three all-embracing categories: hunting, gathering, and the cultivation of domestic crops, or horticultural pursuits. But many traditional Kayapó pursuits—and doubtless those of countless other indigenous groups—do not obey these useful but arbitrary Western divisions of labor.

Consider the Northern Kayapó's prowess as tropical gardeners—not just of familiar domestic plants but of certain semidomesticated and wild plants as well. To supplement their forays into the rain forest for wild animal and plant foods, the Kayapó patiently tend vegetable gardens that are located near their houses or dispersed around the villages in small openings that have been laboriously cleared and burned from the forest. In these rather unexceptional gardens they cultivate assorted domestic crops, from manioc and yams to squashes and fruit trees and beans.

Yet the Kayapó are an extremely mobile people, venturing on foot on periodic hunting, fishing, and food-gathering excursions. They travel on the remnants of what was apparently once a vast network of meandering footpaths that interconnect their villages with a constellation of preferred hunting, fishing, forest food-gathering, and agricultural areas.

Village vegetable gardens are decidedly immobile repositories of food, and much of their harvest, particularly the root crops, would be a burdensome load for foot travelers. As a result, the Kayapó systematically sow certain varieties of hardy domestic plants along their labyrinth of local trails, which are said, even today, to stretch thousands of miles. Over time, their labors produced gardens more suitable to a semi-nomadic forest people: long threadlike "trail gardens" that, while just as fixed as the ones back in the village, nonetheless are ever at the fingertips of hungry Kayapó trekkers.

In times past, this vast labyrinth of trailside plots must have represented a significant food resource. Even today, *a single contemporary Kayapó village, by conservative estimates, probably has 500 kilometers of trails that average 2.5 meters wide and are planted with yams, sweet potatoes, many other varieties of edible tuberous plants, medicinal plants, and fruit trees.*

Moreover, Kayapó gardeners—as if in defiance of the Western classifications of plant species as exclusively "wild" or "domesticated"—do not confine their cultivation strictly to the common tropical horticultural crops. They routinely retrieve useful wild plants directly from the surrounding rain forest, then carefully replant them in their sun-dappled forest gardens, close to campsites strung beadlike along the region's tangle of trails. In these *artificial resource concentrations, or "forest fields,"* the pragmatic Kayapó are known to nurture at least fifty-four different *wild* plant species, ranging from wild manioc and yams to bush beans.

Here, with the desirable forest plants grouped together in compact stands, the Kayapó travelers temporarily at the campsites can conveniently gather their edible roots and other gifts. By systematically transplanting plants native to the forest into these human-designed "forest fields," the Kayapó, says Darryl Posey, are practicing *a type of ecological strategy largely overlooked by Western science.*

These and other successful Kayapó strategies of shaping the natural world suggest, concludes Posey, that *indigenous cultures are a valuable human resource that offers a rich and untapped source of information about the natural resources of the Amazon Basin.* In combination with complementary Western scientific ideas, they hold the promise of *a new path for ecologically sound development of the Amazon.*

Human Greed and Pollution Will One Day Destroy the World [10]

MALAYSIA:
Chewong

Time, however, is growing short. Nature's machinery is being demolished at an accelerating rate, before humanity has even determined exactly how it works. Much of the damage is irreversible.

—Paul Ehrlich, ecologist [11]

One day soon, say the Chewong people, who live in the dwindling tropical rain forests of peninsular Malaysia, Tohan, the creator of the first human beings, will once again destroy all life on earth.

But Tohan will not perform this cyclic planetary purification out of arbitrary anger or spite. He will cleanse the face of Earth Seven—the familiar realm of ordinary animals and plants and human beings—only because once again, humans have neglected their responsibility to care for its lands and life-forms.

Tohan could not possibly love living things more. After all, was it not he who provided the first human beings—a man and woman—with *njug,* or breath, after orchestrating the creation of *both sexes simultaneously and in an identical manner?* And was it not Tohan who, with the help of the *bi asal*—the Original People who existed before mere mortals—retrieved the precious seeds of fruit-bearing trees from lofty Earth Six—the cool, idyllic dwelling place of the *bi asal,* whose underside forms the skies of ordinary Earth Seven? Was it not he who sprinkled those seeds over the great rain forests of Earth Seven so that human beings could harvest their seasonal bounty?

But now, when Tohan sees excessive human abuse of Earth Seven, he must act, as he has in the past. The moment he feels that the world has become *kama,* or too dirty, he will simply turn his beloved Earth Seven upside down.

In a cosmic juggling act, Tohan will sweep the entire surface of Earth Seven clean. All life on earth will be drowned and destroyed, so that it can be replaced by newly created populations of animals and plants. The rugged green rain forests of Malaysia will be instantly leveled to a stark, barren plain. And from this will rise a fresh topography of untrammeled hills and valleys and river beds upon which new human beings will hunt and fish and grow gardens of rice and tapioca and plantain.

The newly minted Earth Seven will sustain the new humans for as long as they generously share the fruits of the lush green forest, as long as they respect and care for its other inhabitants, and as long as they perform sacred rituals to maintain its fragile balance. But if Tohan discovers that these humans too have squandered his gifts—if he sees that once again there are *too many people, too many deaths, too much blood from killing animals, and too much urine and faeces* and that this has again made Earth Seven *very hot and unhealthy*—then he will once again unleash his vast powers of destruction.

Before he does, he will, as always, whisper soft words of warning of world's end to all surviving Chewong, as well as other neighboring Orang Asli, or indigenous peoples. Then, as the cyclic cataclysm unfolds, he will transform them into *flower buds and fly up to Earth Six,* leaving those human beings who tormented Earth Seven to suffer the final pains of extinction.

5

Animal Powers

The Kinship of Humans and Beasts

A Candid Conversation Between Two Species
The Man: *I am the predilect object of Creation, the center of all that exists. . . .*

The Tapeworm: *. . . You are exalting yourself a little. If you consider yourself the lord of Creation, what can I be, who feed upon you and am ruler in your entrails? . . .*

The Man: *. . . You lack reason and an immortal soul.*

The Tapeworm: *. . . And since it is an established fact that the concentration and complexity of the nervous system appear in the animal scale as an uninterrupted series of graduations, where are we cut off? How many neurons [nerve cells] must be possessed in order to have a soul and a little rationality?*

—Santiago Ramón y Cajal, Nobel Prize-winning neuroanatomist[1]

For most of the time that human beings have inhabited the earth, they have been hunters. As paleolithic hunters, they developed an assortment of life-sustaining spiritual, material, and strategic arts and accumulated a detailed knowledge of their environment and of the animal species in it. They stalked mammoth, elk, bison, and other great quarry tens of thousands of years ago, using meticulously crafted arrow points. They trapped and fished, employing ingenious implements and techniques, in order to capture smaller wild game for food. Even today, in an often harsh and unforgiving world increasingly dominated by modern technology, tiny islands of neo-traditional existence remain. There are places, however imperiled, where hunters sometimes still venture out, much as they have in the past—into lush tropical Malaysian or Amazonian jungles, across sun-baked Australian or African grasslands or plains, along ice-choked Arctic shores—in order to supplement their diets with the high-quality protein of freshly killed animal flesh.

Survival based on hunting demands an intimate understanding of the natural history of wild animals. It requires a familiarity with the minute details of their daily activities and habitat preferences. It depends upon a keen sense of their breeding cycles, migratory patterns, and feeding preferences. It relies upon finely tuned insights into their modes of communication, their sensory capacities, the seasonal changes in their behavior and appearance, and their peculiar vulnerabilities to human approach and attack. Such breadth and depth of knowledge grants the hunter a degree of daily intimacy and potentially long-term empathy with the mental lives and survival experiences of fellow animal species that might otherwise be unimaginable.

To the modern life scientist, such an enduring and intimate association between two dissimilar organisms (in this case, human predator and prey) is broadly known as symbiosis, regardless of whether its effects are ultimately beneficial, damaging, or negligible to the parties. The relationship between predator and prey, in which a larger animal of one species kills and devours a smaller one of another species, is only one possible variation on the theme of symbiosis. Because the outcome of predation is lethal to one of the two parties by definition, it is easy to assume that such a relationship is entirely destructive to the "victimized" prey species.

But ecologists have long observed that over the long term the dynamics of a symbiotic relationship between predator and prey populations tend not to be unilaterally destructive. Rather, over time, the initially negative effects of predators upon prey populations actually become positive in an evolutionary sense as the weakest and most vulnerable members are disproportionately killed. Gradually, the two species adjust and adapt in response to the persistent selection pressures and their survival needs.

The ecological basis for such reciprocal evolutionary adjustments is straightforward. The two species—however divergent their form, habits, and evolutionary pasts—share through symbiosis a mutual "interest" in each other's evolutionary success. If the trophic, or food-chain, relationships within the ecosystem of which they are part are to survive and prosper, *both* populations—predators *and* prey—must, over time, survive and prosper.

This fundamental ecological principle is no less applicable when the predator in question is not a polar bear, a peregrine falcon, or a voracious piranha, but Homo sapiens—the greatest predator the natural world has ever known. Something quite different is operating in this case, however. While human hunters are no less biologically bound than other predatory organisms to engage in an elaborate, reciprocal, and multigenerational genetic "dialogue" with the animal populations that they pursue, kill, and feed upon, they are exquisitely gifted with the mental capacity to ponder the possible meanings of the enduring symbiotic bonds between species.

Scientists tend to focus almost exclusively upon trying to describe the outward manifestations of such interspecific bonds *objectively* by cataloging the behavior of individual animals, tracking changes in gene frequencies, and charting population fluctuations. The traditional subsistence hunter, while keenly aware of at least the most visible aspects of some of these same interactions, is decidedly more eager to explore the *subjective,* or internally based experiences involved—of *being* a predator, for instance, or of *identifying* with prey. The hunter is challenged not simply to slay his prey but to try, within the context of the spiritual values and practices of his culture, to come to terms psychologically with a number of potentially disturbing moral contradictions.

He feels, for instance, the central dilemma of having to kill, disembowel, and devour a wild creature that possesses a physical form, sensory organs and viscera, a behavioral repertoire, and an ancestral past that closely resembles his own—indeed, that he believes is animated by the same sacred vital spark, or soul, that animates human beings. He feels the subsequent dilemma of eating a beast's sweet, pungent flesh while at the same time feeling a measure of genuine pain at having snuffed out its precious life. And he feels the dilemma of praying for the health and well-being of the life-form (or unborn generations of its kind) in the presence of the bloodied, perhaps still warm and trembling carcass slain by his own hand.

Yet as a result of the knowledge and experiences they glean from their culturally distinct viewpoints, individual human beings can feel and openly express genuine love for the animal species with whom they are locked in symbiotic embrace. Even in the midst of a modern biologist's "objectivity" and emotional detachment from his animal subjects, he can sometimes experience the impulse to renew humankind's deepseated and perhaps ultimately irrepressible capacity to be drawn to, somehow identify with, and even feel visceral concern and affection for fellow animal species.

The compassionate life scientist and the traditional subsistence hunter may well have in common the same innate, profoundly human affinity for other life-forms that E. O. Wilson, the distinguished Harvard entomologist and evolutionary field zoologist, refers to as "biophilia." Could it be that the passionate spontaneous bursts of awe, startling familiarity, overwhelming appreciation, and even reverence for his wild animal subjects springs from the same ancient wells of shared humanness from which the hunter draws as he struggles to spiritually atone for the taking of animal life?

Wilson's notion of biophilia—of an inherent love and sense of kinship with all forms of life on earth shared by all human beings—stands as a bold, if perhaps heretical, affirmation of this view. *To explore and affiliate with life is a deep and complicated process in mental development,* he has written. *Our existence depends on this propensity, our spirit is woven from it, hope rises on its currents.*

On Frightening Children 2

NORTH AMERICAN ARCTIC:
Barren Grounds Inuit

One eye, one bulging eye, the technological scientific eye, was willing to count man as well as nature's creatures in terms of megadeaths.
—Loren Eiseley, anthropologist[3]

A small group of Inuit children was playing near their family's camp, their ringing chorus of laughter rising up over the flat tundra landscape. As they chattered and busily gathered stones to build tiny benches on which to sit, a woman from their community, who was gathering moss nearby for fuel, took care to step quietly so as not to disturb the playful throng.

But as she drew closer to the cluster of children, who were by now completely preoccupied with their play, she could no longer restrain herself. She stopped directly behind them and clapped her hands suddenly, as loud as she could, to playfully frighten them.

But the fear she inspired in the unsuspecting children had an effect that she did not intend. They were so frightened that *they grew wings and rose up from the ground and turned into* nikjatut *(willow grouse) and flew away.*

Filled with remorse at having so terrorized the innocent little children, the woman sought the aid of fellow villagers in bringing the children back. The rescuers *went after them in vain but never caught them.*

Today when they hear the sudden flurry of willow grouse wings in flight, the Barren Grounds Inuit are sometimes reminded of those startled youngsters who were thoughtlessly changed into feathered fowl. For all the *nikjatut,* they say, *come from those frightened children.*

It may not be easy to divine from this modest tale precisely how traditional Barren Grounds Inuit are inclined to look upon their own offspring or upon other forms of life that share the tundra. At one level, it seems to enshrine the Inuit notion—shared, if not always acted upon, by countless other cultures around the world—that children are extraordinarily precious members of society; that they are exquisitely alert, sensitive, and conscious of their surroundings; and that they are extraordinarily vulnerable to maltreatment or emotional abuse by adults who refuse to give them the profound respect and affection to which they are unconditionally entitled.

Beyond this, the story hints that the Barren Grounds Inuit viscerally sense a kinship with the wild animal species whose fates intersect daily with their own. By seeing in the timidity and hurried flight of the willow grouse the same panic, fear, and trembling that their own offspring might express in the face of sudden terror, the Inuit seem to confirm that these winged creatures possess an equivalent moral standing in the universe. The willow grouse, mirroring their children's own capacity for suffering, must therefore be treated with much the same compassion they would show their children.

The deep, culturally sanctioned empathy for other animal species implicit in this and other Inuit stories sometimes collides with hunting peoples' traditional dependency upon freshly killed animal flesh. At some level, the Inuit hunter must confront considerable psychological pain in the process of slaying prey that he believes are endowed with the vitality, sentience, and sacredness inherent in his own human kin.

This was made clear to the Danish explorer and ethnologist Knud Rasmussen during a remarkable conversation with an Inuit man named Ivaluardjuk as they walked out on the ice-strewn hunting grounds outside Lyon Inlet. The Inuit hunter said, reports Rasmussen:

The greatest peril of life lies in the fact that human food consists entirely of souls. All the creatures that we have to kill and eat, all those that we have to strike down and destroy to make clothes for ourselves, have souls, like we have, souls that do not perish with the body, and which must therefore be propitiated lest they should revenge themselves on us for taking away their bodies.

Could it be that with such tales as that of the transformation of children to willow grouse, the Inuit constantly remind themselves of the vital spark and innate vulnerability to pain that is shared, despite appearances, by human beings—young and old—and willow grouse alike?

The Gifts of the Northern Wind [4]

CANADIAN SUBARCTIC:
Waswanipi Cree

*If the race of men were as old as the race of
grebes, we might better grasp the import of his
call. Think what traditions, prides, disdains, and
wisdoms even a few self-conscious generations
bring to us! What pride of continuity, then, im-
pels this bird, who was a grebe eons before there
was a man.*

—Aldo Leopold, ecologist[5]

The traditional Waswanipi hunter says that success in hunting
is not entirely his own doing. A successful kill can partly be
attributed to the willingness of the particular moose or beaver
or whitefish itself to lay down its life so that Waswanipi
people can live. Beyond the generosity of the animals themselves, the hunters say, *chuetenshu,* the north wind, *also gives
them what they need to live* during the long, harsh months of the
Canadian winter.

The Waswanipi hunters know that the north wind and the
souls of their prey are neither capricious nor passive but are
dynamic indications of the hunters' current moral standing in
the "eyes of nature." The north wind and the animal spirits
operate in a reciprocal relationship with the hunters' actions—
today and in the past—and thereby provide a way that the
vast nonhuman membership of the natural world can monitor
hunters and mete out punishment based on the quality of
treatment it has received at their hands.

In the process, these forces of nature have the power to
grant the spiritually diligent Waswanipi hunter access to the
vital, meat-laden game animals upon which his community
depends. In fact, in their generosity, they have been known
to offer the hunter perhaps the ultimate gift: a prey animal

that, in the midst of frantic flight, undergoes a magical paralysis and, frozen in time, awaits, almost eagerly, the hunter's fatal shot.

One traditional Cree hunting song, performed at the beginning of the caribou season, is supposedly particularly meaningful to those who routinely hunt caribou.

> *When I hunt caribou,*
> *I feel as if they are standing still,*
> *Even if they are running away from me,*
> *I feel as if they are standing still,*
> *How easy it is when I go to kill caribou.*[6]

In exchange for the fickle bounty of flesh, fur, and bone that the north wind and the animal spirits offer him, the Waswanipi hunter has an eternal obligation to act responsibly. The hunter's duties toward his prey may seem rather simple, but in fact they are burdensome and profound—as are the potential consequences, should he fail to fulfill them.

He is bound, for example, to *use what he is given completely.*

He must *act respectfully towards the bodies and souls of the animals by observing the highly structured procedures for retrieving the animal, butchering it, consuming the flesh and disposing of the bones and remains.*

He must *kill animals swiftly and avoid causing them undue suffering.*

Should he ever devise hunting tools and techniques that enable him to kill many more animals than he can reasonably use, he is obligated neither to *kill more than he is given,* nor to show the ultimate disdain for his living prey—*killing them for fun or self-aggrandizement.*

The living circle of reciprocity that connects the Waswanipi hunter, his quarry, and the *chuetenshu* is, as the traditional hunter well knows, more than a poetic figment of the human imagination. It is deeply rooted in the ecological realities of the natural world. It reflects, however imperfectly, a dimension of the timeless bond between man and beast and nature—one that lingers, as always, just beyond the limits of human language and powers of description.

Like other time-tested elements of traditional Waswanipi knowledge about nature, it represents two truths in one, an ecological and an ethical vision. Unlike "objective" Western scientific ways of knowing, it simultaneously encodes a description of vital recurrent patterns in nature, along with the knowledge of how to sustain these over long periods of time. For as the responsible Waswanipi hunter has been instructed by his elders, *the body of the animals the hunter receives nourishes him, but the soul returns to be reborn again, so that when men and animals are in balance, the animals are killed but not diminished, and both men and animals survive.*

Each Species Sees the World Through Its Own Eyes [7]

MALAYSIA:
Chewong

A careful study of sensory capacities reveals the fact that almost no two species have exactly the same [sensory] capacities. . . . Each animal has its own Merkwelt (perceptual world) and . . . this world is different from its environment as we perceive it, that is to say, from our own Merkwelt.

—Niko Tinbergen, Nobel Prize–winning animal behaviorist[8]

Since their mythical beginnings, the Chewong people of Malaysia have willingly shared the tropical rainforest ecosystem with myriad other life-forms. Over time, Chewong society has given rise to a singular vision—one at once pragmatic and poetic—of the fundamental similarities and differences between what Westerners would refer to as "human" and "nonhuman animals."

This perspective on animals emerged gradually over many centuries and hundreds of human generations. It was shaped by the patient observation of daily, real-life encounters with wild creatures. So it is hardly surprising that Chewong mythology and nature lore are rich in keenly observed details on the habits and natural history of local fauna. In its profound grasp of the innate biological capacities of different species, it often seems to complement some of the most sophisticated insights of modern animal behavior and ecology.

The Chewong hunter, like the modern evolutionary scientist, does not view human beings as innately superior to other animal species. No published Chewong account of the mythic creation of the First Animals parallels modern science's evolutionary narratives of the origin of life on earth some 3.5 billion years ago. But the Chewong language itself helps keep humankind in proper biological perspective.

The Chewong cosmos does not harbor a sense of human superiority. In fact, their language apparently does not even possess a term for that all-inclusive category "nonhuman animals." The Chewong do, on occasion, use foreign words for "animal" that they borrow from the dominant Malay language. And in their own language, they recognize certain categories of morphologically similar animals, such as *kawaw* (birds), *kiel* (fish), and *talòden* (snakes).

Nonetheless, within their traditional communities, many Chewong grant each animal in the Malaysian rain forest its own particular name and distinctive identity. The conspicuous absence of an all-embracing term for "nonhuman" creatures suggests that, in the world of the Chewong, *human beings are only one species among many different kinds of animate creatures.* As a result, the Chewong simply *do not divide the world into human versus the rest of nature and supernature.*

In this sense, the Chewong vision of the totality of the natural world parallels that of mainstream evolutionary biology. Both the Chewong hunter and the modern zoologist would agree that, in terms of fundamental needs, capacities, and origins, human beings are truly animals and are intimately related to all other forms of life.

By refusing to partition the natural world arbitrarily into "human" and "nonhuman" hierarchical components, Chewong society freed its collective imagination to explore the vast, uncharted terrain of "animal consciousness" or "animal thinking," as some modern biologists call it. They attach great significance to the notion that each species has its own perception of reality—an animal "worldview," circumscribed by the limitations of its brain and central nervous system, that is every bit as valid and complete as that of humans. They are keenly appreciative of the fact that each kind of animal in the rain forest is equipped with its own singular array of senses on which it must rely to interpret the topography and flow of events in its world. To communicate this understanding, the Chewong have created an ingenious, succinct, and biologically apt metaphor.

Different conscious beings, say Chewong elders, possess different *med mesign,* or *different eyes.* In other words, each animal species in the rain forest inherits a set of *med mesign different from those of other species.*

This is true, the Chewong acknowledge, for the *siamang,* or Malaysian black gibbon. There is a *siamang way* of perceiving the world. A *tiger way.* A *fruit bat way.* A *hornbill way.* A *monitor lizard way.* A *tapir way.* An *anteater way.* A *slow loris way.* An *elephant way.* A *water snail way.* Thus the distinctive sensory worlds and apparatuses of each sensitive and exquisitely adapted animal species within the lush Malaysian jungle is fully acknowledged and respected.

The idea of the vast *relativity of perception* among the rain-forest fauna, a full-blown, culturally sanctioned empathy for other species, is orally enshrined in traditional nature-wisdom as a cornerstone of Chewong ecological perceptions and ethical values. This knowledge permits the Chewong to instantly identify with fellow life-forms, to imaginatively transform human "realities" into animal ones. It is part of the lives of all members of Chewong society, not just a knowledgable elite; it informs their relationships with animals and illuminates their moral obligations in their attitudes and daily activities.

From Chewong beliefs in animal and human *med mesign* arises an extraordinary degree of empathy and respect for other species along with an implicit environmental ethos that places enormous value on maintaining the proper relationships with such experientially gifted animal kin. Chewong society's attitudes toward their fellow species may have facilitated their efforts to discern meaning in animal actions and interactions, no matter how cryptic, mysterious, or cruel they might otherwise appear. The behavior of every creature— including humans—is seen as a reflection of its basic biological heritage, repertoire, appetites, and needs.

Embedded within the Chewong notion of animal *med mesign* is the conviction that what each creature sees through its eyes constitutes a "truth" that is equivalent to that of human experience. In the Chewong cosmos, as anthropologist Signe Howell puts it, *as far as members of a particular species are concerned, the world that they view is the true one.* Because the desires and behaviors of each species, however unsettling or even threatening to humans, arise naturally from its vision of the world, the Chewong are inclined to judge them compassionately.

In one Chewong tale, for instance, a family that unknowingly offends the spirits by eating a meal containing both monkey flesh and fruit (a dietary taboo known as tiger *talaiden*) is relentlessly pursued by a ravenous tiger. This is no ordinary tiger but a deranged human being who has lost his humanity and become a bloodthirsty beast by donning a feline cloak and has transformed its human *ruwai,* or soul, into a tiger's.

Bongso, the cool-eyed shamanic Chewong hero, is gifted with the singular ability to *see in every other world without losing the perspective of his own.* He eventually succeeds in saving the terrified family by impaling the tiger with a trap made of sharp spears deep in the forest. He transforms himself into a gibbon to carry the great carcass through the treetops back to the village, then places it on the ground. As the villagers look on, he blows sacred smoke on the slain beast's head and asks it, *"Why did you want to eat us?"*

Like the Chewong themselves, the creature had been driven to eat "meat" by its very nature, simply in order to survive. But while the Chewong perceive "meat" as the wild game that they stalk in the forest, the malicious man-eating tiger, no longer endowed with a kindred human soul, perceives fleeing human beings as "meat" and is compelled to attack them.

The tiger is momentarily revived by Bongso's shamanic powers. *"I don't remember,"* whispers the dying beast in reply to his question. *"All I wanted was meat. When I looked at you, I only saw meat."*

One of the cultural "prices" of such interspecies dialogue and empathy is that Chewong must try each day to abide by a litany of sacred rules governing ethical human relationships with animals. These sacred rules grant enormous freedom for each species to pursue its own peculiar strategy for survival; at the same time, it is considered a serious betrayal when the rules are transgressed by thoughtless or ignorant humans.

In the end, only one individual within traditional Chewong society has the capacity to travel between different animal realities, consciously retaining complete memory of the experience. The shaman, or *putao,* alone is able *to see, when in the different non-human and superhuman "worlds," in the same ways as members of those worlds see their reality, without losing his ability to see as a human being at the same time.*

The Chewong shaman and the least anthropocentric, most daringly imaginative of modern ethologists share a certain understanding of wild animals. Both possess a profound understanding of the dynamics of other species' lives and a deep respect, even awe, for each life-form's sensory singularity. Both share the view that the internal "realities" of all animal species, however difficult to fully fathom, are equally worthy foci of human curiosity, reverence, and contemplation—not just our own familiar and effortlessly accessible *human way.*

Animal Behavior 9

AFRICA:
San Bushmen

Human consciousness and subjective feeling are
so obviously important and useful to us that it
seems unlikely that they are unique to a single
species. This assumption of a human monopoly
on conscious thinking becomes more and more
difficult to defend as we learn about the ingenuity
of animals in coping with problems in their nor-
mal lives.

—Donald R. Griffen, animal behaviorist[10]

So acute are the Bushmen's powers of observation of the ways of wild animals in their local environment that their knowledge reinforces the profound respect for the capacities and needs of other species that underlies traditional San Bushman society.

Much of the Bushmen's understanding of animal lore is pragmatic. They rely, for example, on the natural toxins secreted by the larva of the beetle *Diamphidia simplex* for the potent poisons with which they tip their arrows, so they possess a thorough grasp of that insect's life cycle. Similarly, Bushmen harbor an undisguised fondness for the occasional sweet delights of wild honey in their otherwise often bland subsistence diet. As a result, they can expound at some length on the swarming activities of local honey-producing bees, their social organization (including the identity and role of the stingless queen, or *captain*) and their basic reproductive strategies. Constantly threatened by mosquito-borne malaria and other parasitic illnesses, they have reportedly devoted *more attention to the life cycles of parasitic arthropods than to any other group,* even if many of the subtleties of the transmission and infection of these diseases eluded their traditional prescientific scrutiny.

The Bushmen's knowledge of animal behavior is astonishingly detailed, beyond the needs of survival-oriented pragmatism and seemingly for its own sake. The Bushman hunter systematically catalogs the majority of local bird species by assigning them specific names. He can expertly reproduce their songs—and not as mere mimicry; he can often pinpoint extraordinarily subtle differences in the songs of birds that are virtually indistinguishable to others. Bushman "ornithology" often includes an intricate understanding of a bird species' reproductive behavior, its nesting habitat, and even its shifting dietary needs. This is useful hunter's lore, but it also expresses the same search for a more complete picture of nature's workings that motivates Western scientists.

Nowhere are the Bushmen's gifts as consummate animal behaviorists more apparent than in their observations of the large predator mammals upon whom they depend and whom they hunt on the south African terrain. Here their knowledge is often unsurpassed. The !ko Bushmen, for example, were long aware that the spotted hyena engaged in occasional predatory behavior, while scientists still mistakenly thought the species fed strictly upon carrion. The predatory behavior was finally confirmed in 1968 by a noted European expert in mammalian behavior.

Bushmen can also give surprisingly detailed accounts of the activities and habits of the porcupine by interpreting the precise patterns of their intersecting tracks left the night before. The porcupine, they note, *lives in lairs which it takes away from ant-bears by contaminating the hole with its own urine. Before copulating, porcupines play extensively at different places. After mating, a union lasts for life.*

As dedicated, full-time "students" of animal behavior—unhindered by the time limitations of research grants or fleeting academic ambitions—generations of San Bushman men and women have transmitted their accumulated insights in

story, casual conversation, and song. Contemporary Bushmen can distinguish a black-and-white genet from a rusty-
spotted genet on the basis of where each prefers to sleep.
They know intimately the dynamics of the bonds between
mother antelope and their young and can readily locate the
camouflaged offspring—or masterfully mimic a mother's call
if they choose.

The endless hours that the Bushmen spend in the company
of wild creatures, unmatched by the vast majority of field
zoologists, grant them a privileged, almost voyeuristic, view
of animal ways. The Bushmen speak nonchalantly of a
wildebeest buck engaged in masturbation; of a herd of eland
rebuffing a wounded fellow eland's repeated attempts to return to the group; of the hereditary status of a gemsbok cow's
matriarchal role in her herd.

The Bushmen are quick to acknowledge that the sensory
capacities of life-forms around them are far superior to their
own. They insist that the wildebeest is superior to all creatures, even the antelope, in its exceedingly keen sense of smell.
The wildebeest's olfactory sensitivity seems even more acute
when the weather is moist—although prolonged rainfall
counters this effect when the warm, moist, upwelling odors
from the rain-soaked soil mask the odor of a stalking hunter.
After a few days of persistent rains, the wildebeest's keen
sense of smell reaches its full powers. Say the Bushmen, it is as
if the sun *pulls up the wet* that blankets the Kalahari afterward,
permitting the distinctive scent of the hunter to penetrate the
others—to *go between the wet.* The odor of the hunter wafts
unobstructed on breezes along the corridor between the damp
earth and the warm, redolent, rising mass of air.

Under such optimal conditions, especially with the help of a
favorable gust of wind, the Bushmen can sometimes detect the
scent of their four-legged wildebeest quarry. But the wary
wildebeest does not require the assistance of a fortuitous gust
of wind to smell the hunter. The reason for this is really rather
simple. For at times, they say perceptively, *a fly may sit on the
hunter and go to the buck, taking the man's smell along. This can*

happen on hot days, when he is sweating, and the antelope will be seen to dart off suddenly.

Ethnologist Hans Heinz, with undisguised admiration, has devoted considerable effort to studying the scientific legitimacy of Bushman knowledge of nature. He confirms the probable validity of this observation: that a wayward fly, rather than a gust of wind, can transmit human odors—in the form of olfactory molecules adhering to its feet—to a nearby wildebeest. Reflecting upon such stunningly subtle and painstakingly acquired observations, Heinz openly confesses that he is *increasingly astonished at the wealth of information* about nature embedded in Bushman society and convinced that Western science and civilization *can learn so much from the Bushmen.*

∿∿∿∿∿∿∿∿∿∿∿∿∿∿∿∿∿∿∿

The Master of the Animals [11]

COLOMBIA (NORTHWESTERN AMAZON): Desana

We are inextricably part of nature, but human uniqueness is not negated thereby. "Nothing but" an animal is as fallacious a statement as "Created in God's own image." Is it not mere hubris to argue that Homo sapiens is special in some sense—for each species is unique in its own way; shall we judge among the dance of the bees, the song of the humpback whale, and human intelligence?

—Edward O. Wilson, entomologist and evolutionary biologist[12]

The Desana of eastern Colombia say that the destinies of the animal species of the tropical rain forest lie in the hands of Vaímahsë, the Master of the Animals.

He is the eternal guardian of the myriad game mammals and birds and fish upon which the Desana depend for a sizable portion of their sustenance. He is owner of *vehkë* the tapir (*Tapirus terrestris*). *Yehsé* the peccary (*Tayassu pecari*). *Urá* the howler monkey (*Alouatta seniculus*). *Semé* the paca (*Cuniculus paca*). *Pamó* the armadillo (*Daspus novemcinctus*). Protector of *nahsé* the toucan (family *Rhamphastidae*). *Angá* the tinamou (genus *Crypturellus*). And *koramahángë* the curassow (*Pipile p. cajubí*). He is master of *vaí-pë* the catfish (*Pseudoplatystoma fasciatum*) and *unyú* the piranha (genus, perhaps, *Serrasalmo*).

But more than this, Vaí-mahsë, the Master of the Animals, is the guardian of all animal species, regardless of their immediate usefulness or disposition toward human beings. He is overseer of *mimí* the tiny hummingbird, *kumú ye'e* the little lizard, and every spider and scorpion and snake in the ancient tropical rain forest.

Vaí-mahsë often appears to the Desana in human form—as a gnarled dwarf, his body dyed distinctively red with paints and scented with the pungent juices of sacred plants. He has also shown up to the Desana in the shape of an inconspicuous lizard—one that lives at the base of huge boulders and tilts its head upward to gaze knowingly, eyes glinting through dry half-closed lids, at the one who chances across his path.

The Master of the Animals is a master of disguise. He can metamorphose into any number of faces and forms in order to monitor and mete out appropriate punishment for the transgressions of human beings against their animal kin. This powerful omnipresence makes Vaí-mahsë perhaps *the most important divine personification for the Desana hunter,* who must please and placate him to enjoy continued good fortunes with his bow-and-arrow and blowgun. All members of Desana society must remember their responsibility to view the fauna of the forest with proper respect.

Although the multifaceted figure of Vaí-mahsë can surface almost anywhere in Desana territories, he seems to have his favorite places. When asked to point out Vaí-mahsë's abode, a Desana *payé,* or shaman, may nod in the direction of a rock formation rising above the forest canopy, where certain dark, labyrinthine caves serve as his *malocas,* or houses. Or the *payé* may mention Vaí-mahsë's *maloca* near the perilous white-water of the Papurí deep beneath the ominous whirlpools between certain rocks, as the underwater spiritual protector of freshwater fish.

Places that are important to the well-being of the animals that frequent them possess a measure of Vaí-mahsë's power—certain water holes, for example, or the foul, muddy wallows of tapirs and peccaries. These sites are treated as sacred wildlife sanctuaries, whose boundaries Vaí-mahsë himself drew in the interest of these creatures. Whatever the precise location of the Master of the Animals' abode, all these sites are considered *sacred and dangerous places* in deference to Vaí-mahsë. When the casual traveler approaches such a sanctuary, he must either pass by in respectful silence or go out of his way to avoid it altogether.

The inherent power of these sacred places is not due solely to the sanctifying presence of the Master of the Animals. They are also the ultimate source of each animal species' reproductive powers and fertility, the repositories of teeming future generations of the unborn, in microcosm.

Within the damp, cavernous, womblike interior of each sacred place, beneath its beloved soils and roiling waters, Vaí-mahsë stands guard over what might best be termed the vital spiritual and biological essence of each species—its fragile, fecund, living marrow, without which it would fade into extinction. In these sacred submerged chambers, the Master of the Animals keeps a watchful eye over the precious and irreplaceable *gigantic prototypes of each species*—their primal earthly ancestors. And he cares, as well, for the teeming hordes of their yet-to-be-born offspring—the countless *thousands of animals—deer, tapirs, peccaries, monkeys, rodents, and many more* [that live] *in a great community similar to that of human beings.*

One of Vaí-mahsë's primary tasks is to spin the great wheels of life in the tropical rain forest. He constantly replenishes his precious stores of animal essences and populations with the life-nourishing souls of Desana Indians when they die. He earnestly negotiates with his spiritual counterpart in human society, the Desana *payé,* or shaman, the terms of exchange between human souls and impending animal births. While in a trance, the *payé* pleads with Vaí-mahsë for the next season's bounty of game animals. In return, he promises to *send to the house of Vaí-mahsë a certain number of souls of persons* after their deaths. These, he knows, are destined to *return to this great "storehouse" of the hills* so that they can *replenish the energy of those animals the Master of the Animals gives to the hunters.*

The Master of the Animals can also inflict punishment on Desana who fail to show proper respect to his animals. A modern Desana shaman told anthropologist Gerardo Reichel-Dolmatoff a remarkable tale of a momentous encounter between a Desana village and the potent spiritual guardians of game species after a local infraction. In the shaman's dreams, the Master of the Animals journeys to the guilty village, masquerading as a generous albeit uninvited and slightly sinister human guest. He arrives unannounced at the river's edge along with a large entourage in a fleet of canoes laden with blowguns, musical instruments, delicious food and drink, and other seductive gifts.

Without telling anyone that the food and drink is impure, he tricks his unsuspecting Desana hosts into gorging themselves on it. The Master of the Animals achieves revenge for his animal constituency when all of the villagers suddenly fall seriously ill. As if under his spell, they find themselves overwhelmed by dreams in which the very creatures upon whose flesh they have, in their gluttony, been feeding loom up before their eyes nightmarishly. The animal masters *make us eat these fish and we eat them in our dreams,* reported the shaman. *All sorts of fish appear in our dreams. All sorts of animals. Also all sorts of birds.*

By threatening the health of the Desana and forcing them to endure visions of avenging animals, the Master of the Animals and his companions compelled them to become viscerally reconciled with victimized species and with the spiritual and ecological cost of failing to honor the terms of their sacred compact. *This is why we dream confusedly,* lamented the shaman. *This is how they diminish our life. This is how we fall ill.*

The task of tracking the fates of different species of animals over time is so complex that modern science is confined, for the most part, simply to sketching their broad contours, using the esoteric vocabulary and mathematical symbols of evolutionary and population biology. But by casting animal species largely in terms of statistical twists and turns, science can strip them of much of their contextual meaning.

When animal populations are reduced to mere numbers, how can they hold human beings accountable for their ecological transgressions? How can animals be seen as anything more than a "harvestable resource"? Who will sing their praises, grieve for their losses, articulate their desires, and negotiate for their legitimate, ecological needs?

With their powerful image of the Master of the Animals, the Desana effectively direct attention to some of the most profound and enduring dimensions of each kind of animal—its origins, its uniqueness, its intrinsic value, its vital links to other diverse forms of life, its inextinguishable right to exist.

The Desana image of "species," however incompletely it has been portrayed here, likely has its own limitations. It may not provide society with the same arsenal of powers to manipulate or predict animal populations, as the modern science of wildlife management does, however imperfectly. On the other hand, it may harbor the precious power to nurture in each member of a Desana community a profound sense of the elemental role of all animal species in nature, and a sharply focused, vital—as opposed to an abstract, diffuse, and lifeless—vision of a "species" from which a host of ecologically sound human values naturally flow.

To the Desana, the spiritual and biological essence of all animals of the local rain forest are distilled within the compact, fertile personage of Vaí-mahsë, the Master of the Animals. Even if one cannot demand from him an instantaneous record of a species in the form of a computer-generated population graph or wildlife status report, within him is embedded each species' "dossier": its sacred origins; its distinctive character, habits, and habitat; its irreplaceable procreative powers and sources.

In this sense, Vaí-mahsë is a most worthy earthly representative and negotiator for the interests of all animals. He provides an urgent voice on behalf of their legitimate long-term needs for well-being and survival. He severely punishes anyone who would weaken, wantonly destroy, or blatantly disregard his diverse constituency. And because Vaí-mahsë embodies *all* that is known about these animal-relatives of humankind— along with *all* that remains mysterious or unknown about them—he has a wealth of wisdom to transmit to ordinary people in his routine, memory-jarring interactions with them.

ᐯᐯᐯᐯᐯᐯᐯᐯᐯᐯᐯᐯᐯᐯᐯᐯᐯᐯᐯᐯ

The Willingness of a Deer to Die [13]

NORTH-CENTRAL CALIFORNIA:
Wintu

Does a frog see—is it aware of visual images, does it know that it is responding? There is nothing whatever that I can do as a scientist to answer that question. That is the problem of consciousness. It is altogether impervious to scientific approach.

—George Wald,
Nobel Prize–winning biologist[14]

In our culture at large—including science—we see ourselves as the best and only possible way of being intelligent.

—Francisco J. Varela, biologist[15]

While pursuing a deer through the sun-scorched foothills to the south of the snowy slopes of Mount Shasta, the Wintu hunter knows that to be highly successful this day, he must somehow reconcile two crucial forces: his skill and his luck.

His *skill* as a hunter is a variable over which he has managed to exercise some control; it arose from his own concrete, hard-won daily experience in this world. It is reflected in his prowess at carving a bow from yew wood and meticulously shaping the jeweled point of his arrow from volcanic obsidian; at expertly tracking the deer's fresh spoor in the rust-red soil; and at releasing his shot at precisely the right instant so that it flies straight into the most vulnerable organs of the fleeing deer, killing it cleanly.

But his *luck* as a hunter—that inevitable serendipity at play in the timely intersection of his own life and a particular deer's—is, in Wintu thinking, an entirely different matter. This difference is evident in how Wintu speak about the world around them and about its natural features and life-forms, including deer.

At dawn, for example, before eating, traditional Wintu often greet the first yellow rays of sunlight and all that they promise for this day, with an elemental, yet eloquent, morning prayer. In it, hopes for a successful hunt represent only one thread.

> *Behold the sun south above.*
> *Look at me down to the north.*
> *Let me wash my face with water; let me eat; let me eat food.*
> *I have no pain.*
> *Let me wash my face with water.*
> *Today let me kill a deer and bring it home to eat.*
> *Look at me down to the north, grandfather sun, old man.*
> *To the south and north I am active.*
> *Today I shall be happy.*

To the traditional Wintu, human experience and skill are capable of affecting only a tiny fraction of nature's immensity. The natural world that lies beyond a person's frail bubble of personal experience is fundamentally *unbounded, undifferentiated, timeless.* So, while individuals may think that by the time they reach old age, they have genuinely altered the world as they interacted with it, this is simply an illusion.

In truth, what they have done is no more than grant fleeting expression to a boundless eternity of ancient, preexisting patterns, relationships, and materials that are all a part of the grand design of the natural world. The individual Wintu, during the course of his or her transient lifetime on earth, merely actualizes *a given design endowing it with temporality.* As a mortal human being, as for other species, his role in the sacred order of the natural world is necessarily constrained. He neither *creates nor changes; the design remains immutable.*

This notion of a vast, orderly, and unchangeable cosmos beyond feeble human sensory limitations has a profound effect upon the Wintu hunter's view of his prospects during a deer hunt. In the first place, while his carefully honed hunting skills are certainly likely to improve his chances somewhat, his luck—or lack of it—is thought to be deeply connected with patterns of nature that lie, dim and unseen but always acknowledged, beyond his personal grasp.

Thus, if he succeeds this day in killing a deer, the hunter can justifiably attribute his success to a mixture of personal skill and temporary good fortune. But if he fails and is forced to walk out of the forest without a freshly dressed carcass slung over his shoulder, it is immediately clear to him that greater forces in nature have favored the life of this deer.

The survival of an animal that his misguided arrow fails to hit can only reflect the enduring order of the vast nature of things, so the luckless Wintu hunter does not complain, *"I cannot kill deer anymore."* Instead, in his wisdom about the workings of the cosmos, he says of this day simply, *"Deer don't want to die for me."*

And, should luck shine upon him and a deer—in an expression of nature's grand design—willingly die for him, the hunter accepts this gift with humility, gratitude, and courtesy. He accepts the deer's sacrifice only because he and his people genuinely need it. And he *utilizes every part of it, hoofs and marrow and hide and sinew and flex. Waste is abhorrent to him, not because he believes in the intrinsic virtue of thrift, but because the deer had died for him.*

By accepting the warm, energy- and nutrient-laden carcass as a supreme gift, and by honoring its willing sacrifice by respectfully handling its physical remains, the hunter confirms and revitalizes the sacred contract between human beings and kindred animals. His empathy for the elegant creature and his sense of its place in the cosmos compels him to communicate with the deceased deer and its unborn descendants with the same reverence with which he addresses his own family members and ancestors.

The relationship between Wintu hunter and deer, between human and beast, is thus horizontal. It is an ancient and familiar negotiation, punctuated by moments of joy and grief, between affectionate equals. In the end, this minute interspecies bond is dwarfed by the sheer size and grandeur of larger, fluid, yet orderly universe, in which the fates of countless other elements are destined daily to intersect.

6

Plant Powers

The Relationship Between Humans and Vegetation

With the turning of the earth, the sun comes up on fields, forests, and fjords of the biosphere, and everywhere within the light there is a great breath as tons upon tons of oxygen are released from the living photochemical surfaces of green plants which are becoming charged with food storages by the onrush of solar photons. Then when the sun passes in shadows before the night, there is a great exhalation as the oxygen (O_2) is burned and carbon dioxide (CO_2) pours out, the net result of the maintenance activity of the living machinery.

—Howard T. Odum, systems ecologist[1]

Plants are extraordinary. . . . No two plants are alike. . . . I start with the seedling, and I don't want to leave it. I don't feel I really know the story if I don't watch the plant all the way along. So I know every plant in the field. I know them intimately, and I find it a great pleasure to know them. [A scientist must have] a feeling for the organism.

—Barbara McClintock, Nobel Prize–winning plant geneticist[2]

Modern biologists are acutely aware of the ancient and formidable debt that humankind owes to the botanical world. They have amply documented the extent to which *all* the earth's life-forms are ultimately ecologically dependent upon plants—from the sea's vast flotsom of minute single-celled algae to great continental forests of tropical and temperate trees, whose broad leaves and coniferous needles seem almost to reach out in their eagerness to have chlorophyll molecules quickened by the sun's rays.

That primal ecological dependency arose quite early in the 4.5-billion-year history of our planet. The first organisms to carve out a living by capturing sunlight for the biochemical assembly line called photosynthesis were probably the blue-green algae, or cyanobacteria (common in pond scums today), that emerged over two billion years ago. Earlier life-forms had been heterotrophic cells—incapable of fashioning their own energy-rich food resources. These largely primitive forms of bacteria were fueled not by tapping solar energy but by chemically cracking large organic molecules that had formed spontaneously when lightning, sunlight, and other forces acted upon the cauldron of the earth's primeval seas. But the pioneering cyanobacteria, like the photosynthetic green plants that would follow them, were capable of assembling their *own* organic food molecules by combining hydrogen atoms from molecules of ordinary water with ambient carbon dioxide molecules. They therefore represented a crucial evolutionary step in biological self-sufficiency.

In time, competition for the earth's finite stores of spontaneously generated organic matter grew fiercer, and bacterial and plant photosynthesis opened up a vast, new, and virtually inexhaustible source of energy to support life. By granting the entire food web of species access—directly or indirectly—to solar radiation, photosynthetic organisms gradually assumed an absolutely indispensable ecological role in the biosphere. They emerged as "producers": the primary food resources on which "consumer" animal species ultimately depend.

The dawn of photosynthesis brought revolutionary changes in the composition of the earth's atmosphere. These would reinforce, in other ways, the primary ecological dependency of all animals—including human beings—on green plants. Photosynthetic organisms, whether blue-green bacteria, marine algae, or more complex seed-bearing terrestrial plants, routinely release oxygen as a waste product. So as the plant kingdom prospered, the oxygen content of the atmosphere rose correspondingly. In effect, the entire gas-enshrouded, blue-green planet heaved a series of great, geologically slow, oxygen-rich sighs.

Over the next two billion years or so, these planetary "exhalations" of free oxygen (in the form of twinned oxygen atoms) continued to transform the gaseous composition of the earth's air. The oxygen content in the atmosphere rose from almost zero to settle gradually, at times unsteadily, at its current equilibrium levels. During this time, the gusts of fresh oxygen generated by green plants opened up countless new evolutionary opportunities for novel life-forms. As the earth became increasingly hospitable to aerobic, or oxygen-dependent creatures, it spawned an astonishing diversity of novel life, including countless varieties of fish, amphibians, reptiles, birds, and mammals (and in the last evolutionary blink of an eye, Homo sapiens).

The ancient ecological bond between human beings and vegetation does not end with our dietary and respiratory reliance on the botanical world. Plants make countless other contributions to planetary ecosystems, which in turn support all human societies. The roots, stems, and leaves of trees and other complex vascular plants serve as great planetary siphons, collectively transporting ground water skyward at such great volumes that they can profoundly influence local weather patterns. The very structure of plants—their cool shade, their towering, gravity-defying trunks, and their natural umbrellas of leaves and branches—provides vital habitats for many of the species upon which humans, directly or indirectly, depend. Even in death, plants exhibit a certain ecological generosity to humankind. They bequeath their physical remains to the land, where hordes of waiting microbes soon render them part of the rich, life-sustaining humus of new soil.

Beyond these essential ecological services, plants provide us with a bounty of nonnutritive renewable resources, ranging from fibrous and leafy structural materials to a vast pharmacopoeia of medicinal substances. They also impinge more subtly on our lives, emotionally and aesthetically, in ways that are impossible to measure. They can offer us solace. Flowers—the often riotously colored reproductive organs of evolutionary advanced plants—adorn our places of worship, accompany us through rites of passage, and embroider our burial sites as embodiments of life's endless fecundity, continuity, capacity for regeneration, and hope. Favored herbs, shrubs, and trees sown in orderly arrays create elaborate gardens—artificial, idealized, miniature ecosystems designed to elicit in us feelings of serenity, security, and peace of mind.

Perhaps nowhere is the unwritten pact between humans and plants more explicit than between farmers and their domesticated crops. Often genetically modified to the point of utter dependency upon their human caretakers for survival, wheat, corn, and other agricultural plant species now share our own biological destiny. Their evolutionary fates have become inextricably intertangled with our own. By domesticating plants, we ourselves have become, in some sense, "domesticated" by them. This marriage, for better or worse, between two species—one animal, the other green plant—has grown out of a long, reciprocal, evolutionary relationship. And like so many other ecological bonds between human beings and vegetation, it can lead to genuine human feelings of love and devotion for living plants.

✿

∧∧∧∧∧∧∧∧∧∧∧∧∧∧∧∧∧∧∧∧∧∧∧∧

Something That Grows [3]

ALASKAN INTERIOR:
Koyukon

*What is it exactly that binds us so closely to living
things? The biologist will tell you that life is the
self-replication of giant molecules from lesser
chemical fragments, resulting in the assembly of
complex organic structures. . . . The poet-in-
biologist will add that life is an exceedingly im-
probable state, metastable, open to other systems, thus ephemeral—and worth any price to
keep.*

—Edward O. Wilson, entomologist and
evolutionary biologist[4]

The Koyukon Indians of the Alaskan interior refer to plant
species collectively as *mindinolyal,* which can be translated as
"something that grows."

Implicit in this Koyukon word is the suggestion that the
essence of the hardy, incredibly tenacious vegetation in this
region of the North American subarctic is its perpetual impulse
toward growth and propagation, often against great environmental odds. Here in Alaska's vast untamed interior, with its
harsh winters and fleeting summers, the northern flora range
from sparse stands of wind- and ice-stunted coniferous forests
to carpets of ground-clinging lichens and mosses on open
expanses of tundra and muskeg. To survive each year, these
ancient plants, like their human Koyukon counterparts, are
compelled to face a cold winter's blast that often lasts seven
months or more. With no more than a brief summer's respite
from the sun's long southerly seasonal swing, green plants
have adapted ingeniously to the local climatic imperative.
They flourish and reproduce at a furious pace before succumb-

ing to the next round of frigid, cold-season temperatures and
dwindling sunlight.

Within the traditional Koyukon cosmos, much of the vast
natural world, including vegetation, is steeped in spiritual
power. *Not only the animals, but also the plants, the earth and
landforms, the air, weather, and sky are spiritually invested.* This
constellation of spirits animates the universe, connects elements to one another and to the past, and provides "eyes" that
tirelessly scrutinize human attitudes and activities. Not only
humans, animals, and assorted natural objects but also a number of plants are endowed with a spiritual essence that invigo-
rates and watches over the material forms in which they
happen now to be clothed.

The spirits of plants, like other spirits, are exquisitely attuned to the well-being of their kind. For example, if a person
displays disrespect toward a birch tree by casually casting
aside wood shavings while making snowshoes, the spirit of
the tree can retaliate. When the person next searches for a
piece of wood, the spirits may hide themselves, making it
more difficult for the person to find them.

The spiritual cores of plants are not alike. They are as distinctive and variable as the outward forms, habitat preferences, and survival strategies of the plants themselves. Like all
life-forms, each plant *was transformed from a human* near the end
of the primordial Distant Time era. In the wake of the cataclysmic world deluge and Raven's heroic Noah-like rescue of
representative pairs of threatened species, each of them underwent a metamorphosis from humanoid to botanical being.

According to the Koyukon, even the humble bracket fungi
that thrive on trunks of rotting trees, shapeless and devoid of
chlorophyll, bear evidence of Raven and the Distant Time.
During one of his creative frenzies, Raven sprinkled globs of
edible fat across the land so that people could obtain food
without effort. But fearing human lethargy, he changed his
plan. Retracing his steps, he urinated on each glob, transforming it into a bitter birch fungus. While no longer edible, it is still
burned to repel mosquitoes.

Despite the continuum of power within the plant kingdom, plant spirits generally judge human beings harshly. They mete out appropriate punishment for human actions that abuse, insult, or waste botanical gifts. The spiritual power attributed to a given plant species does not necessarily correspond to its size, potential danger, or usefulness within the Koyukon subsistence economy. In fact, the contribution of local edible plants to the diets of contemporary Koyukon communities may be quite small and may have never exceeded ten percent of their total diet even in the traditional hunting-and-gathering life in the past.

Moose, caribou, salmon, and other local game that the Koyukon prize are permanently imbued with spiritual power arising from their passage through the mythical time of world creation known as the Distant Time; so too are plants imbued with the sacred. In the traditional Koyukon scheme of things, plants' spiritual roots descend deep in the primordial soil of the Distant Time. Just as the latent spiritual residue from the Distant Time within each animal carries with it profound human obligations and responsibilities, so does the sacred dimension inherent in plants. A plant's role in the vast network of natural interactions may seem minor. But vegetation, in all its spartan Northern diversity, imposes an ethos of interspecies honor and respect upon each generation of Koyukon that hews its fibers, smells its fragrant blossoms, and savors its sweet fruits.

Ts'ibaa—the white spruce—is an evergreen tree that thrives on well-drained soils of mountain slopes and riverine valleys, reaching a height of up to one hundred feet. It harbors within it a potent spirit known as *biyeega hoolanh,* an expression of its mythical Distant Time connections. Most plant spirits are viewed as relatively minor forces in nature, but *biyeega hoolanh* rivals the strength even of some of the most spiritually potent game animals, such as bears and wolverines. This may be partly a reflection of the white spruce's pivotal importance to the Koyukon as a crucial source of fuel for heat and for curing hides, of wood for carving, and of pliable roots for weaving baskets. The importance of the white spruce within the traditional Koyukon cosmos is confirmed in the Koyukon language, which contains at least *forty terms for describing parts of trees and kinds of wood, terms used mainly or exclusively for this species.*

To Koyukon sensibilities, the spiritual powers of a mature white spruce tree tend to be *concentrated in its boughs and top,* or crown. The spruce's crown, known as *ts'iba tlee* or "spruce head," was traditionally employed by shamans during healing ceremonies to "whisk" away a patient's illness. A Koyukon hunter, bone weary after long hours of trudging through snowdrifts to check his trapline, might go out of his way to spend the night under a familiar, tall white spruce tree, remembering well his elders' admonitions that the spirit of this regal representative of *mindinolyal* almost certainly *will take care of you.*

Kk'eeyh—the paper birch tree—is also considered to be steeped in *biyeega hoolanh,* or spiritual power, as a result of its origins in the Distant Time. With its characteristically shaped leaves, shed like clockwork each fall, and the stark whiteness of its trunk, whose bark peels off in strips, this common deciduous tree is beautiful and of great practical value to the Koyukon. Its distinctive pale bark is harvested, without serious harm to the living tree, during the warm months of the year and is neatly folded into baskets and other containers. Its hard, tightly grained wood is used for Koyukon tools of survival such as snowshoes, sleds, and canoes because of its durability. Its logs are one of the most highly regarded heating fuels in Koyukon country.

But the *biyeega hoolanh* of the paper birch tree is more than a crude spiritual measure of economic value. Its diffuse, built-in, moral imperative prescribes the limits of human exploitation of a species. Because of their respect for the paper birch and its shared links with the Distant Time, the Koyukon observe sanctions that prohibit the inappropriate harvesting of birch bark in winter *because this leaves the tree naked to the cold and will bring on frigid weather.* In fact, the best way for human beings to harvest bark from the birch is to do so with consummate concern for the tree's comfort. Ideally, the Koyukon physically carry the birch log inside their home, carefully *thaw it, strip the bark, and then bury the log under the snow to protect it from exposure to the cold.*

Such gentle, kindly, even reverential treatment of a plant underscores the traditional Koyukon empathy toward vegetation. It reveals a genuine acknowledgment of the perceived "sufferings" of plants and even a degree of personal identity with them. Alaskan anthropologist Richard Nelson, who has lived with the Koyukon and sensitively recorded their ecological perceptions, would go a step further. The Koyukon gestures of respect toward plants reveal a deep empathy for plants' capacity to experience, at some level, the same sort of agonies and indignities that humans sometimes are forced to endure. Nelson suggests that this emotional capacity is believed to linger in a plant *for days, months, or years, depending upon the organism* after it has been slain or harvested. Because the Koyukon believe that *living things do not die immediately when they are "killed" or cut down,* human beings are obliged to treat logs and branches and even tiny discarded chips of wood with some of the reverence they would normally accord the whole living organism. Individuals who do otherwise are likely to *have bad luck,* states Nelson, *just as they can lose their luck with the animals.*

Some plants reveal so clearly and unmistakably their humanlike sensibilities and their links with the Distant Time that their spiritual kinship with humans can scarcely be missed. These connections are often expressed as stories. According to one such tale, *mink-man,* a primordial human-animal figure of the Distant Time, approached a group of human-plant figures known as *tree-women. Mink-man's* mission was not a pleasant one. His solemn duty was to inform the *tree-women* that Raven, the sacred transformer spirit who happened to also be husband to each of the *tree-women,* had just died.

Upon hearing this sad news, each of the *tree-women* expressed her profound sorrow by inflicting a superficial flesh wound to her body. Through these wounds, their "skin" was disfigured in a way that persists today in the texture and hue of the bark of the particular kind of tree that each of the *tree-women* became following a sacred metamorphosis.

One of the grieving *tree-women* was transformed into an alder—a deciduous tree that bears tiny cone-shaped seeds and prefers the moist soils beside rivers. When this particular *tree-woman* heard *mink-man*'s tragic news, *she cried and pinched herself until she bled.* When she was transformed into a modern alder tree, her distinctively colored bark oozed a bloodred juice, which the Koyukon traditionally used as a red dye.

In this way, the Koyukon are forever reminded of the suffering of the *tree-woman* who was the Distant Time ancestress of the alder trees now scattered across Koyukon lands. At the same time, the primordial unity of plants and animals with humankind in the Distant Time (revealed, for example, in the alder's bloodred juices) underscores the rightful place of vegetation in the enduring order of things.

The *geega,* the common bog blueberry bush, forms lush thickets among local muskegs and provides the Koyukon with tasty and nutritious berries every season. Like a number of other fruit-bearing low-lying bushes, the *geega* are steeped in a sacred power that requires no elaborate storytelling or reference to the Distant Time to explain.

In the Koyukon vision of nature the ordinary bog blueberry, and all berry plants, possess extraordinary spiritual powers for no other reason than this: *They grow close to the earth and are nurtured directly from it.* In their tight embrace of the land, berry plants also hold the potent spiritual warmth of *sinh tala*—that *most fundamental of all spiritual powers* that *emanates from the earth's surface.*

Islands of Forest [5]

AMAZONIA:
Kayapó

I am trying to save the knowledge that the forest
and this planet are alive, to give it back to you
who have lost the understanding.

—Paiakan, contemporary Kayapó
Indian leader[6]

Liquidating old-growth forests is not forestry; it is
simply spending our inheritance. Nor is planting
a monoculture forestry; it is simply plantation
management and plantation management is all
we are currently practicing. . . . Restoration for-
estry is the only true forestry. We use the forest—
remove products and nutrients—and then we
restore its vitality, its sustainability so that we
can remove more products in time without im-
pairing the forest's ability to function. . . . Any-
thing else is not forestry.

—Chris Maser, biologist and sustainable
forestry consultant[7]

Looking out across the sweeping chlorophyll-green panorama
of a tropical rain forest in the remote Xingú River watershed of
central Brazil—across its towering multitiered stands of trees,
its rain-wrinkled hillsides, its patches of grassland—it is easy
to assume that the fabric of the natural world has scarcely been
altered by the generations of Kayapó that continue to survive
here.

True, there are some visible scars of traditional Kayapó
activities upon this seemingly pristine Amazonian scene. Human handiwork is unmistakable in the geometric design of a
Kayapó village—its neat circle of family dwellings arranged

around the pivotal communal men's dwellings. Small, methodically weeded vegetable gardens lie adjacent to the houses, and in the distance are larger swidden field gardens. The Kayapó have claimed these rudimentary clearings from the ever-encroaching wave of lush tropical vegetation at the rain forest's edge with machetes and controlled burnings. In them, bananas, corn, manioc, and assorted other fruits and vegetables thrive on thin tropical soils that are temporarily enriched by the release, by fire, of minerals and nutrients previously bound up in the leaves, stems, and branches of the tropical rain forest's vegetation.

Kayapó communities are adept at altering the ecosystem around them in ways that are invisible to most Western eyes. One of the most intriguing of these is the painstakingly slow but nonetheless effective Kayapó technique of reforesting savannah.

A key Kayapó reforestation strategy is to renew clumps of trees in small patches of forest of variable size scattered across open savannah. These dynamic "islands of forest" adrift in surrounding savannah "seas" are known locally as *apêtê*. Most Western observers have assumed that *apêtê* arose through the familiar ecological process called succession—a natural, predictable, progressive sequence of stages in the composition and appearance of a grassland ecosystem. It was widely assumed that savannah gave birth to *apêtê* in much the same way that a freshly cleared patch of temperate forest is taken over first by fast-growing weeds, then by shrubs, and finally by mature trees—all without the slightest human intervention.

But in the Kayapó savannah lands, especially in the grassy areas that the Kayapó regularly frequent, areas of *apêtê* arise by human design. In fact, astonishingly enough, up to three-fourths of the little islands of forest—each of different size, shape, and stage of maturity—have been deliberately placed there by Kayapó hands.

The basic Kayapó reforestation strategy is as ingenious as it is simple. They create miniature replicas of existing forest islands in the grasslands, complete with fertile soil and young plantings. They tend them for a time with the same care that they lavish on their vegetable gardens. They generally do this in August and September—the first months of the local wet season. After the plants in the artificial *apêtê* sites take root and begin to flourish, they are left unattended to grow and reproduce on their own, through the natural processes of ecological succession, into mature groves.

The traditional Kayapó recipe for regenerating forest islands in a treeless expanse of savannah involves the following steps:

❖ First, they gather leaves and branches and pile them into a compost heap. After the rotting vegetation has sufficiently decomposed, they smash it with sticks into a finer mulch.

❖ They carry the mulch to the savannah planting site—ordinarily, a dishlike depression in the soil that will trap rainfall. They sprinkle it with earthen debris from termite mounds and ant nests, as well as a dash of living termites and ants themselves. (The nest debris presumably fertilizes the soil. The Kayapó say that the insects, deliberately taken from mutually hostile colonies, are so intent on battling one another that the tender young shoots of the new plantings are left relatively unscathed.)

❖ They pile the resulting mixture into a mound measuring one to two yards across and a foot or so deep. They place a variety of wild plants from the nearby rain forest onto this fertile soil.

❖ In the months ahead, members of a family will pass by the site en route to their more distant garden fields. They will pause to care for the young flora of the forest islet, which is termed *apêt-nu* at this immature stage. They continue to add plantings along the periphery of the islet to increase both its size and its botanical complexity.

In time, these *apêt-nu* become *apêtê*. The frail, artificial islets of vegetation, stimulated by wild seed dispersal and other natural processes as well as human intervention, develop into true *apêtê,* consisting of tall, shade-lending trees.

Within these ever-expanding stands of trees is a bounty of wild herbs and bushes planted by the Kayapó. These provide villagers with useful food, material, and medicinal products.

The Kayapó harvest hundreds of kinds of roots, leaves, and nuts; some 250 different kinds of wild fruits; and more than 650 different medicinal plants from the tropical rain forest. Over a period of years, as the *apêtê* grow still larger— expanding by a few acres in a decade—they serve other needs as well. Mature forest islands provide precious habitat, conveniently close to the homes of Kayapó hunters, for prized game birds and mammals. They have served as defensive cover for fierce Kayapó warriors. They harbor the secret medicinal gardens of powerful Kayapó shamans. And, on occasion, they provide a measure of privacy for young Kayapó lovers.

The Kayapó are rewarded in two principal ways for their exceedingly patient labors of savannah reforestation. They gain a strategically placed patchwork of self-sustaining woodland "gardens," stocked with scores of useful wild plant and animal species. And, in ways we can scarcely imagine, they receive the more intangible pleasure of seeing their beloved *apêtê*-dappled savannah lands endlessly rejuvenated and visually renewed—despite the demands of generations of Kayapó hunters and food-gatherers.

ᴧᴧᴧᴧᴧᴧᴧᴧᴧᴧᴧᴧᴧᴧᴧᴧᴧᴧᴧᴧᴧᴧᴧᴧᴧᴧ

Cutting the Cane People[8]

MALAYSIA:
Chewong

One exercises justice or injustice to plants and
animals as well. . . . Plants and animals also
have a right to unfolding and self-realisation.
They have the right to live.
—Arne Naess, environmental philosopher[9]

Since time beyond memory, the Chewong of peninsular Malaysia have ventured into the verdant tropical rain forests to harvest the useful parts of wild plants. They synchronize their hunting and gathering activities with the annual cycle of the rain forest. Their lives are attuned to the ripening of durian, rambutan, and countless other edible fruits within the forest, to the seasonal abundances of fleshy mushrooms and starch-laden roots that thrive in the moist soils of the forest floor, and to the forest's bounty of natural building materials—sturdy saplings for the framework of their huts, broad *attap* leaves for the waterproof roofing, flattened bark or split bamboo stems for the floors.

One of the most useful gifts of the rain forest is the resilient stem of certain cane plants. The Chewong skillfully work these into plaited burden-baskets for carrying loads on their backs, finely textured mats to sleep on, and small pouches for carrying tobacco. In recent years, the demand for these materials has increased from non-Native Malay neighbors, and the villagers in impoverished Eastern Chewong communities have begun to sell them forest fiber such as *seg manao,* or malacca cane. By carrying bundles of malacca cane down the narrow dirt road to Lanchang, a cluster of clapboard shops on the road to Temerloh, they have earned meager cash incomes to supplement their imperiled hunting, gathering, and slash-burn agricultural way of life.

But in the face of growing markets, the temptation to increase their harvests of cane dramatically and to commercialize them has raised difficult questions for traditional Chewong. They know too well that the cane stands in the forest represent something far more important than "natural resources" passively awaiting human exploitation. To the traditional Chewong, the cane plants—*seg manao*—like all species in the rain forest, possess *ruwai,* or souls. In fact, the Chewong believe that the spiritual essences of cane plants are divine *"people"*—mythically metamorphosed into rustling leaves and fibrous stalks. Malacca cane is thought to be entitled to the same sort of deep respect, even reverence, accorded to blood kin.

Over the centuries, the high intrinsic value that the

Chewong have traditionally placed upon cane has probably helped to limit the size of their harvests. At least until recently, it has helped discourage the Chewong from greedily overharvesting, even in the face of rising commercial cane prices in the Malaysian economy, and even though most Chewong families living on their traditional lands are poor, malnourished, and could desperately use the additional cash income.

Not long ago, according to anthropologist Signe Howell, the temptation simply became too great for several young Chewong boys. Overwhelmed by the desire to sell enough cane and agila wood to purchase previously unimaginable luxuries such as biscuits, batteries, and transistor radios, the boys began to chop down the "cane people" in earnest. When nothing cataclysmic befell the irreverent youth, some of the adult members of the Chewong community joined them in this pillage—always fearful of retribution from the forest spirits for their willful destruction of so many plants.

Before long, one villager told his neighbors about a terrible dream he had had about their mistreatment of the malacca cane. In it, true to Chewong tradition, he encountered several *bi inhar*—the all-seeing spirit beings who dwell invisibly in certain waterfalls, mountaintops, and other sacred places and who are the departed souls of long-deceased *putao,* or shamans. *"We are very angry with all of you,"* one of the *bi inhar* had said sternly to the dreamer. *"For you have gone into the forest and, acting like thieves, stolen from us—beings whom you have always honored and granted great respect."*

To the dreamer's astonishment, however, the *bi inhar* made no mention of the missing stands of malacca cane that the Chewong had whisked off to market in nearby Lanchang. Rather, the *bi inhar* accused the Chewong of a quite different crime. *"We are angry with you,"* continued the *bi inhar, "for stealing all of our 'SWEET POTATOES.' "*

Suddenly, the meaning of the strange dream became clear to the guilt-ridden dreamer. Its message meshed beautifully with the deep-seated Chewong belief that *each* species in the rain forest—not just human beings—possesses *med mesign,* a vision of the world that is as legitimate and "true" as any human interpretation.

The dreamer realized that the villagers' belief that the malacca cane plants are "people" was not entirely correct. True, to the *hot eyes* of mortal Chewong, the cane did look like nothing more than clusters of long-stemmed vegetation. But that had simply been a human illusion. To the *cool eyes* of the wise *bi inhar* spirits, the same plants took on a quite different appearance. Through the spirits' eyes, the cane looked like a familiar staple vegetable growing in their garden; in the world in which the *bi inhar* live, the plants were sweet potatoes! Thus, *when the* bi inhar *encountered humans cutting down the cane, they saw porcupines digging their sweet potatoes!*

The dreamer's reevaluation of the events galvanized some of the more traditional members of the Chewong community. They fervently believed that the *cool eyes* with which the *bi inhar* spirits saw the world normally veiled to mortal humans were, in fact, the eyes of powerful deceased shamans and that they perceived the *true* nature of things.

Inspired by the dream's revelation, the Chewong villagers decided that while their greed hadn't yet destroyed what they had thought were "cane people," they had nonetheless acted most irresponsibly. The dream had taught them that the cane stands actually played a more important role than any of them had imagined—a role invisible to ordinary *hot eyes.* The plants were not simply "cane people" but the sacred sustenance of the beloved *bi inhar* "people" who watched over the Chewong in sickness and in health. Thus, the cane plants were even more worthy of Chewong respect than they had previously been.

Because the *bi inhar* viewed the cane as laboriously cultivated "sweet potatoes," they were naturally enraged at the villagers sneaking into their "gardens" and stealing them. The *bi inhar* expressed the same rage that the Chewong felt when they zealously defended their own slash-and-burn gardens of sweet potatoes, tapioca, and plantains against the maraudings of hungry wild animals.

The Chewong then decided to change their ways. While they could not, out of necessity, completely abandon their commercial harvests, they showed a renewed respect for the cane plants. They expressed this by honoring the powerful *bi inhar* owners of the cane. Each night before they ventured into the forest in search of cane, they paused in their village and performed a simple cane-harvesting ritual. In one of their elevated stick huts, they would pray and burn scented wood chips in ceremonial bowls filled with glowing embers. In this way, they offered sacred smoke to the *bi inhar* as a gift in exchange for the cane they would cut the next day.

As the pungent incense spiraled up into the starry night, the Chewong felt assured that the *bi inhar* spirits would *eat this smoke.* When smoke reaches the mysterious, hidden realm where the *bi inhar* live, it is instantly transformed into a delicious food. Their words of prayer, too, were borne aloft upon the same rising plume of smoke. *"Peace upon you, upon you peace. Excuse me,"* offered one Chewong villager, in a prayer of thanksgiving and hope that continued for nearly an hour. *"I know very little, I have not studied enough,"* he added humbly.

With this ceremony, the Chewong have modified their traditional beliefs about nature in a way that allows them to survive in a changing and often hostile modern world. At the same time, this new tradition allows them to communicate with the *bi inhar* spirits of their past. They view this rejuvenated relationship, however fragile, as reciprocal. The *bi inhar* serve as guardians of all life and all landforms in the rain forest—including even the modest malacca cane plant. Because the incense smoke that carries human words to them is also their food, the *bi inhar* depend upon the Chewong and their nocturnal prayers for sustenance.

The Chewong pray fervently to sustain the *bi inhar,* trying not to harvest more malacca cane than they need for their children to survive. In return, the *bi inhar give protection and help* to the beleaguered Chewong. At the same time, they give protection and help to every other life-form on earth. Their poignant ritual contains a deep understanding of the interdependency of humanity and nature and a profound message for Western society.

∧∧∧∧∧∧∧∧∧∧∧∧∧∧∧∧∧∧∧∧∧∧∧∧

The Honey Tree Song [10]

SARAWAK, MALAYSIA:
Dayak

The mutualistic connections between many plants and animals created by pollination systems are important in binding the machinery of nature into a functional whole.
—Paul Ehrlich, ecologist[11]

To the Dayak peoples of Sarawak—that remote, mountainous province on the island of Borneo, greened by dense tropical vegetation and dissected by countless rivers—song may be the preferred medium through which human beings attempt to foster a proper balance with the forces of nature.

The Dayak singer draws upon his or her particular creative gifts and composes rich, poetic songs and chants, often with startling images and juxtapositions that seem to harmonize the full range of stages and experiences in Dayak life. Dayak songs embrace a rich variety of forms: purely secular songs of courtship, praise, or grief; sacred songs—some exceedingly personal—fashioned from prayers, dreams, or revelations; and soothing lullabies, solemn chronicles, and sweet seductions.

The most beautiful Dayak songs emerge from the lips of the singer as genuinely creative works of art that almost miraculously integrate and illuminate some of the most precious elements of the traditional Dayak world, as experienced by the individual, the community, and the wider world of nature.

One such song is known as the "Honey Tree Song." Sung

by Raseh Amang Ampih, a member of a Bidayuh-speaking Land Dayak community called Kampong Mentu Tapuh, it was recorded by American poet Carol Rubenstein in 1972. Like most of the indigenous peoples of Sarawak, the Bidayuh-speaking peoples cultivate rice, a variety of garden vegetables, and other crops in transient, fire-razed patches on steep mountain slopes. Their harvests of tropical slash-and-burn agriculture are often supplemented by forays into the forests in pursuit of wild deer, monkeys, and other animals, as well as betel nuts, fruits, and numerous other edible plants.

To these people, one of the forest's most cherished edible gifts is honey. It is extracted at considerable peril from the hives of wild bees, in the uppermost branches of stupendous tropical trees. Wild honey is generally harvested by a young male villager during the course of a ritual that takes place in the dark of night.

The ritual begins as the bold youth ascends the massive trunk of the targeted tree by laboriously chiseling out footholds as he climbs. As he ascends, he carries a fiery torch whose billowing smoke stupefies the restless horde of bees above. Far below, villagers encourage him in his daring quest, their faces illuminated by a fire they have kindled at the base of the tree in order to engulf the smoke-stunned bees from above.

Perspiring heavily, the young man continues his slow skyward journey up the honey tree. His journey parallels in some ways the village shaman's spiritual flights of ecstasy. It also resembles the mythical ordeal of Sebauk, the boy-hero of the Dayak, who once climbed so high up a tree that he reached the treetops of the mirror-image rain forest in the upside-down world above. There dwelled the Grandfather of the Moon and the Grandfather of the Seven Stars, the original guardians of agricultural knowledge.

As he continues toward the hive, the young man sings his personal version of "The Honey Song." He sings it gently as a prayer, not only to appease the restless bees, but to celebrate the impending bounty of honey. The song confirms that honey is one of nature's endless gifts, even though its harvesting is perilous for the Dayak, and it asks that bees and honey be renewed so that future generations of Dayak might enjoy them.

His song is laden with images that poetically fuse the present with the timeless mythic past. He sings of hearing the sounds of forest beetles and crickets. He sings of his ancestors. And he sings of this towering honey tree's first stirrings of life as a small seed planted by a *short-quilled porcupine and his wife, planted by a pheasant on the edge of the jungle, planted by a moonrat on the edge of a hill.*

"*Go back, bees, go back,*" he calls to the hive, now just above his sweat-soaked head. "*Return, soul, together with me return,*" he continues, with these lyrical words transforming his worldly food-gathering activity into a far more profound journey.

Finally, he arrives at the hive and after several minutes gently subdues the bees with smoke from his torch. He extends his hand into the smoke-shrouded hive, much as the boy-hero Sebauk gained sacred knowledge about agriculture from the mirror-image rain forest.

Similarly, the village shaman, during his ecstatic healing flights, reaches out for the far more elusive "honey" of his patient's lost soul. The youth, like the shaman, descends laden with sweet dripping honey and joyfully embraces his catch— *feet linked with feet, hands with hands linked.*

Song has the power to bring a measure of harmony to the vast, multidimensional Dayak cosmos. The very act of singing breathes life into the network of subtle interconnections between human beings and the entire natural world. Song somehow *links* all things in nature together, in the process of honoring and participating in nature's sacred, mysterious whole.

Here among the Dayak peoples of Sarawak, as in so many other indigenous communities around the world, plants have great spiritual status. In spite of its numbing omnipresence in the dense rain forest, the earth's lush, living mantle of green foliage is not taken for granted. It is joyously given a measure of the reverence and esteem accorded to the most precious and beloved of game beasts.

The enduring bond between human beings and vegetation reflects a timeless appreciation of the natural world and of the vital ecological and spiritual importance of plants to humankind. Indigenous societies around the world have long been fully cognizant that green plants, in all their wondrous variety of habitats and forms, play an absolutely fundamental role in the larger patterns of nature as they tirelessly grow and regenerate beneath the sun's life-generating rays. Native knowledge of this primary ecological interdependency among plants, animals, and humans, along with a sense of their ancient and shared creation stories, must contribute to the widespread Native belief that the botanical realm, or at least some portion of it, is permeated by the sacred.

7

Sacred Space

The Relationship Between Humans and Land

Land, then, is not merely soil; it is a fountain of energy flowing through a circuit of soils, plants, and animals. . . . An ethic to supplement and guide the economic relation to land presupposes the existence of some mental image of land as a biotic mechanism. We can be ethical only in relation to something we can see, feel, understand, love, or otherwise have faith in.

—Aldo Leopold, ecologist[1]

In the spiritually detached Western view of nature, land is lifeless. It is inert, a two-dimensional physical surface (if we exclude a third dimension, which grants rights of access to urban high-rises above or to mineral or water rights below)—to be surveyed, subdivided, and zoned. It is a commodity—valuable but no more "sacred" than a stack of cedar logs, a heap of coal, or any other economic resource. It is a financial investment—to be bought, "developed," and resold (hopefully at a handsome profit) by shuffling official titles and deeds.

Still, Western civilization is not totally devoid of a sense of what might be called the inherent "sanctity" of land, of a dimension of holiness or inviolability to the land. If we in the modern, industrialized West have historically relegated "sacred places" to the margins of our spatial existence, we have not yet entirely forgotten them.

Our traditional places of worship have long been viewed as consecrated ground. When we step over the threshold of a majestic spire-peaked cathedral and kneel reverentially in its cavernous stone chambers, we have, if we are believers, crossed an imaginary boundary between the secular and the sacred.

When Western nations wage war, they sometimes reveal the existence of sacred terrain. They may take great pride in their efforts to direct terrible weapons of destruction away from civilian populations as well as from supremely sacred sites such as churches and synagogues, religious shrines, cemeteries, hospitals, fine arts museums, and other exalted, if not always overtly "sacred," cultural places.

Even today, in some quarters, Western tradition endorses a primordial connection between agriculturists and the lands that they cultivate. While modern farmers may no longer refer to their lands as sacred, they may still unabashedly proclaim their undying "love of the land."

Beginning with the first stirrings of the American conservation movement in the late eighteenth century, Westerners have displayed a willingness to set aside and protect geographic spaces that are judged precious and irreplaceable natural sanctuaries for wildlife. By publicly lobbying for vast, pristine tracts of land to be perpetually protected as wilderness areas or national parks, some of the forerunners of the modern North American environmental movement were arguing, in essence, for a collective sanctification of nature.

Certain relatively untrammeled places, they maintained, ought to be reserved by national consensus as precious—not just as refuges for vulnerable wild species but also as sustenance for the human spirit. In 1901, the pioneering American conservationist John Muir lovingly referred to California's Sierra Nevada range as "benevolent, solemn, fateful, and pervaded with divine light." He was essentially calling for an historic if secular expansion of the vestigial Western notion of the sacredness of land.

American historian J. Donald Hughes has explored the cultural differences between American Indian and European concepts of land and offers a succinct cross-cultural definition of the sanctity of geographic place.

Sacred space is a place where human beings find a manifestation of divine power, where they experience a sense of connectedness to the universe. There, in some special way, spirit is present to them.[2]

Can a residual glimmer of the sacredness of geographic space also be found in Western science? At first, such a possibility seems far-fetched. By its very mode of uncompromising intellectual analysis to arrive at quantifiable and verifiable truth, science seems destined to "de-sanctify" the universe, to, in effect, systematically suck the "sacred juices" from the earth.

But few biologists would deny that at some point—perhaps more than once—in their lives, as they scrutinized the natural world, they have experienced a natural setting in a way that compelled them for a time to look upon it in a more reverential light. If theirs were not literally "religious" experiences, they were still epiphanies of a sort. They offered unexpected flashes of ecstatic and intuitive—yet clear-eyed, perceptive, and concrete—understanding of the underlying evolutionary and ecological unity of nature, revealed within the microcosm of a living landscape. These epiphanies have been partly inspired by each scientist's rich accumulation of detailed microscopic and macroscopic insights into the wondrous workings of the natural world.

Even under science's unflinching gaze, the land itself at times reveals qualities that can only be described, if metaphorically, as "sacred." Science's extraordinary images of the earth reveal landscapes to be vast, artful visual fusions of time and space. By pinpointing the processes through which the world's ecosystems evolved and by educating our eyes and minds, science can make our natural surroundings speak to us in ways that can render them deeply meaningful to us. By elevating our understanding of the natural world and its myriad, intertwined lives, science can even be said to, in some sense, sanctify nature for some of us.

Geographic places around the globe, such as the Galapagós Islands, are almost mythical in their significance to evolutionary science and stand as monuments to past eras of unparalleled biological creativity, transformation, and loss. Science recognizes towering mountain peaks as former inland oceans, now high above sea level and far removed from modern saline seas yet still cobbled with the fossilized remains of primordial marine life. Science sanctifies the ancient African rift valleys that cradle the subterranean bones of our origins, our shared humanoid ancestors. And it tutors us in the stirring tale of life's past, etched in pastel layers of sedimentary stone and waiting to be read in visually evocative geological wounds in the earth's crust such as the Colorado River's Grand Canyon.

Such aesthetically inspiring and ecologically or evolutionarily significant places on earth can represent, in some sense, the "sacred spaces" of modern science. These sites offer us an extraordinary intimacy with nature's orderly processes and interconnected designs and remind us of the timeless connection between landforms and all life.

Science's bright, "objective" light has provided us with increasingly elegant conceptual mirrors of nature. It has teased away a number of the vital living threads that bind the biosphere's intricate, interconnected flows of energy and matter into a single ecological whole. It has revealed this planet as the shared birthplace of all species and our only true home.

Yet in spite of such unifying insights, by its very nature scientific knowledge seems incapable of finally confirming human beings' responsibility for maintaining the integrity of the land. Science's "freeze-dried" abstract visions of the natural world are stripped of meaning and bereft of clues as to human environmental conduct, indeed are morally mute. And so we find ourselves, in times of crisis, compelled to search for less spiritually reticent ways of being in nature. We look longingly to other traditions that permit us to honor and protect the earth and openly proclaim the most precious places and processes of the natural world holy, in ways that complement the most precious insights of modern science.

~~~~~~~~~~~~~~~~~~~~~~~~~~~

The Sacred Microcosm of the Navajo Hogan [3]

AMERICAN SOUTHWEST:
Navajo

Modern man, the world eater, respects no space and no thing green or furred as sacred. The march of the machines has entered his blood.
—Loren Eiseley, anthropologist[4]

The Navajo hogan* is a spacious, dome-shaped dwelling, constructed of logs and mud, that gracefully complements the seasonal weather regimes and stark sandstone contours of the desert country of the American Southwest. It has long served as both shelter and theater for a wide range of activities in the lives of Navajo people—from cooking, weaving, sleeping, and childbearing to storytelling and ceremonial singing and prayer. To the Navajo, hogans are *not just places to eat and sleep, mere parts of the workaday world;* they occupy *a central place in the sacred world.*

The spiritual sanctity of the hogan has its roots in Navajo origin myth. The heroic acts of creation were carried out by First Man and First Woman, after their emergence upon the earth from the darker realms far below. One of their deeds was to build and bless the first ceremonial house, or hogan, on the earth's surface. There, protected by its skylike domed roof and surrounded, as far as the eye could see, by sterile waters, the primal pair fashioned the first fragile life-forms with which to populate the earth's untrammeled crust. Because the hogan—then and now—is a *microcosmic structure which stands at the center of the world, at the emergence place,* it came to symbolize the universe in its totality.

The hogan's sacredness permeates every feature of its design. From a mythical Navajo perspective, its very architecture matches in miniature the vast architecture of the universe. The hogan can be superimposed mentally upon the blue dome of the sky, which its dome-shaped roof reflects. Its flat dirt floor corresponds to the surface of the earth itself. Each of the four upright wooden pillars that support the roof is aligned and clearly identified with one of the four cardinal directions. The Navajo mind tends to link these directions together in a fluid "sunwise" flow—from east to south to west and finally to north—so that, when it is appropriate to do so, human motion can reverently mimic the sun's path. The single entrance to the

---

* This account is based on the contemporary form of the Navajo hogan, which apparently had its origins in the late nineteenth century. An earlier design, we are told, had a conical, forked-pole form. In either case, the plane formed by the intersection of the earth's surface and the Navajo hogan was a circle.

hogan faces east, in homage to the *sole opening of the world,* which lies in the east.

Sacred Space Its geometric form is central to the sanctity of the Navajo hogan. Traditionally, the house's outermost perimeter is always in the shape of a circle. In more recent hogan designs, the circle is also inscribed by the inner walls. In Navajo cosmological parlance the circle resonates with symbolic cosmic significance. The horizon, the great visible boundary between the edge of the earth and the edge of the sky, is circular. The daily trajectory of the sun through the firmament is circular. The radiant yellow disk of the sun, nature's annual cycles of growth and fertility, and the climatic turning of the seasons, are circular. And the path that the Navajo walk as they move in a sunwise direction inside the hogan, chanting and praying to restore the earth to the natural state of dynamic balance and environmental beauty called *hózhó,* is also circular.

The hogan's inherent sacredness is joyfully proclaimed in many Navajo stories, prayers, and songs. Much of Navajo life is lived within these sheltered spaces that are identified with the distant beginnings and outermost dimensions of the cosmos, and their influences are felt everywhere in Navajo culture. They are evident, for example, in this fragmentary refrain taken from a Chief Hogan song recited by the well-known Navajo Blessingway singer Frank Mitchell:

> *Howowo 'ai yeye 'aiye!*
> *It is a sacred house that I have come to,*
> *It is a sacred house that I have come to,* holaghei.
> *Now I have come to the house of the Earth.*

And the hogan's influences are apparent in one Navajo's description of the harmony of materials and messages within the sacred cosmos of the humble hogan:

The hogan is comprised of white shell, abalone, turquoise, and obsidian, bringing the home and the sacred mountains into one unit. The home is also adorned with the dawn, the blue sky, the twilight and the night—the sun in the center as the fire.

Could a sensitive modern ecologist—driven by a heartfelt passion for the beauty and well-being of the natural world—possibly conceive of a personal living space whose symbols and design features embody so effectively, and daily remind him of, the elegant scientific vision of the universe?

ΛΛΛΛΛΛΛΛΛΛΛΛΛΛΛΛΛΛΛΛΛΛ

How Humans, Spirit Power, and the Land Create a Living Whole [5]

CENTRAL BRITISH COLUMBIA:
Gitksan

Creation itself therefore, i.e. all evolving nature including the human brain and human psyche, logically takes on a relative degree of sacredness not present in dualistic thinking where the things that are most sacred are set apart in another form of existence.

—Roger Sperry, Nobel Prize–winning neurobiologist [6]

In traditional Gitksan society, a newborn baby emerges into the sanctuaries of two principal life-shaping social institutions. Based upon the lineage of the mother, a child will be granted membership in a particular Gitksan clan and house.

The hereditary clans number four: Giskaast, or Fireweed Clan; Lax Gibuu, or Wolf Clan; Lax Xskiik, or Eagle Clan; and Laxseel/Lax Ganed, or Frog Clan. Each clan contains a number of much more closely related kinship groups called houses—a name that reflects the fact that, as recently as last century, everyone in each house shared a single communal dwelling within a Gitksan community.

Each Gitksan house bears its own name, identity, and shared history. Its *ayuks,* or traditional crests, express these and are displayed at feasts as physical representations of the great formative events of the group's past: its mythic birth throes, its ancient military victories and defeats, its long legacy of supernatural dialogue, and its adventures with the forces of nature, ancestral life-forms, and local features of the land-scape. The crest is the fruit of a direct, ongoing communion with the natural world over a period of more than five thou-sand years, as the Gitksan have thrived amid the jagged snow-capped mountain ranges and thunderous, salmon-choked rivers of the British Columbia interior.

Each Gitksan house is the proud heir and owner of an *ada'ox.* This is a body of orally transmitted songs and stories that acts as the house's sacred archives and as its living, millennia-long memory of important events of the past. This irreplaceable verbal repository of knowledge consists in part of sacred songs believed to have arisen *literally from the breaths of the ancestors.* Far more than musical representations of his-tory, these songs serve as vital time-traversing vehicles. They can transport members across the immense reaches of space and time into the dim mythic past of Gitksan creation *by the very quality of their music and the emotions they convey.*

Taken together, these sacred possessions—the stories, the crests, the songs—provide a solid foundation for each Gitksan house and for the larger clan of which it is a part. According to living Gitksan elders, each house's holdings confirm its ancient *title to its territory and the legitimacy of its authority over it.*

In fact, so vital is the relationship between each house and the lands allotted to it for fishing, hunting, and food-gathering that the *daxgyet,* or spirit power, of each house and the land that sustains it are one. The spiritual connection between the Gitksan people and their traditional territories is captured in the totem poles, whose skyward spires of hand-carved human-animal crests recount the history of each house. In the memorable words of Delgam Uukw, a Gitksan, and Gisday Wa, a hereditary Wetśuwetén chief (spoken in 1987 in support of their ongoing land claim suits against Canadian govern-ments), each Gitksan totem pole *re-creates, by reaching upward,* the link with the spirit forces that give the people their power. This lovingly fashioned pole stands firmly upon sacred Gitksan soil, its face etched with the memories and dreams of its collective owners, *its roots spread out into the land, thereby linking man, spirit power, and the land so they form a living whole.*

For us, states Delgam Uukw, *the ownership of territory is a marriage of the Chief and the land. Each Chief has an ancestor who encountered and acknowledged the life of the land. From such encounters come power. The land, the animals and the people all have spirit—they all must be shown respect. That is the basis of our law.*

ΛΛΛΛΛΛΛΛΛΛΛΛΛΛΛΛΛΛΛΛ

Red Kangaroo Dreaming [7]

CENTRAL AUSTRALIA:
Aranda

A land ethic, then, reflects the existence of an ecological conscience, and this in return reflects a conviction of individual responsibility for the health of the land. Health is the capacity of the land for self-renewal. Conservation is our effort to understand and preserve this capacity.
—Aldo Leopold, ecologist[8]

Bone-dry river beds and grassy plains fan out from the northern flanks of the rugged Macdonnell mountain ranges of central Australia. Here the red kangaroo, *Macropus rufus,* is no ordinary marsupial to members of the venerable Krantji Kangaroo clan, who trace their spiritual lineage to this totemic figure.

These Northern Aranda people are Australian Aborigines whose traditional homelands encompass the parched region. To them the powerful, fleet-footed red kangaroo is also a beloved ancestor, shaper of the landscape, and immortal being of that timeless, instructive, and never-ending epoch of creation and earthly transformation widely known as the Dreamtime, Dreaming, or Creation Time.

During the Dreaming, according to one Aranda story, great herds of red kangaroos sometimes assembled on a grassy, mountain-fringed, idyllic plain. Here, surrounded by bees, bandicoots, birds, and other kindred animals and plants, the kangaroos talked to the mulga parrots, their paternal aunts and trusted allies. During daylight hours, the watchful parrots cry out to arouse the sleeping kangaroos if hunters happen to venture too near. When night falls, all the animals return to a deep, subterranean realm, where, metamorphosed back into human form, they gather together until dawn. The kindly mulga parrots, now transformed into women, bring the humanoid red kangaroos skin bags filled with cool water, which they have earlier laboriously flown from afar. At dawn, the entire Dreamtime congregation ascends to the earth's surface, where they resume their animal forms and habits.

Today, in this vast undulating landscape of scrub mulga woodland, and desert plain, no place is more sacred to the Red Kangaroo clan than a single, small natural spring known as Krantji. This spring is nothing less than the *pmara kutata,* or everlasting home, of Krantjirinja—their Original Ancestor, the leader, or "chief," of their Red Kangaroo clan. Out of the cool depths of the spring's perennial waters, they say, *sprang into life Krantjirinja himself, who was a true kangaroo.*

Krantjirinja emerged from the subterranean earth-womb as a fully formed red kangaroo, endowed with the animal's massively muscled body and hind limbs. But he was clearly no ordinary kangaroo. During daylight, as he grazed effortlessly upon the lush green herbs and grasses surrounding the sacred spring, he retained his animal form. But with the setting of the searing sun, Krantjirinja took on a human form. After decorating his transformed body with bold white geometric patterns fashioned from tufts of down feathers, he danced and sang in ecstasy until dawn.

To the Aranda, Krantji spring is sacred because it is the aperture through which the Red Kangaroo chief made his first appearance on earth after the *awakening of the ancestors from their eternal sleep underneath the sheltering crust.* It is also sacred because Krantjirinja's presence continues to animate this place, to pulsate from it, in ways that challenge the human imagination and that permeate the natural world. His creative, life-rejuvenating powers seem to imbue Krantji spring with a life of its own.

Beneath its sun-dappled waters, say the Aranda, an ancient sunken shield has lain for centuries. Beneath this shield are several sacred stone slabs known as *tjurunga.* It has long been the traditional duty of each generation of the Red Kangaroo clan to ceremonially honor and care for these stones, not simply because they are passive symbols of the clan's enduring bond with the red kangaroo but because they are remnants of the living tissue of Krantjirinja, their common ancestor. In this sense, the *tjurunga* at Krantji are *visible embodiments of some part of the fertility of the great ancestor.* They are biological reservoirs of reproductive energy from which *all kangaroo ancestors arise in batches,* emerging first in *the form of kangaroos,* then assuming *human bodies.*

And what of the Red Kangaroo chief Krantjirinja himself, that eternal figure who oscillates so effortlessly from marsupial to man? The Aranda point to him as the *living essence* of the Dreamtime unity of the two species. But how can ordinary language—Aranda or English—possibly capture the extraordinary focus, the commonality, the timelessness that Krantjirinja brings to the clan lineages?

The Northern Aranda themselves have not yet provided us with a definitive published account of their vision of Krantjirinja's crucial role in the cyclic processes of nature. But the well-known Australian anthropologist T.G.H. Strehlow spoke Aranda and traveled deep into traditional Aranda territory in the company of Aranda elders. In his classic text *Aranda Traditions,* published in 1947, Strehlow hinted at some of the possible layers of meaning in Aranda images of the Original Ancestors. As he struggled to communicate the arcane aspects of Aranda thought on this pivotal theme, he often relied upon

some of the most powerful and evocative images and metaphors of modern science, ranging from cell biology to atomic
physics.

Every cell of the original ancestor, Strehlow wrote, *is a living
human being.* Whether one speaks of the ancestral Witchetty
Grub (a larval form of a local insect), the ancestral Bandicoot (a
local marsupial), the Red Kangaroo, or some other totemic
figure of shared human and animal Dreamtime origins, *every
cell in his body is potentially either a separate living witchetty grub,*
bandicoot, or red kangaroo, respectively—*or a separate living
man of the witchetty grub totem,* Bandicoot totem, or Red Kangaroo totem. The Original Ancestor is the ancestor of all living
human beings in his totem clan *and* of all living animals of his
kind. Within each clan, human and animal are bound together
by common descent, mutual concern, and shared destiny.

During the course of a particular ancestor's heroic, land-
sculpting journey on, under, or above the earth's virginal Creation Time surface, the ancestor left in its wake a sacred,
eternal, living spoor. Rock formations, trees, water holes, and
other features that dot the local terrain mark ancestral Dreamtime passages, record their dramas, and entomb many of its
principal characters, as if in slumber. At the same time, these
sacred places are centers of nature's reproductive powers.
Each hero's Dreamtime journey is permanently etched in the
earth's crust in a trail (in Strehlow's poignant phrase, with a
nod to modern embryology) of *potential life-cells which are only
waiting for an opportunity to assume some visible, corporeal form.*

In this sense, the vitality of the Red Kangaroo ancestor
inhabiting Krantji spring is at once spiritual and ecological. His
story is a reflection of the Aranda peoples' Dreamtime origins
and religious duties, and of the primal, cyclic, life-perpetuating
processes of the natural world. In at least one of his aspects,
Krantjirinja embodies the essence of nature's life force and
fertility, the primordial, pervasive, and perplexing life-stuff
that animates all living things. He possesses an element of the
elusive vitality that pulsates in the mulga parrot's cries, that
causes the pale yellow bloodwood-tree blossoms to burst

open, and that fuels the mad, unseen mitotic cell divisions of a red kangaroo fetus developing within the sanctuary of its mother's pouch.

Their knowledge that the local terrain is a sacred map of their animal ancestor's journeys gives members of the Red Kangaroo clan an extraordinary sense of participation in the workings of local ecosystems. If local big-game populations dwindle, for example, the Aranda hunter can communicate directly, through ritual and prayer, with the forces of nature that have thereby placed his existence in peril. Radiating out from Krantji spring along the Dreamtime trails of the clan-animal ancestor are indelible geographic points where human beings can communicate with the *sum total of living human and animal fertility.*

More than this, the hunter's understanding of the Creation Time connections between the topography of the land and nature's mysterious regenerative powers allows him to work in harmony with the forces of fertility. As Strehlow suggests (fusing an image from modern physics with one from modern biology), he can *create the animals he needs with ease, simply by rubbing a portion of the rock representing the changed body of the ancestor with a stone; for every atom of that rock is a potential animal.*

There is breathtaking beauty in the Northern Aranda notion of Red Kangaroo Dreaming—of a shared totemic ancestor whose Dreaming tracks across the earth artfully intersect with, illuminate, and animate the lives of human beings, red kangaroos, and countless other life-forms and processes.

Indeed, during their heroic Creation Time treks across the landscape, the ancestors left a trail of words and musical notes as well as indelible physical footprints, permanently etching their stories in the earth. Generations later, by devoutly singing the appropriate sacred song, a totemic clansman could reliably navigate for days along these great Dreamtime tracks. In the process, the land would be rejuvenated, memories of totemic ancestors would be ritually rekindled, and reunions with faraway kinsmen would take place along the ancient Dreamtime spoor of stone, story, and song. *In theory, at least, the whole of Australia could be read as a musical score,* Bruce Chatwin states succinctly, in his book *The Songlines. One should perhaps visualize the Songlines as a spaghetti of Iliads and Odysseys, writhing this way and that, in which every "episode" was readable in terms of geology.*

But beyond lending a sense of spirituality and cosmic order within the Aboriginal world, can these ancient beliefs convey genuine ecological insights into the workings of nature?

In December 1980, A. E. Newsome, a wildlife biologist and a respected authority on the natural history and ecology of the red kangaroo, published a brief but remarkable article that calmly suggests that Aranda Red Kangaroo stories might harbor considerably more scientific meaning than skeptics had imagined. In his cautiously worded paper "The Eco-Mythology of the Red Kangaroo in Central Australia," published in the journal *Mankind,* Newsome reported on an intriguing *congruence of myth and reality.* In fact, the Northern Aranda stories about Red Kangaroo Dreaming and the sacred spring at Krantji, he wrote, *may have an underlying ecological rationale.*

Relying upon living Aboriginal elders and Strehlow's classic Aranda texts, Newsome meticulously pieced together segments of the meandering Dreaming trails evoked in certain Red Kangaroo stories. He matched sacred Aranda sites mentioned in accounts of the mythological journeys of the ancestors with actual physical locations.

Although Krantji was not the only sacred site where Aranda hunters sought to ritually renew precious red kangaroo populations, some of the most important increase ceremonies were carried out here. Always, the Aranda approached Krantji *in silence and reverence,* eyes closed, fingers feeling their way along familiar facades of rock—*already having laid down their weapons some ways off to indicate to the ancestors their homage and peaceful intent.* By disarming, the hunters offered a friendly signal not only to their ancestors but to the kangaroos. For *there was no hunting near ceremonial sites:* kangaroos themselves were sacred and protected here.

Upon approaching the Krantji spring—apparently located in a narrow stone crevice near a distinctive rock formation covered with gleaming white limestone—the members of the Red Kangaroo clan performed their primary task. They struck sacred rocks and trees in the vicinity, knowing that *every grain dislodged arose as a kangaroo when next it rained,* and singing to Krantji:

> *Be fruitful in the ancestral embrace,*
> *Filled with game for the use of men!*

The red kangaroo, a herbivore, leads a nomadic existence, patiently pursuing seasonal abundances of edible green plants as they arise. In this part of central Australia, it depends most heavily upon the green plants that flourish along the moist, shady drainages of rivers and creeks. Throughout the year its most reliable staple is *Eragrostis stifolia,* a grass known locally as "Never-Fail" because of its hardiness in the face of recurring drought.

Because of its dietary preferences, the red kangaroo's range follows rather closely the patterns of high soil moisture created as waters drain the lower slopes and adjacent plains of the northern Macdonnell Ranges. During dry spells, the animals tend to congregate near river beds and plains, where grasses still thrive. After the seasonal rainstorms they fan out more, feeding on fresh greenery that stretches into drier savannahs and mulga-tree woodlands.

Aboriginal tales of the Dreamtime travels of Krantjirinja and other kangaroo ancestors during the Creation Time, Newsome found, revealed a sophisticated grasp of red kangaroo ecology. A map of the ancestors' overland trek near Krantji—breathing life and form into the landscape as they went—corresponded with uncanny precision to maps of the preferred habitats of red kangaroo, which Newsome had painstakingly assembled by scientific study. Conversely, a map of the subterranean portions of the ancestors' Dreamtime journeys, during which their radiant powers are diminished, corresponded neatly with expanses of desert lands largely inhospitable to red kangaroo populations.

This striking complementary relationship between orally transmitted Creation Time cartography and modern data on red kangaroo populations, concluded Newsome, could hardly be serendipitous. On the contrary, he stated,

The ancient Aborigines who created these legends must have been well acquainted with the ecology of the red kangaroo, and appear to have passed that knowledge into the mythology to be hidden by allegory.

Traditional Aranda beliefs about the sacred site called Krantji appear to represent a remarkable fusion of ecological and spiritual knowledge. They encode genuine ecological truths about the population dynamics and dietary preferences of local red kangaroos. At the same time, unlike sterile scientific findings, they contain a moral code mandating irrevocable human responsibility to honor and nurture those precious, life-sustaining animal populations in perpetuity.

A taboo against hunting red kangaroos in areas surrounding sacred clan-totemic sites like Krantji is, in effect, a potent conservation tool. These sacred places are often located along the overland Dreaming trails of the ancestors, corresponding to prime red kangaroo habitat. Embedded in ancient Aranda spiritual knowledge of the origins and eternal fecundity of the red kangaroo is a potentially powerful environmental ethic that must have ensured, wrote Newsome, that the *red kangaroos were protected near their best habitat.*

By periodically paying homage to the Original Ancestor of the red kangaroo, Aranda hunters established, in essence, spiritual and ecological "reserves" for this species. Over generations their sustained reverence was probably rewarded. Sacred songs, dances, and prayers performed in such sanctuaries sustained and even seemed to renew local kangaroo populations, just as if precious particles of dust from beloved sacred kangaroo sites like Krantji *became a kangaroo when next it rained,* as Strehlow's account puts it.

In essence, concludes zoologist Newsome, *the Aborigines had so fashioned their beliefs that they had a high chance of success.* Such a poignant marriage of spirit and ecology is inconceivable without a profound, enduring sensitivity to the *real* workings of the natural world over great expanses of time. Over millennia, by seamlessly combining ancient spiritual insights into the human psyche with painstakingly accumulated knowledge of the concrete structures and processes of nature, Aranda thought and memory seem to have given birth to a "land ethic" in the truest, most holistic, sense of that term. For the traditions surrounding the Red Kangaroo Dreaming at Krantji, to the extent that we understand them, equip human beings with a profound emotional and ecological connection with the rest of creation and, as a result, with, in Aldo Leopold's apt phrase, an "ecological conscience"—a responsibility to conserve forever *the capacity of the land for self-renewal.*

The Heart of Our Mother Earth

ARIZONA:
Hopi

*The Earth is the birthplace of our species and, so
far as we know our only home. . . . We are close
to committing—many would argue we are already committing—what in our language is
sometimes called Crimes against Creation.*
—"Preserving and Cherishing the Earth: An
Appeal for Joint Commitment in Science
and Religion," a public statement signed by
astronomers Carl Sagan and Freeman
Dyson, atmospheric scientist Stephen
Schneider, and biologists Peter Raven,
Roger Revelle, and Stephen Jay Gould,
among other distinguished scientists

To outsiders, the ecological perceptions and land ethics of First
Nations sometimes seem rather elusive, subtly veiled in ceremonies and Creation stories or in linguistic, symbolic, and
experiential barriers to their understanding. But Westerners
can scarcely ignore the thrust of Native nature-wisdom when
a Native community issues a public statement in defense of the
land. Often such environmental statements have been addressed to people around the world, in the language of the
dominant society and in utter desperation. Westerners should
consider their words as generous cross-cultural gifts to educate
them about the destructiveness of their workaday worlds. On
the other hand, they are also often bold, contemporary reaffir-
mations and reformations of Native thought and identity.

One lucid public proclamation of Native attitudes toward
traditional lands is reprinted here in part. It was originally
issued by Lomayaktewa, Starlie, Mina Lansa, Ned Nayatewa,
Claude Kewanyama, Jack Pongayesvia, Thomas Banyacya,

Sr., David Monogye, and Carlotta Shattuck, under the title "Statement of Hopi Religious Leaders." The respected Hopi spokesperson Thomas Banyacya graciously gave us permission to quote from the undated five-page mimeographed statement, signed by these Hopi religious leaders, the official interpreter, and the recorder, while we were interviewing him at his home in the Hopi village of Kykotsomovie, Arizona, in March 1990. Its heartfelt words and values, we feel, require no commentary:

Hopi land is held in trust in a spiritual way for the Great Spirit, Massau'u. Sacred Hopi ruins are planted over the Four Corners area, including Black Mesa. This land is like the sacred inner chamber of a church—our Jerusalem.

The area we call Tukunavi (which includes Black Mesa) is part of the heart of our Mother Earth. Within this heart, the Hopi has left his seal by leaving religious items and clan markings and plantings and ancient burial grounds as his landmarks and shrines and as his directions to others that the land is his. The ruins are Hopi's landmark. Only the Hopi will know what is here for him to identify—others will not know.

This land was granted to the Hopi by a power greater than man can explain. Title is invested in the whole make-up of Hopi life. Everything is dependent on it. The land is sacred and if the land is abused, the sacredness of Hopi life will disappear and all other life as well.

The Great Spirit has told the Hopi Leaders that the great wealth and resources beneath the lands at Black Mesa must not be disturbed or taken out until after purification when mankind will know how to live in harmony among themselves and with nature. The Hopi were given special guidance in caring for our sacred lands so as not to disrupt the fragile harmony that hold things together. . . .

To us, it is unthinkable to give up control over our sacred lands to non-Hopis. We have no way to express exchange of sacred lands for money. It is alien to our ways. The Hopis never gave authority to anyone to dispose of our lands and heritage and religion for any price. We received these lands from the Great Spirit and we must hold them for him, as a steward, a caretaker, until he returns.[9]

Bone Country [10]

NORTHERN AUSTRALIA:
Murngin

*Conservation is a state of harmony between men
and land. By land is meant all the things on, over,
or in the earth. Harmony with land is like harmony with a friend; you cannot cherish his right
hand and chop off his left. That is to say, you
cannot love game and hate predators; you cannot
conserve the waters and waste the ranges; you
cannot build the forest and mine the farm. The
land is one organism.*

—Aldo Leopold, ecologist[11]

High in the eastern region of that blunt, peninsular, north-
ernmost nub of Australia—the place called Arnhem Land—
dwell the Aboriginal people known as the Murngin. Here in
Arnhem Land's rugged, rain-strafed landscapes—its pale
weathered cliffs of naked, bonelike sedimentary rock; its thunderous waterfalls; its sun-baked thickets of rainforest vegetation; its great fetid swamps, choked with decaying vegetation
and creased by the gliding forms of ravenous crocodiles—here
the Murngin look upon their traditional lands as the ultimate
spiritual, evolutionary, and ecological source of their lives.

Their elemental sense of blood kinship and primordial oneness with the land is kept constantly alive in Murngin hearts
and minds by social institutions. Like many other Australian
Aboriginal peoples, Murngin society routinely assigns community members to a particular clan—a traditional group
united by a deep solidarity with designated objects or animal
and plant species.

170   The Murngin believe the potent clan bond is inherited
through one's father's lineage from ancient Creation Time

ancestors. Invariably, the bond extends far beyond specific animal ancestors—the sacred spiders and bats, boulders and billibongs—into the land itself. Branching out into Arnhem Land's tortured terrain like a diffuse plexus of fine blood-bearing capillaries, it nourishes the earth—and is in turn nourished by the earth.

Each totemic clan is the proud owner of its own estate, a divinely apportioned area of the landscape encompassing major and minor ceremonial sites. The clan's Creation Time origins and obligations mandate these sites. In addition to bearing eternal collective responsibility for its sacred territory, the clan is endowed with a repertoire of *sacred songs, rites and paraphernalia that* [have long] *constituted the title deeds to the territory.*

So spiritually potent is a clan's sacred land that it is believed to have the power of insemination. Every human fetus conceived within its boundaries—even by transient parents journeying from the tropical interior to the seacoast—is thought to be quickened somehow by the land. Thus, the person into whom the fetus eventually develops is eternally bound to the land where the conception took place. The person also becomes bound to the often burdensome primary duties to the clan, regardless of the person's place of birth. In this manner, *one man's conception totem can be another man's patrilineal*—that is, paternally inherited—*clan totem.* This lifelong Aboriginal bond with the land deepens the individual's sense of responsibility for kindred Dreamtime spirits and spaces.

The Rrarigurak Gurumba Gurumba clan, a Murngin totemic group, tells a story that offers a vivid glimpse into the Murngin's extraordinary sense of connection to their land. According to Australian anthropologist Nicolas Peterson, this clan traces its roots to an ancestral hero named Kurko Akowar—a divine masculine human-canine figure of the Dreaming epoch. This ancestral Male Dog-Man, Kurko Akowar, determined the character of the clan's sacred land-base.

The sacred landholdings of the Rrarigurak Gurumba Gurumba clan border the expansive, stagnant waters of Arafura Swamp. Within the estate's boundaries are diverse terrains: lowland tropical rain forest, ridges faced by steep cliffs and cut by gurgling streams, and on higher ground, dry plateaus greened by hardy eucalyptus trees.

During the Dreaming era, Kurko Akowar was transformed into the shape of a man. He burst through the earth's surface from the dark, cavernous underworld, with the aid of his enormous penis. He emerged with great force at a place marked today by a huge boulder in a stream bed, near the stream's source. As he emerged, he created the stream, which gushes like semen down a forested slope to enrich the low, languid waters of Arafura Swamp.

Then Kurko Akowar clambered down the steep, two-hundred-foot-high escarpment, where he had made his dramatic entrance, to the great swamp. He left behind a monumental spoor as a reminder to his descendants of his passage, and with each incident in his journey he transformed the topography of the earth. The marks that he made upon the land were much like the footprints, blackened campfires, and holes that mortal humans leave behind, or the broken shells, bones, and other debris they heap into garbage piles. They differ only in scale. Each time Kurko Akowar paused to rest, the weight of his body formed a crater that created quiet pools in the stream. When he paused to defecate, his excreta became the precious deposits of white clay that the Murngin still use in their ceremonies.

Finally, Kurka Akowar returned to the rock where he had first emerged and reentered the womblike opening in the earth where the stream had its source. There, according to the Rrarigurak Gurumba Gurumba clan, he dwells today before the flames of a subterranean fire—the sacred Murngin symbol of women and their reproductive power.

Kurka Akowar's remarkable earth-shaping travels are recalled by the clan in design, ritual, and song. But clan members have no need to examine cryptic emblems or ponder the details of stories and songs to remember the Dreaming odysseys and antics of Kurka Akowar and other ancestral heroes. They are permanently encoded, for those with eyes to see and understand them, in the local flora, fauna, and geological features of the land, especially at the locations where Dreamtime ancestors like Kurko Akowar first appeared. These sacred places, sporadic upwellings of an unseen subterranean current that ultimately animates all forms of life, are the primary *foci of collective clan sentiments that lie at the core of the relationship of the people to the land.*

Local regions of the earth's surface, then, are integral not only to traditional Murngin ancestry, kinship relationships, and identity but also to the Murngin mind. From their perspective, the landscape itself and its distinctive colors, odors, and contours functions as a living extension of the human brain. Not unlike the areas of the brain that chemically encode and store memories, the land here is a living repository of the past—replete with cryptic messages, cues, and moral reminders from the Dreamtime era.

In the absence of written words and permanent man-made monuments to bolster fickle human memory, the Murngin and other Australian Aborigines traditionally have relied on the script of sacred geography. To them, the land itself is a living, ever accessible repository of their memories of the Creation Time order that has long sustained them. Within their worldview, place itself is the mnemonic of significant events and of personal and group history.

This pivotal notion of place is so deeply ingrained in Murngin sensibilities that it is discernible even in routine greetings. When two Murngins first meet, they ask about each other's geographical roots. The identity of a Murngin man or woman can be shaped by both the clan totem and the conception totem; a person will ask a stranger about both.

When a Murngin man encounters a stranger, he might first ask in which sacred territory he was biologically conceived: *"From which water do you come?"*

Then he asks the stranger about the sacred territory of his hereditary totemic clan. The question is simple and direct, and in its anatomical metaphor, it unambiguously expresses the potent, formative role that the Murngin associate with the hereditary landscape.

Sacred Space

"*Where,*" he asks, probing the depths of the other's identity, "*is your bone country?*"

8

Time as a
Circle

Responding to the Rhythms
of Nature

The increase of disorder or entropy with time is
one example of what is called our arrow of time,
something that distinguishes the past from the
future, giving a direction to time.
— Stephen Hawking, astrophysicist[1]

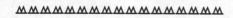

A society's conception of time is one of the pillars of its world-view, its shared ideas and images that grant order and meaning to the universe. Time is the concept that binds together what might otherwise appear to be a chaos of cosmic elements and events. It exposes causal relationships and associations between events and explains their relative permanence or impermanence. Time can even reveal, by extrapolation, the future forms and destinies of things. Time is, in some sense, the warp and weft of the whole cosmic tapestry; and the human imagination, with its culturally sanctioned freedoms and restraints, is its weaver.

Within a given community, time provides the rhythm by which stories of mortal individuals and the earth unfold. It is the lens through which we see and chronicle all natural phenomena. Thus, the way that a people views the passage of time—the particular "geometry" that they assign to time—plays a crucial role in shaping their relationship with the natural world.

The phrase "time's arrow" captures the essence of the conventional Western concept of chronological time, at least psychologically. Deeply embedded within it is the idea that time is linear, sequential, and unidirectional, like an arrow, speeding away from the taut bowstring that launched it toward its unseen target, never to retrace its trajectory. Both past and future are potentially infinite.

This arrowlike model of time is a foundation of Western civilization and thought. Linear time underlies our most cherished notions of "progress"—our collective faith in the inexorable, incremental refinement of human society, technology, and thought. Linear time, the spinal column of Western notions of history, neatly aligns the jumble of past human experience that might otherwise seem unsettling or devoid of meaning into an orderly, chronological procession of sequential events, each "officially" assigned its own measure of "importance."

Western science, an integral part of the Western worldview, is similarly dominated by the notion of linear time. Despite brilliant detours by Albert Einstein and other twentieth-century physicists into time's more subtly abstract aspects, such as its astonishing elasticity, time's arrow continues to serve as the mainspring for much of modern scientific thinking.

Modern astrophysicists calculate the chronological ages of distant stars based on the colors of their spectral light. Modern geologists assess the chronological ages of certain kinds of rock by using the predictable decomposition of radioactive Uranium-238. And modern evolutionary biologists chronicle the sequential emergence of diverse forms of life by collecting fossil imprints in earthen layers of known age or by monitoring minute molecular "clocks" in the form of fickle chemical bonds in DNA and other genetic molecules.

Yet science can also be said to recognize, if secondarily, a quite different quality of time, one whose "geometry" can be described as circular and recurrent. While the notion of circular time might at first seem paradoxical, even heretical, it permeates our daily lives. Many familiar rhythms of the natural world, such as the passing of the solar seasons, the fluctuations of predator and prey populations, and the replication cycles of DNA can be seen as eloquent expressions of cyclical time operating within a grander framework of linear time.

The pervasiveness of "time's circle" in nature is no accident. Many recurrent rhythms of biological processes can be traced to the shifting influences of the sun and the moon, which have served as celestial "heartbeats" throughout the evolution of life on earth. Our tilted planet's annual orbit around the sun reliably divides the year into predictable seasons. The earth's axial spin results in a daily regimen of sunrises and sunsets, days and nights. The moon orbits monthly around the earth, and its shifting gravitational urgings produce corresponding tidal ebbs and flows in the earth's water.

Such primary rhythms set into motion a host of secondary fluctuations in light, temperature, and humidity that reverberate through the natural world, profoundly affecting all organisms. In response, evolutionary forces have often shaped the sensory capacities of species to capitalize on these rhythms, sometimes even equipping them with remarkably accurate internal biological "clocks."

The seasonal changes of a deciduous forest in north-central North America reflect circular time, as the leaves of its maples, beeches, and other trees change color, are shed, then are replaced each year. The shells of tiny, coastal shore-living fiddler crabs undergo periodic color changes that are biologically cued by daily and lunar light-dark cycles. Tobacco, soybeans, and countless other plants begin to flower only after their daily dose of sunlight has reached a threshold level conducive to successful seed production and germination.

Starlings, finches, and many other birds display similar reproductive synchrony with twenty-four-hour, or circadian, sunlight rhythms. Many mammals—flying squirrels, hamsters, antler-crowned elk and deer, and even human beings—exhibit patterns of growth, metabolic activity, and behavior that reflect the rhythmic pendulums of the natural world.

Biologists are keenly aware that in some sense nature is rooted in circular time, even as linear time's relentless arrow, and the cosmos's inexorable increase in entropy, or disorder, continue unabated in the background. Viewed up close and prescientifically, the recurrent natural rhythms of circular time could quite legitimately be perceived as primary, life-affirming cycles. To many Native peoples, some of these cycles have always been sacred, worthy of the most profound veneration, and steeped in signs and significance for all humankind. Through ancient nature-honoring rituals, the primeval cycles of nature—and circular time itself—are symbolically renewed, and rendered "eternally present"—in essence, timeless. Far from being reduced to abstractions, they are personally and collectively *experienced* as living ecological and spiritual circles of time.

There is a place in Native and Western worldviews for both linear and circular time. But Western society and Western science have historically tended to put enormous emphasis upon the former, often relegating the latter to the margins of our daily lives, values, and experiences. Native societies, by contrast, have traditionally embraced manifestations of circular time in the universe, sanctifying them with their rituals and their awe. We in the West are inclined to look out upon a vast panorama of linear, profane time, punctuated, if we are fortunate, with little more than a transient sense of a spiritually and ecologically charged "timeless" dimension of nature. To Native eyes, the same universe is temporally unified by a vast continuity of personal glimpses—by vision quests, songs, and ceremonies, by dreams and creation stories—into the sacred whirlpool of timeless cosmic, or mythic, time.

These ancient, hard-won indigenous images of nature's sacred cycles and of human obligations to maintain them need not threaten cherished Western visions of time. But they could provide useful common ground between Western and indigenous thought. They could help to guide Westerners toward a scientifically sound vision of circular time: a psychologically integrating, rather than fragmenting, fusion of time's circular and linear aspects. What we might call time's "spiral" could help transform our society by transforming our views of ourselves.

Viewed in the context of "spiral time," traditional Native tales of world creation and catastrophe, of mythic heroics and follies, might be seen in a new and more respectful light. While we are not suggesting that these could serve as some sort of mystical "crystal balls" for reliable predictions of our ecological future, many of these wise and "timeless" tales are applicable to all humankind and are capable of helping us mesh the ticking of our modern mechanical clocks with the simultaneous spin of nature's seasons. While they cannot precisely predict recurrent human crises and dilemmas, these cross-cultural stories often contain revelatory insights into human nature and the natural world that can help to awaken the possibility that familiar patterns of the past—great cycles of growth and decline, birth and death, ecological devastation and renewal—can, and perhaps will, re-emerge.

AAVVVVVVVVVAAVVVVVVVVVVVM

A Year of Caribou Moons [2]

NORTH AMERICAN ARCTIC:
Barren Grounds Inuit

*Life began a long time ago. The date of the event
is unknown, but it was at least three thousand six
hundred million years before we were born.
Numbers as large as this are anesthetic and
paralyze the imagination.*

—James Lovelock, British chemist[3]

The Barren Grounds Inuit of north-central Canada mark the passage of time by the cycle of seasons during the solar year and the corresponding patterns of life cycles in the local environment.

The Inuit mark the onset of this natural cycle not with a celestial event such as a solstice or a full moon but with the life-affirming arrival of the beloved caribou herds to their lands in May. In their traditional world, the caribou is the most important species. Its spectacular seasonal movements provide the Inuit with periodic supplies of meat, hide, antlers, and other material resources vital to their survival in the harsh landscape. In the Inuit cosmos, time is expressed as the ancient intersection of the migratory caribou's annual life cycle with the life of the Inuit community—underpinned by the moon's silent cadences.

According to Igyugaryuk, an Inuit man interviewed by

Knud Rasmussen early in this century, a year in the life of a Barren Grounds Inuit community is measured in sixteen stages. Each stage is intimately associated with a recurrent lunar or biological event in the regional surroundings. Together, they constitute a circle—a chronological and ecological whole that is at once celebratory, reassuringly repetitive, as subtly supple as nature itself, and incandescent with the periodic patterns of growth and regeneration.

Ate'rwik is the first month of their year. Its Inuit name is translated as the *moon in which the caribou go down* from the forests in the south to Baker Lake (approximately early May).

The second month, *avitaq,* or *the divided moon,* is a time of transition. Both snowless and snow-carpeted terrains, both thawed and frozen waters, are routinely encountered in the local landscape (approximately June).

Kanralak is the time of *caribou skins with two kinds of hair,* when new hair growth appears beneath the old in the coats of caribou (approximately early July).

*Atayn—the one with the open mouth—*is the season when the Inuit begin to observe young fledgling birds sitting in their nests, their mouths hungrily agape (approximately late July).

*Tuktunigfik—the moon in which the caribou come—*is initiated by the coming of new caribou herds from a nearby region of lakes and plains (approximately August).

Akuglerorfik is *the moon in which the caribou have a medium coat.* It conveys the time, keenly recognized by Inuit hunters, when the coats of the caribou are neither extremely short or extremely thin (approximately late August or early September).

*Ameraiyarwik—the moon in which the caribou antlers lose their skin—*expresses a more dramatic change in the lives of the caribou (approximately late September).

*Nikliha'rwik—the moon in which it begins to be cool—*is the time when fragile sheets of ice begin to form on small pools of standing water (approximately early October).

Similarly, *hikoha'rwik,* or *the moon in which the big lakes begin to cover over,* commemorates the initial freezing-over of larger bodies of water (approximately late October).

Nuliarwik is *the moon in which the caribou mate* (approximately November).

Katagarivwik is *the moon in which the antlers fall from the caribou bulls* (approximately December).

Itlivik is *the moon in which something is laid in,* when fetuses begin to form in pregnant caribou cows (approximately late January and early February).

*Aungniwik—abortion month—*is marked by extremely frigid temperatures. Because of the severe dietary restrictions imposed by extreme cold and deep snow cover, many caribou cows suffer miscarriages (approximately late February and early March).

*Tarquenaq—the nameless moon—*is thought to be an especially dangerous month, when human beings are exposed to extraordinary risk of hunger and are therefore particularly obligated to obey spiritual teachings and taboos (approximately March).

*Tukiliarwik—the moon in which the caribou must begin to go through the country—*is when the southern herds, having grown restless, are beginning to migrate northward (approximately April).

The Barren Grounds Inuit year concludes with *imingnar-qivwik—the moon in which the roofs fall down.* The warmth of the sun, increasingly overhead and more potent by now, begins to melt Inuit dwellings of ice and snow (approximately early May).

It, in turn, flows fluidly again into the first Inuit month—*ate'rwik, the moon in which the caribou go down—*as the solar-driven life cycles of the precious caribou begin anew, like the lives of the human beings who depend upon them.

In this way, the Inuit pay homage not only to primary celestial rhythms in their universe but to the more subtle and imprecise ecological rhythms in the visible patterns of life, experience, and memory upon the surface of the land.

Swan Time 4

NORTHEASTERN BRITISH COLUMBIA:
Dunne-za (Beaver)

And so they live and have their being—these
cranes—not in the constricted present, but in the
wider reaches of evolutionary time. Their annual
return is the ticking of the geological clock. . . .
[And] the sadness discernible in some marshes
arises, perhaps, from their once having harbored
cranes. Now they stand humbled, adrift in
history.

—Aldo Leopold, ecologist[5]

The lives of the Dunne-za, a traditional hunting people of the forested Canadian subarctic, have always moved to a circular rhythm. In fact, the circle is so central to their ecological and spiritual visions that their cosmos is replete with living loops, each interacting with every other, each resonating with and within a grand, all-embracing circle of time.

Canadian anthropologist Robin Ridington, who has studied and written about the Dunne-za since 1964, offers several eloquently simple illustrations of the recurrent Dunne-za image of the time-mediated circle.

During the transmission of sacred knowledge from one generation to the next, the wise Dunne-za elder and the tender Dunne-za youth *circle around to touch one another.* The Dunne-za hunter, during his revelatory dreams about the animals he is destined to stalk, kill, eat, and honor, *circles around to touch his game* as he sleeps.

In the same way, the burning disk of the sun *circles around to touch a different place on the horizon with each passing day.* And it also *circles from northern to southern points of rising and setting.* So, too, during the spring breeding season, courting pairs of grouse flaunt their feathers flamboyantly and act out their deep-seated prenuptial passions in the circular choreography of their mating dances.

So do pale flocks of migrating swans, their great feathered wings beating slowly, turn overhead in collective circles before they *fly south to a land of flowing water when winter takes the northern forest in its teeth of ice.*

And much as the sun curves across the sky from dawn to dusk and shift slowly southward during the transition from summer to winter, so, too, the mind of the wise Dunne-za Dreamer circles while his *body lies pressed to earth, head to the east, in anticipation of another day's return.*

Dunne-za Dreamers are gifted members of the community who take ecstatic journeys on their songs in order to *dream ahead for everybody.* They are acutely aware of the parallels between their spiritual trajectories and those of feathered swans. The Dreamer soars aloft on perilous circular voyages to the unseen world of his ancestors, then returns wiser and reborn; so the swan periodically takes winged, sky-piercing flight in its spectacular fall migration to unseen southerly realms, only to return revitalized the following spring. In the words of Charlie Yahey, a modern Dunne-za Dreamer:

> *Even swans, when they have hard luck in the fall time*
> *and start to starve, they can just go right through the sky*
> *to heaven without dying.*
> *Swans are the only big animals that God made*
> *that can go to heaven without dying.*

The incandescent sun and the consciousness of the ecstatic Dreamer, who *is able to leave his body on earth and fly like a swan along a trail of song that is* Yagatunne, *the Trail to Heaven,* might be said to *shine on one another,* thereby mutually illuminating each other.

The Pulsations of Cosmic Time [6]

AMERICAN SOUTHWEST:
Navajo

The cosmological arrow of time . . . is the direc-
tion of time in which the universe is expanding
rather than contracting.

—Stephen Hawking, astrophysicist[7]

Traditional Navajo men and women, like human beings everywhere, experience a linear dimension of time in their daily
lives: in the chronological passage of years between birth and
death, and in the unbroken procession of the generations of
their ancestors.

Within the microcosm of a Navajo's life, time is represented
symbolically as a straight line (with perhaps occasional detours) or as an angular, snakelike, zigzagging line. A Navajo
term for *eternity* expresses it as *until I die of old age, until my
period has completely passed.*

At a cosmic level, however, the Navajo notion of time sheds
such mortal, human-centered illusions and manifests itself in
the purity of a circle. Within the vastness of the whole universe, the underlying cyclical nature of time is apparent to
spiritually attuned Navajo in the dynamic flow of events and
processes in nature.

Cyclic time appears in Navajo stories in the universe's pattern of *long-term expansions and contractions on a cosmic scale.*
This recurrent process began in the mythical, primordial past,
when the freshly formed earth and sky were forced and
stretched outward from the original center. It will be followed,
so the Navajo say, by an opposite phase when the world
springs back to this cosmic center of creation—culminating in
a *perfectly symmetrical, pulsating movement over the whole period.*

Cyclic time is also revealed in creation stories surrounding
the heroic adventures of the ancestral Holy People. First Man,

First Woman, and other original beings made their way up to the earth's surface from a dark primal place within the core of the nurturing earth. They emerged from a sacred opening in the earth's surface, then dispersed across the land in all directions, expanding the Navajo presence in the new world. In the great mythic cycle, the souls of deceased Navajo continuously return there. In this way, life and death, mythic and temporal time join together in time to grant order to the natural world.

Inside the sacred first hogan, First Man, First Woman, First Scolder, Blackgod, Coyote, and other primary beings orchestrated the creation of the primeval earth, clothing it in a diversity of newly quickened life-forms and positioning the celestial bodies overhead. They also set into motion the cycle of the seasons. After sculpting a miniature version of the world on the hogan's floor, First Man sketched a circular diagram of the solar year, dividing it first into halves, summer and winter, then further subdividing each half into twelve separate months.

But, according to one creation story, upon seeing the year made up of so many months, First Scolder protested. *"The time is too long, twelve here and twelve there, that will never do,"* he cried. *"Instead, put six here and six there."* According to another story, the Holy People spun the circle of months by assigning them such evocative names as *slender wind* (November), *month of delicate leaves* (April), and *month of enlarging seeds* (August). They blessed each of them and designated them as phases of the great cycle of growth and reproduction of all life on earth—as recurrent times *when mountain sheep mate, when deer shed their antlers, when antelope drop their fawns, when fruits ripen.*

While Navajo cosmology suggests that the *overall* [cosmic] *time of the present reality is circular,* it does not say that nature's familiar cyclic rhythms will serve forever as the drumbeat of the universe. To the contrary, many Navajo believe that humankind is living quite precariously, considering our accelerating abuse of the very natural world that has always sustained us, during the current cosmic cycle. Eventually, *within a number of human generations* the Earth and all its inhabitants will experience another period of cataclysmic collapse.

Such Navajo prophecies of the imminent destruction of the world as we know it may be disturbingly unwelcome news in some quarters. Within a traditional Navajo context, however, they can also be seen as strangely comforting, for they are one more expression of a great cosmic symmetry—a circle at once beautiful, terrifying, and sublime.

ᴧᴧᴧᴧᴧᴧᴧᴧᴧᴧᴧᴧᴧᴧᴧᴧᴧᴧᴧᴧᴧᴧᴧ

The Consequences of Time's Circle on Cause and Effect [8]

CENTRAL BRITISH COLUMBIA:
Gitksan and Wetśuwetén

Each age searches for its own model of nature. For classical science it was the clock; for nineteenth-century science, the period of the Industrial Revolution, it was an engine running down. What will the symbol be for us? . . . [Perhaps] a junction between stillness and motion, time arrested and time passing.

— Ilya Prigogine, physicist and
Isabelle Stengers, chemist[9]

Today, the Gitksan and Wetśuwetén people are joined in a heroic, century-long struggle to gain legal title to some twenty-two thousand square miles of their traditional homelands located in the mountainous interior of British Columbia. To them, *time is not linear but cyclical.*

In their eloquent opening statement to the Supreme Court of British Columbia on May 11, 1987, the Gitksan and Wetśuwetén patiently attempted to clarify how their culture's notion of circular time gives rise to a notion of cause and effect that is fundamentally different from the one by which Western civilization functions.

In the dominant Western worldview, hereditary chiefs testified, time is linear. An event gives rise to another event only as time moves forward along a unidirectional time line. But in the traditional Gitksan and Wetśuwetén cosmos, time must serve as the medium not only for mundane events and natural phenomena but for visionary dreams, shamanic journeys, and other, such rapturous experiences that defy time and thus form a circle. As a result, traditional Gitksan and Wetśuwetén believe causality is curved and follows a correspondingly circular path.

In daily life this circular vision of time gives to the Gitksan and Wetśuwetén a shared sense of identity and history. It contributes to their ethics and to the recurrent obligations they have to the natural world, and it explains experiences within that world. Their notion of a cyclic world destiny differs fundamentally from Western notions of history as a progressive unfolding of causally linked events and achievements. In their circular conception of cause and effect, the seasonal pulsations of nature, the lives of ancestors long dead, and the world-shaping transformations of the mythic era of creation have a continuous, powerful influence upon the present. *Events of the "past" are not simply history but are something that directly affects the present and future.* This places a heavy ethical responsibility for "right action" on the Gitskan and Wetśuwetén, in much the same way that Buddhists and Hindus view the effects of one's actions as reverberating far beyond the boundaries of a single life or generation.

The whole Gitksan and Wetśuwetén cosmos spins around this axis of circular time and causality. According to the testimony of the hereditary chiefs, it underlies their most cherished beliefs about the primordial connections that bind human beings and all other life-forms on earth together. To the spiritually attuned Gitksan and Wetśuwetén eye, human beings do not stand apart from or above other forms of life. They are part of a vast, multilayered, cosmic whorl of life cycles; the natural world emerges as an unbroken *continuum between humans, animals, and the spirit world.*

The great cycle of life and death that links the deeds and destinies of individual human beings with the natural world also defines relationships between people and prey. Where Western society looks upon wild animals as "natural resources," the Gitksan and Wetśuwetén see them as kindred beings that will ultimately be reincarnated just like humans, if their spirits are treated with proper respect.

The Gitksan and Wetśuwetén believe that the vital spiritual core of humans and animals can linger on after an individual's death. But this takes place only *if the spirit is treated with appropriate respect,* the hereditary chiefs maintained. If, in defiance of traditional codes of conduct, a careless hunter fails to honor properly the physical remains of an animal he has slain, the spiritual fires still flickering within the animal's blood-flecked carcass will refuse to be reborn. The animal's spirit will decline to sacrifice itself again in order to feed and clothe human beings, and future populations of its kind will decline.

Animals and fish are viewed as members of societies which have intelligence and power and can influence the course of events in terms of their interrelationship with human beings. By means of the circle of reincarnation, these forms of life have a causal role in the creation of the future and the present. A hunter's actions also interact with the perpetual *cycles of existence,* and the consequences of his choices "circle back" to influence his family's and community's ability to survive in the years ahead. Human beings cannot elude their obligations to ensure the well-being of the land and its inhabitants without dire consequences. Time causally links the past, present, and future and binds human beings to the prescriptions of wise ancestors and timeless tribal codes of conduct. The circular shape of Gitksan and Wetśuwetén time and causality guarantees that the consequences of each human deed or misdeed will career through the curved cosmos and communicate with the inner- and outermost reaches of time.

Time Measured by the Forests We Have Eaten [10]

VIETNAM:
Mnong Gar

*If it is true that the sun, the seasons, the waters,
and human life itself go in cycles, the inference is
that "there is time for all things," something
different to be done at each stage of the cycle. . . .
Only when we realize that nothing is new can we
live with an intensity in which everything becomes new.*

—Northrop Frye, literary critic

To the Mnong Gar, a contemporary indigenous people who have long inhabited the remote, undulating highlands of south-central Vietnam, time's passage is measured in terms of the cutting and regrowth of familiar patches of tropical forest.

The Mnong Gar, known as Phii Brêe, or "Men of the Forests," to their neighbors, are seminomadic, slash-and-burn agriculturalists, who represent the most ancient cultural stratum of Indo-Chinese populations in this region. They live, for the most part, along the banks of the Middle Krong Kño River, whose turbulent waters cascade down from this mountain fastness of densely forested hillsides, valleys, and plateaus to flow into the great Mekong River, as it meanders through the irrigated rice paddies of southern Vietnam's more densely populated coastal lowlands toward the sea.

Here the Mnong Gar erect small hamlets, mere clusters of thatched huts and longhouses adjacent to clearings, or *miir,* that they have laboriously cut from the encroaching jungle. In these temporarily nutrient-rich patches of tropical soil, they plant rice and other vegetable staples, supplementing them with, among other things, the flesh of fowl and water buffalo. In time, as the fertility of their gardens wanes, the mobile

Mnong Gar gather their modest material possessions and move to a new, more promising site within their traditional territory, where they promptly construct new shelters and sow fresh crops.

In time, this passage through their traditional territory eventually takes them back to the original forest opening, now overgrown, that they had earlier abandoned. Typically, a Mnong Gar community does not return to the same site for perhaps ten to twenty years. But they will not have forgotten the small gash in the forest that had once sustained them. In fact, as recently as the 1950s, according to Georges Condominas, a French anthropologist who has lived with and studied the Mnong Gar, their primary method of monitoring time depended upon their precise memories of the geographic location and appearance of each such clearing they had created in the jungle. Observes Condominas: they had *no method whereby they log the passing of time other than by referring to the wooded areas they clear and burn off in succession to make their annual plantings.*

To the Mnong Gar, time is not an abstraction; it is personally and collectively experienced. It is not linear, universal, or subject to official standardization; it is cyclical, local, and inextricably a part of the recurrent natural processes of growth and decline, of life and death, of the forest. As a result, the same solar year is routinely given a different name by each Mnong Gar village, reflecting each community's unique vision of that period of time and its utter ecological dependency upon a particular grove of trees and its underlying gift of soil. *For in that period each will have "eaten" a section of its own domain.*

For example, in the village of Sar Luk, a community of 146 inhabitants when Condominas lived there during the late 1940s, the Mnong Gar assigned the year "1949" (that is, the agricultural season stretching from late November 1948 to early December 1949) this luminous name: *We ate the forest of the Stone Spirit Gôo.* A similar nomenclature is used to name each Mnong Gar year. The first part of a Mnong Gar year-name—*Hii saa brii,* Mnong Gar for "We ate the forest of . . ."—is an acknowledgment that the forest sustains human beings and, in effect, must be partially "devoured" by them. The second part—"the Stone Spirit Gôo"—refers to the location of a particular piece of forest floor that provided the Mnong Gar with fertile garden soil for perhaps two seasons. Thus, *the same term serves to denote two years separated by one or two decades.*

By weaving the fate of the forest that "feeds" them into their traditional systems of reckoning time, the Mnong Gar people have, in effect, institutionalized their awe and respect for the land. They slash and burn jungle because they must sow crops to feed their children and maintain the sacred continuity with ancestors. But, in the process, they express their abiding devotion to their sacred lands, and, at the same time, map both the events of their lives and the physical landscape itself by commemorating each such transient stand of trees in a cyclic, biologically-based formulation of time.

Their deep reverence for the forest, along with their reluctance to "gorge" excessively on its gifts, is revealed in their practice of preserving certain pristine groves of old-growth forest absolutely untouched. Such a mature stand of trees is recognized by the entire community as a sacred forest sanctuary: it is *the habitat of the Spirits and, for that reason, is never touched by the rice planter's axe.*

Mnong Gar love of the land is not, of course, restricted to forest. It is all-embracing. In September 1949, Condominas witnessed a traditional nature-renewal ceremony in the neighboring village of Sar Long. It is aptly called Nyiit Döng, or the Great Festival of the Soil, and includes elaborate prayers honoring the Spirit of the Earth, the Spirit of Soil, and other elements of nature, along with musical processions, flat-gong orchestras, domestic animal sacrifices, and festive giant—bamboo pole raising rituals. During one of the crucial, life-restoring rituals of the Great Festival of the Soil, a holy man sings a resonant song, or "gong saying," that *retraces the origins of the world.* It offers a glimpse into a Mnong Gar vision of the shared spiritual roots, temporal unity, and ecological integrity of a balanced natural world:

> *In the beginning of time, there was only a land of mud,*
> *the land of Nduu and Ndoh.*
> *In the beginning of time, there was only a land with earthworms;*
> *seven alone crawled upon it.*
> *In the beginning of time, there was only a land with bamboo shoots;*
> *a single* dlei *clump grew on it.*
> *In the beginning of time, there was only a land with wild*
> *vegetables; a single plot of ground they covered.*

Later, participants in the Great Festival of the Soil, bearing offerings of bamboo-tubes filled with rice beer and handfuls of rice and buffalo meat, pass in single file to a clearing in the forest where their gardens are located. Before quietly returning to the village, they offer this poignant prayer of gratitude to the Earth whose verdant forests they have "eaten," like generations of Mnong Gar before them.

> *I feed thee, Spirit of the Earth*
> *Spirit of the Forest, of the Green Trees,*
> *Spirit of the Forest,*
> *Spirit of the Village Sites;*
> *decree that the Paddy grow,*
> *that the Fire devour.*
> *Leading my younger brothers,*
> *leading my elder brothers,*
> *tomorrow, and the day after tomorrow, I will again act*
> *in the same way.*

wwwwwwwwwwwwwwww

9

World Renewal

Maintaining Balance in the Natural World

Early in the history of life, Nature began to shape new species to fit into habitats already occupied by other species. Never since the Archaean Period has a living thing evolved alone. Whole communities have evolved as if they were one great organism. Thus all evolution is coevolution and the biosphere is now a confederation of dependencies.

—Victor B. Scheffer, marine mammalogist and author[1]

We are at a moment both of profound change in the scientific concept of nature and of the structure of human society as a result of the demographic explosion. As a result, there is a need for new relations between man and nature and between man and man. We can no longer accept the old a priori distinction between scientific and ethical values.

—Ilya Prigogine, Nobel Prize–winning physicist, and Isabelle Stengers, chemist[2]

What can modern life science teach us about the responsibility we bear for ensuring the well-being and continuity of the natural world?

After decades of studying the natural world, the modern ecologist portrays nature with the broad brushstrokes of systems and population ecology. Over time, a vast communal canvas emerges on the ecologist's easel, a colorful scientific pastiche of countless living ecosystems in flux: sketches of slender, wave-pummelled coastal shore ecosystems, populated by rafts of drifting microscopic algae, undulating kelp beds, and tenacious rock-clinging invertebrates; arctic tundra ecosystems, spanning distant horizons and carpeted with patches of lichen and miniature, frost-stunted forests; dark abyssal sea bottoms, where strange cool-blooded fishes swim in silence and hordes of tiny shellfish rest patiently, mouths agape, beneath a rain of debris from brighter waters above.

But where in these artful scientific models are ordinary individuals likely to learn *anything* about their ethical obligations for protecting this patchwork biosphere and its dynamic ecological equilibrium? No hint of an environmental imperative is embedded in the ecologist's ingenious intellectual descriptions.

Science's supposedly "value-free" mode of inquiry and outlook renders it ill equipped to offer moral guidance for how we *ought* to relate, individually and communally, to the intricate "machinery" of nature that it unveils. *Natural philosophy, states Harvard entomologist E. O. Wilson, has brought into clear relief the following paradox of human existence. The drive towards perpetual expansion—or personal freedom—is basic to the human spirit. But to sustain it we need the most delicate, knowing stewardship of the living world that can be devised.*[3]

197

Despite the limits of scientific wisdom, a clear understanding of ecological principles and processes can greatly illuminate decisions we make every day that affect the fates of ecosystems all over the world. Ecology is replete with intriguing images (if not stern moral imperatives) of how the myriad life-forms within a healthy ecosystem—including Homo sapiens—interact in fruitful biological (if not philosophical) harmony.

The modern science of ecology has a great deal to say, at least implicitly, about the integral role of natural processes that might metaphorically be referred to as ecological "gratitude." These are the built-in circuits and mechanisms in ecosystems through which the living parts, in effect, "give something back," or contribute to the overall harmony of the system. Systems ecologists refer to these circular pathways as positive and negative "feedback loops." They are circular flows of energy or matter that perform vital homeostatic, or "self-correcting," functions for the system by either accelerating or decelerating other ecological processes.

The invisible clouds of carbon dioxide that humans and other oxygen-breathing creatures routinely excrete as gaseous "waste" are, in a very real sense, in moderation, ecological "gifts"—bursts of positive feedback—to the flora of the biosphere. The carbon dioxide molecules eventually go on to stimulate photosynthesis in the leaves of plants—ultimately generating new vegetation for plant-eating creatures to devour. In the same sense, the farmer who carefully covers his fields with organic manure and other fertilizers before sowing crops is offering an ecological "gift" of nutrients and minerals to this agricultural ecosystem.

Ecology also has much to say, albeit indirectly, about the notion of "sacrifice" in nature. By means of feedback loops, a mature tree in a tropical forest ecosystem can help perpetuate its own kind, as well as its fellow species, by gradually relinquishing its energy- and mineral-laden leaves. These leaves enrich the meager forest-floor soils so that new seedlings can grow. Another tree within the same forest routinely "sacrifices" a portion of its fruit bounty to clown-beaked toucans; the turtle, a portion of its leathery eggs to marauding rodents; the tapir, its warm, blood-infused flesh to the poison-tipped darts of an Amazonian hunter's blowgun. The hunter, as well as his kin, will eventually yield to the same stern unspoken ethos of ecological sacrifice, however reluctantly, when his body becomes a feast for teeming populations of various decomposing organisms.

Finally, the science of ecology waxes metaphorically eloquent on the intrinsic value of ecological "sanctuary." Embedded in even the most sterile conceptual and mathematical models of nature that modern ecologists conjure up lies an unspoken recognition that certain geographical spaces, species, and processes within the whole may be exceptionally critical and vulnerable to damage.

An Atlantic coastal estuary, for instance, with its spectacular seasonal influxes of shrimp, crab, and fishes may be so vital as a nursery area for future generations of marine fauna that it might be absolutely essential to the well-being of the whole coastal ecosystem to protect it as a breeding "sanctuary." Similarly, a few groves of trees high in the mountains of central Mexico may turn out to be an absolutely critical terrestrial reserve that guarantees the survival of the migratory monarch butterfly on its transcontinental pathway.

But if science can point out concepts of gratitude, sacrifice, and sanctuary that are pivotal for a global environmental ethic, it has so far been incapable of reliably instilling in people a deeply felt environmental conscience. Can science encourage human beings, with their often selfish inclinations and fleeting attention spans, to periodically pay homage to these implicit ecological values? In industrial societies so intoxicated by science-driven technological leverage over nature, and so prone to unbridled excess, can we enforce a set of values that honors the cyclic processes of the natural world and is dedicated to their revitalization? Where can we hope to find contemporary counterparts to ancient Native "world renewal" ceremonies that can unify public sentiment and ecological insight into a common spirit- and science-confirming sense of the "sanctity" of nature's life-generating features and balance? And what social institutions might help channel a latent impulse to celebrate and reaffirm the ancient, unwritten pact among all species, etched in our shared DNA sequences and our terrifying mutual dependencies?

The very success of science in our lifetime in granting modern industrial societies unprecedented power has left those societies psychologically dissociated from their natural surroundings and spiritually adrift. Yet even if science is silent on the subject of human beings' moral obligations to the biosphere, it can offer illuminating insights into the moral choices that confront us. It can alert individuals, scientists and nonscientists alike, to the awesome complexities and unities of the physical universe. By so doing, it can help awaken human hearts to a visceral sensibility for the whole. And perhaps in Native perspectives on nature, we will begin to find a morally responsible "sacred ecology" to complement our conveniently human-centered, "value-free," secular and scientific one.

~~~~~~~~~~~~~~~~~~~~~~~~~~~~~~~~~~~~

Caring for the Land 4

NORTH-CENTRAL CALIFORNIA:
Wintu

One of the penalties of an ecological education is that one lives alone in a world of words. Much of the damage inflicted on land is quite invisible to laymen. An ecologist must either harden his shell and make believe that the consequences of science are none of his business, or he must be a doctor who sees the marks of death in a commu-

nity that believes itself well and does not want to
be told otherwise.

—Aldo Leopold, ecologist[5]

When a society looks upon nature as endowed with integrity and completeness, with the sense of shared ancestry and kindred spirit one experiences in loving human relationships, it is hardly surprising that its people feel a profound sense of empathy for the earth's suffering when it is exploited or abused.

Non-Native peoples have intensely exploited traditional Wintu lands in northern California over the past two centuries: the feverish mining for gold and copper ore; the large-scale commercial logging of vast evergreen forests; the construction of steel railways, spinal highways, huge hydro-electric dams and, behind them, great reservoir lakes.

A wanton destruction of mountains, rivers, and forests often accompanied such purported milestones of American progress. But for many Wintu Indians, a personal sense of the earth's pain has persisted. Especially to the most sensitive Wintu survivors, these incursions could only be viewed as bloody wounds on a sentient earth's body.

During the early decades of the twentieth century, a Wintu shaman, an elderly woman from the Bald Hills area named Kate Luckie, tried to convey her own sense of personal loss and belief in impending world catastrophe. Her words, recorded by ethnographer Cora Du Bois in her 1935 monograph *Wintu Ethnography,* seem to seethe with the palpable anger and pain that one might feel upon seeing a member of one's own family brutalized, repeatedly, for another's gain:

When the Indians all die, then God will let the water come down from the north. Everyone will drown. That is because the White people never cared for land or deer or bear.

When we Indians kill meat, we eat it all up. When we dig roots, we make little holes. When we build houses, we make little holes. When we burn grass for grasshoppers, we don't ruin things. We shake down acorns and pine nuts. We don't chop down the trees. We only use dead wood.

201

*But the White people plow up the ground, pull up the trees, kill
everything.*

*The tree says, "Don't. I am sore. Don't hurt me." But they chop it
down and cut it up.*

The spirit of the land hates them.

*They blast out trees and stir it up to its depths. They saw up the
trees. That hurts them.*

*The Indians never hurt anything, but the white people destroy all.
They blast rocks and scatter them on the ground.*

*The rock says, "Don't! You are hurting me." But the white people
pay no attention.*

*When the Indians use rocks, they take little round ones for their
cooking. The white people dig deep long tunnels. They make roads.
They dig as much as they wish. They don't care how much the ground
cries out.*

*How can the spirit of the earth like the White man? That is why
God will upset the world—because it is sore all over. Everywhere the
White man has touched it, it is sore.*

Such words of heartfelt indignation are entirely appropriate
to the cultural context of a Wintu world that defines the bond
between human beings and their fellow creatures as one of
reciprocal affection and communication, based on ancient
shared origins. Seen in this light, environmentally destructive
acts are far more threatening than mere breaches of territorial
boundaries; they are murderous assaults upon a loved one's
"person." The connection between the Wintu and their traditional lands is one of blood kinship, and within this elemental
social bond, as in healthy human relationships, moments of
grief and sorrow tend, over time, to be counterbalanced by
ones of ecstasy and joy.

A Prayer to the Inner Forms of the Earth [6]

A Prayer
to the Inner
Forms of the
Earth

AMERICAN SOUTHWEST:
Navajo

Our ability to perceive quality in nature begins, as in art, with the pretty. It expands through successive states of the beautiful to values as yet uncaptured in language. The quality of the crane lies, I think, in this higher gamut, as yet beyond the reach of words.

—Aldo Leopold, ecologist[7]

The ancient ancestors of the Navajo people emerged from the dim multilayered subterranean realm where chaos reigns to a surface world of animals, plants, and human beings. This world had been created in a wondrous natural state of all-embracing equilibrium that the Navajo refer to as *hózhó*. Fertile, teeming with life, and endlessly self-perpetuating, the upper earth and its freshly transformed flora and fauna was an integrated living system, breathtakingly beautiful in its riotous display of color and form, in its inherent ecological harmony, and in its resilience.

The Navajo word *hózhó*—ultimately perhaps untranslatable into English—embodies the radiant array of physical, biological, and spiritual attributes central to their perception of the natural world and of humankind's proper relationship to it. It is a sacred word, steeped in ecological as well as aesthetic, religious, and moral meaning. It encompasses (without being limited to) aspects of Western notions such as blessing and beauty, harmony and order, goodness and happiness. And it stands in counterpoint (but is not totally isolated from or immune to) notions of ugliness, chaos, disorder, evil, and despair.

The overarching purpose of Navajo ritual is *to maintain or restore* hózhó. Its central theme, with countless variations, appears to be environmental renewal—the revitalization and restoration of all of nature, from the earth's mortal inhabitants and stone-strewn southwestern landscapes to the outer celestial reaches of the cosmos. To this end, Navajo culture is gifted with an extraordinarily rich repertoire of religious symbols and ceremonies.

The vast body of Navajo religious knowledge mirrors the complex, interrelated structures and functions of nature itself. Its prayers, songs, mythical tales, ritual prescriptions and practices (all traditionally committed to individual memory) have an internal cohesiveness and interconnectedness in which no single ceremonial complex is supreme. Nonetheless, the ceremony called *hózhóójí* or Blessingway is, in the succinct phrase of Navajo elder Long Moustache, *the spinal column of all songs.* According to Sam Gill, an American scholar of comparative religion, a reasonable literal translation of the Navajo term for Blessingway is *the way to secure an environment of perfect beauty.*

The Blessingway ceremony is deeply rooted in ancient Navajo notions of the mythic origins of the world. It was first used, says Frank Mitchell, a highly respected Navajo Blessingway singer, *to place Earth and Sky in a position facing each other.* It was given to the Navajo by their ancestors as a vehicle for human action and as an expression of their responsibility to see that all things in the natural world are *in their proper places, as assigned in the acts of creation.*

At the heart of the Blessingway ceremony are a number of chants and recitations. These are often addressed reverentially to the sacred, living, humanoid, spiritual forms that dwell within all objects and processes—most noticeably in all things living. The animate forms inside all things are sacred, placed there by the spiritually potent Holy People, who made their first appearance on earth in primordial times, long before there were Navajo people. In some sense, these interior forms are the embodiments of the Holy People.

The so-called "Navajo Prayer to the Internal Forms of the Earth," also known simply as the "Earth's Prayer," is a pivotal world-rejuvenating prayer to the vital spiritual core of each element in nature. The proper recitation of its sacred passages returns the environment in its totality to a primal state of hózhó. Through its reenactment, the *original acts of creation are repeated and the world is re-created.*

This ultimate human act of transspecies altruism and environmental renewal lends meaning to the Blessingway ceremony. For Blessing (*hózhó*) *is synonymous with proper order. There is a "way" for everything and that "way" is blessed because it was so decreed in sacred history.* Thus, in the minds of many traditional Navajo, the "Earth's Prayer" resonates throughout the whole world and across boundless expanses of time, summoning forth the sacred beauty and innate harmony that existed in the primordial earth during the era of creation.

The text of so weighty a prayer is long and structurally complex. Within the Blessingway ceremony, the Earth's Prayer is invoked for two principal aims. First, *it associates and identifies the person praying with the inner life forms of the earth*—thereby connecting that individual with the life-sustaining network of interrelationships within the natural world. And second, it *describes the condition of blessing,* or *hózhó, which is the consequence of these relationships.*

The first aim is addressed by a portion of the prayer that verbally connects sacred points on the body of the one who is praying with those of the ancestral Holy People—and hence with the humanoid inner spiritual forms *which all living things must have within them.* The prayer invokes each of the nine pairs of inner forms of the earth: Earth and Sky, Mountain and Water Woman, Darkness and Dawn, Evening Twilight and Sun, Talking God and Calling God, White Corn and Yellow Corn, Pollen and Corn Beetle, Changing Woman and White Shell Woman, and finally Long Life and Happiness.

Embedded in this part of the prayer is a rich litany of references to diverse elements of nature—to rain, clouds, rainbows, and sunlight, and to the sacred pollen of corn plants—gracefully interwoven and interlinked from one spoken stanza

to the next. Here are two stanzas of the prayer, directed to
Earth and Sky, linking the sacred soles of the supplicant's feet
with these human-shaped forms:

*Earth's soles where dark cloud, male rain, dark water,
  rainbow lie across them with pollen, that same dark cloud,
  male rain, dark water, rainbow lies across my soles with
  pollen as I say this.*

*Sky's soles where dark mist, female rain, blue water,
  sunray lie across them with pollen, that same dark mist,
  female rain, blue water, sunray lies across my soles
  with pollen as I say this.*

The second aim of the prayer is the declaration of blessing,
and it is contained in the second portion of the prayer. It seeks
to bring *hózhó* to the entire universe, and the one who prays
deliberately dispatches it to the far corners of the Navajo
world. In Western literary tradition, the microcosm of a single
grain of sand can resonate with the meaning of the whole
cosmos; just so in Navajo prayer the blessing of a tiny part of
the universe is sufficient to bless the whole. This symbolic
extension is evident in the following passage, where the image
of an ordinary songbird (whose blue color evokes happiness,
fertility, and dawn) conveys blessings along each of the cardinal directions to the Earth's inner form:

*Before Earth with small blue birds it is blessed,
  with small blue birds before me it is blessed as I say this.*

*Before Earth with small blue birds it is blessed,
  with small blue birds behind me it is blessed as I say this.*

*Before Earth with small blue birds it is blessed,
  with small blue birds below me it is blessed as I say this.*

*Before Earth with small blue birds it is blessed,
  with small blue birds around me it is blessed as I say this.*

Navajo prayers to the Earth reveal a profound empathy for nature and its various forms, even an ecstatic identity with and a religious veneration of them. These very qualities would be essential to any meaningful science-compatible ceremonies of "world renewal" that Western societies may, by urgent necessity, be compelled to create in the decades ahead.

∿∿∿∿∿∿∿∿∿∿∿∿∿∿∿∿∿∿

Dancing to Renew the World [8]

AMAZONIA, BRAZIL:
Kayapó

When man becomes greater than nature, nature, which gave him birth, will respond.
—Loren Eiseley, anthropologist [9]

The rapid growth of human populations, extensive poverty, and ignorance of ecological principles that are causing the destruction of the tropical rain forest during our lifetimes promise to drive to extinction something approaching a quarter of the world's biological diversity before our grandchildren have the chance to learn about it.
—Peter Raven, botanist[10]

When the Kayapó gather to dance in the sacred ceremonial circle, they know they are dancing to preserve and sustain the structure and integrity of the entire natural world.

Kayapó dances generally begin in the evening, just as another sacred circle—the fiery, scorching tropical sun—completes its curved passage across the tree-punctured western skies. The Kayapó continue dancing to the intoxicating rhythm of drums, chants, and pounding feet until that sun has circled back behind the huge horizontal sky disk overhead to spill its fluid amber light on the dawn.

This heady ceremonial mix of sacred song, dance, and sleeplessness can elicit markedly altered states of consciousness, in which participants *become aware of the non-lineal realm of dynamic power that unifies all time and space.* These sporadic outbursts of intense, viscerally felt ecstasy seem to *tap into a central power source to carry energy to the rituals.* By ancient consensus, these experiences are precious personal conduits to the vast, dimensionless Cosmic Time that underlies and lends order in the Kayapó universe; each ecstatic experience seems to lighten the group's awesome, world-renewing burdens. At the same time, a surge of energy through one fortunate dancer visibly confirms to the others the presence of the sacred source.

The principal aim of traditional Kayapó communal dance ceremonies is *to insure the cyclical movement of time,* out of a profound sense of personal and collective duty. In the words of ethnographer Darryl Posey, the *ceremony is a* raison d'être *for the Kayapó* because *they believe that without the performance of the prescribed rituals, the world would collapse: crops would not grow, children would not be born, the sun and moon would cease to travel across the sky.*

Human Overpopulation [11]

COLOMBIA (NORTHWESTERN AMAZON):
Desana

The very first requirement for ecological stability is a balance between the rates of birth and death. . . . Always, in any living (i.e. ecological) system, every increasing imbalance will generate its own limiting factors as side effects of the increasing imbalance. . . . But the imbalance has gone so far that we cannot trust Nature not to overcorrect.

—Gregory Bateson, anthropologist[12]

The fate of other species inhabiting the biosphere, according to the Desana, is inextricably bound to that of human beings. Because most life on earth draws upon a single, common reservoir of reproductive energy—one with a finite capacity— every human activity that consumes a portion of this energy renders it unavailable for other life-forms.

Thus, any suggestion that human populations can expand exponentially without simultaneously diminishing the future prospects of other creatures is sheer folly. Nature fuels the continuity of life on earth by apportioning a fixed quantity of reproductive energy to diverse life-forms. By necessity, it will balance the fragile equations of global distribution of this lim- ited available energy, regardless of whether human beings are aware of the effects of their actions upon the reproductive future of fellow species.

The fundamental Desana truth that no species is an island imposes a heavy ethical burden upon human society. It sug- gests that any excessive consumption or exploitation of na- ture's precious, exhaustible stores of reproductive energy will seriously affect the survival of nature's entire, interconnected energy system. It imposes upon humans a conscious obliga- tion to limit their energy use so that other forms of life will be assured of their rightful share of nature's rigid budget of en- ergy. It suggests that unrestrained sexual activity, as well as the rapid growth in population that would likely result from such an unbridled expression of human passions, is irrespon- sible.

The need for human sexual and reproductive restraint is particularly important to the Desana hunter because his rela- tionship with animals is at once exceedingly intimate and forever in fragile equilibrium. But it also applies to the world- wide human community, whose daily existence depends equally upon the fortunes of other forms of life and whose survival is at stake in both a biological and a spiritual sense.

With astonishing clarity and imagery, the Desana world- view embraces the timeless ecological truth that human births, for all their personal pains and pleasures, do not take place in splendid isolation. In some sense, each represents (as does the emergence of new life in *any* species) the active siphoning off of a small quantity of precious energy from the vast, yet finite, reserves of vital biological capacity upon which the entire natural world ultimately depends.

The modern population ecologist may prefer to frame this pivotal truth quantitatively—in terms of rising birth rates and falling death rates; in terms of the reduced capacities of pollution-degraded habitats to support animal and plant, as well as human populations; or in terms of increased competition among species for fixed food resources—rather than in the Desana shaman's vivid hydraulic imagery of a closed system of interconnected biological energy pools and flows. But the central messages of scientist and shaman are complementary, rooted in much the same soil of daily observation and familiarity with the processes of healthy, living ecosystems.

Science sees this ecological truth from afar, without forging an unimpeachable moral imperative for all humankind. By contrast, Desana nature-wisdom is steeped in rewards and punishments to ensure that human beings respect the fundamental biological and spiritual links between their own reproductive behavior and the fate of all creatures in the rain forest. All members of traditional Desana society—not just the all-seeing shaman—are expected personally to understand that, in the words of anthropologist Geraldo Reichel-Dolmatoff, *the retention and accumulation of human sexual energy is not only conceived as a conscious control of the [human] birthrate but has as its equally important goal the conservation of a broad margin of sexual potential in which the game animals can participate.* And they are expected to act accordingly.

Human Responsibility for Nature [13]

NORTH-CENTRAL UNITED STATES:
Dakota Sioux

For their development children need the respect and protection of adults who take them seriously, love them, and honestly help them to become oriented in the world.
—Alice Miller, psychiatrist[14]

In the Black Hills region of North Dakota, in the years before the vast herds of wild buffalo disappeared, the Dakota Indians understood the meaning of human responsibility—collective and individual—for all things in the natural world.

In the traditional Dakota world, human responsibility for nature flowed out of a deep-seated sense of shared origins and even blood kinship with all elements of the cosmos. Dakota men or women never assumed such responsibilities voluntarily; rather, each child possessed them from birth. Every human action reverberated throughout the person's immediate family, as well as throughout the vast network of relationships within the natural world. One's duties to parents, siblings, children, and other kin were on a par with one's duties to the natural world.

In his book *My People the Sioux,* published in 1928, Luther Standing Bear wrote that the Dakota often went to great lengths to teach children that in nature *there was no complete solitude.* They made sure the children knew that wherever they went, they would be greeted by the warm, reassuring presence of local life-forms, geological features, and natural forces, which were often as trusted, familiar, and communicative with them as members of their families back home. Through this process, wrote Standing Bear, Dakota children came to an early understanding that *we are of the soil and soil of us,* that *we love the birds and beasts that grew with us on this soil,* and that a bond existed between all living things because they all *drank the same water and breathed the same air.*

Standing Bear's ringing aphorism *we are all one in nature* was not meant merely metaphorically. In traditional Dakota society, each child ventured out into the real world and personally discovered and experienced the fullness of this truth. Each had a duty to try to *pierce deeper into the mystery of universal oneness* by carrying out prescribed rituals or enduring arduous ordeals. These were designed to instill in young people a lifelong, visceral sense of profound humility before Wakan-Tanka, the awesome life-generating powers coursing through the universe, and of utter abandonment of self in the vast, all-embracing boundlessness of nature.

Dakota men and women were required to undergo a rite of purification in which they used the aromatic smoke of burning sweet grass, wafting up into the heavens like a silent prayer, to cleanse their spirits and render the *four-leggeds, the wingeds, the star people of the heavens and all things as relatives.*

For adolescent Dakota boys, the personal vision quest was a mandatory rite of passage to manhood and environmental consciousness. During this solitary sojourn into the mountains, a boy spent several days naked, vulnerable, and fasting as he awaited the arrival of animal-spirit allies who might help him to develop and actualize his understanding of the spiritual and ecological unity of nature. For it is possible that such knowledge is born only of solitude.

Traditionally, during ceremonial preparations for a boy's departure, an elder filled a sacred pipe with tobacco, gestured to the cardinal points of the cosmos, and offered a prayer for the boy's successful journey and for new levels of insight into Dakota duties to nature. *"O Wakan-Tanka,"* he prayed, *"grant that this young man may have relatives; that he may be one with the four winds, the four Powers of the world, and with the light of the dawn. May he understand his relationship with all the winged peoples of the air. . . . Our Grandmother and Mother (earth) . . . this young man wishes to become one with all things. . . . For the good of all your peoples, help him!"*

The Suffering of Trees [15]

MALAYSIA:
Chewong

While we assume there is a design behind the
physical reality, science can't really tell us any-
thing about the designer, the nature of God, or
God's relationship with human beings.

—Paul Davies, mathematician
and physicist[16]

The Chewong believe that in an ancient time beyond memory, the trees of the tropical rain forest could talk.

Nor was the power of speech restricted to the most beautiful and majestic of the primordial flora. It was not unique to the *gol* or the *tangòi* tree, whose crowns sometimes soar fifty yards or more above the damp forest floor and echo with the cries of gibbons; nor did it reside only in the trees whose milky, smooth-barked trunks are buttressed by sturdy weblike growths of living wood at the base and that rise out of the shadows like ghostly spires to support the forest's lush umbrella of leaves.

On the contrary, *every* tree in the forest could speak. And so could every vine, every thorn bush, every flower. Back in those primordial times, all life-forms on Earth Seven (the earthly realm of ordinary existence) were endowed with a precious *ruwai,* or state of consciousness. From *ruwai* flowed the capacity of all beings for language, the communication of ideas through the spoken word.

Back in that misty epoch, it was simply inconceivable that a human being would chop down a tree. If a person attempted to do so, the sentient trees would vocally challenge their human assailant and defend their interests. They would angrily confront a human who tried to bludgeon and mutilate their fellow beings. Worse, wounded trees would *cry out in pain whenever they were cut down, so no one would do this.*

Some contemporary Chewong insist that upon hearing the trees' terrified cries, their ancestors could not bear to cut them down. The early Chewong were deeply moved by these trees with their *ruwai,* their ability to sense pleasure and pain, and their extraordinary power of speech. They developed a profound empathy for the trees' pain, empathy that has remained enshrined in Chewong society for countless centuries. This sensibility evokes a time that predates, until relatively recently, the Chewong's contemporary habit of slashing and burning trees to clear land for agriculture, a time of a simpler, less intrusive hunting, gathering, and foraging way of life.

Over time, however, the sensibilities of the rainforest flora diminished, as did the sensibilities of the Chewong themselves. No longer, claim some Chewong, must they avoid spiritually offending or physically injuring or torturing a tree. The spiritual domain of the local flora has contracted, and today, only a handful of plants still possess the spiritually animating *ruwai* and hence remain fully conscious of human activities. Among them are the tall, stately *gol* and *tangòi* trees; the *dòg* tree, which long provided the Chewong with raw materials for cloth and with precious poison for their blowguns; various bamboos; and an assortment of important medicinal and ceremonial plants.

Some trees—those bearing vital nuts and fruits in certain seasons—are *imbued with* ruwai *only at certain times of the year.* When the edible fruit of the durian tree ripens in June, or when the fruit of the *payòng* tree ripens in September, the Chewong know that the spirits of these life-forms are watching over them. The seasonal ripenings signal that the *ruwai* of the fruits and blossoms have voluntarily descended from the cool, invisible realm of Earth Six (whose underside forms the sky of Earth Seven) high above to dwell, for a time, in the familiar rain forests on Earth Seven. Here on Earth Seven, the visiting *ruwai* graciously wait for the fruit to ripen, enduring the physical discomforts of the forest's searing heat and stifling humidity, simply *so that humans may eat some fruit.*

There is, say the Chewong, an endearing reciprocity in their relationship with these spiritually endowed botanical life-forms. The Chewong are obligated to honor the spiritual es- sence of particular trees, guided by the terrible knowledge that these trees still have a divine spark, an exquisite vulnerability to pain, and a memory that connects them directly to that earlier era when all trees could shout, sigh, and weep.

In return, the *ruwai,* or souls, of these trees consciously try to control, through their periodic journeys to and from lofty Earth Six, the seasonal appearance of the wild fruits, in an effort to help the Chewong who depend on them. This the trees do out of empathy for the living descendants of the Chewong who first respected the sufferings of their ancestor trees.

"They want to help us," say the Chewong, in words that convey the deep interspecies gratitude and religious reverence that seems to flow naturally from a bond between biological and spiritual equals. "They *do not want people to be hungry, and so act accordingly."*

∧∧∧∧∧∧∧∧∧∧∧∧∧∧∧∧∧∧∧∧∧∧∧∧

Bringing the Buds to Life [17]

NEW MEXICO:
Tewa (Eastern Pueblo)

*The indescribable innocence and beneficence of
Nature—of sun and wind and rain, of summer
and winter—such health, such cheer, they afford
forever! . . . Shall I not have intelligence with the
earth? Am I not partly leaves and vegetable
mould myself?*
—Henry David Thoreau[18]

In late February, the night sky in northern New Mexico bris- tles with bright stars, and the dry, adobe-hued foothills beside the ancient Rio Grande are still lightly dusted with snow. At this time the medicine men of San Juan Pueblo gather quietly in the south plaza, the sacred center of this contemporary Tewa village. It is time once again for them to perform the arduous spiritual *work* of *re-seeding mother earth navel,* on behalf of their Tewa kin and *all* of humankind, on behalf of all forms of life and all creation.

The sacred ceremonies are part of a series of nine major spiritual *works* performed every year. Together, the nine *works* of the annual cycle constitute an elegant and complex series of life-sustaining, world-renewing, and community-affirming spiritual activities. Scheduled in loose synchrony with the local cycle of seasons, ranging from the unfurling of new shoots, leaves, and blossoms in spring to the corn harvest in autumn to the waning of the sun's light at winter solstice, the ceremonial cycle serves as the heartbeat of Tewa society. The responsibility for seeing that this annual wheel of spiritual duties turns (guaranteeing that nature's cycles spin with it) lies in the Made People, the formally initiated members of the Tewa spiritual community. The Made People are the earthly representatives of the First People, the supernatural residents of the primal subterranean abode beneath Sandy Place Lake. By reenacting annual *works* as part of their ancient and sacrosanct obligations, the Made People harmonize the relationships between human beings, animals, plants, and every other element of the vast, interconnected cosmos.

Now, in the dying days of winter, a month or so before the spring equinox, this *work* is part of a ceremonial prelude to the coming agricultural season, when life-sustaining corn, beans, squash, and other vegetables must be lovingly coaxed from the bone-dry soil. It is an attempt to spiritually reawaken the still-slumbering natural world of late winter and an earnest human plea to the earth to revolve the seasons so that the Tewa can live and their children flourish.

This late-winter spiritual ceremony is called Bringing the Buds to Life. Like the eight other *works* of the Tewa calendar, Bringing the Buds to Life consists of traditionally choreographed, daylong bouts of intensive prayer, song, and ritual, performed at four-day intervals by each of the eight sacred societies of San Juan Pueblo. These groups of Made People include: the complementary Summer and Winter moiety, the Women's, the Hunt, the Scalp, two Clown, and the Bear Medicine societies.

Bringing the Buds to Life is a *work* fundamental to the spiritual and biological well-being of the natural world. Detailed knowledge of the spiritual events it encompasses therefore remains a carefully guarded secret of the Made People. Any attempt by an improperly prepared outsider to record, analyze, and report on the time-honored subtleties of the ceremony, however well-intentioned, would be as futile and as destructive to Tewa spirituality as trying to understand the essence of "butterfly-ness" by capturing and dissecting a butterfly.

We are fortunate that the eminent American anthropologist Alfonso Ortiz, a Tewa and an active member of San Juan Pueblo community, has granted us a glimpse of some aspects of the Bringing the Buds to Life ritual in his book *The Tewa World*, a classic study of the spiritual and social foundations of his people.

On this late-February night in the starlit plaza, the assembled members of the Bear Medicine Society approach a loosely arranged circle of stones. This rock structure is actually a shrine of surpassing sacredness, which the Tewa call the *navel of mother earth*. It represents the exact spiritual and geometric center of the Tewa universe, and beneath it lies the ultimate subterranean source of nature's fertility. It stands as a sort of umbilical connection between fragile human existence and the mysterious, rhythmic upwellings of nature's bounty.

One of the medicine men steps close to the sacred *earth-navel* opening. Reaching deep within himself for the personal strength and courage he has learned from the Medicine Society, he symbolically *inseminates* Mother Earth by gently placing precious seeds into a womblike chamber in the sacred shrine. So potent are the powers at work among the shadowy figures that for an instant the medicine man transforms this humble world-renewing ritual into a breathtaking act of magic. As he kneels to insert his plant seeds into the chamber, his arms seem unusually long. The aperture seems to expand, as if to accept his gift. He appears to thrust his seed-laden hands much deeper than the shallow shrine pit before him, extending his arms *right into the ground* so that they *deposit the seeds deep within the earth,* through a world-penetrating *shaft or tunnel within the navel which leads straight into the earth and its womb.*

Tewa elders call this awesome feat of human-mediated fertilization *putting in the squash.* They are profoundly aware, however, of the cosmic implications of such supernaturally sanctioned human interventions, intended to harmonize and to impel nature's cycles. In the weeks ahead, *putting the squash* into *the navel of mother earth* will be followed and reinforced by related ceremonies performed by the seven other Made People societies.

After all eight societies have performed the ceremonies that constitute Bringing the Buds to Life, other equally important ceremonial tasks will remain to be performed during the course of the year. Among them will be Bringing the Leaves to Life, which begins the vernal equinox, and Bringing the Blossoms to Life, which begins shortly thereafter. Each of these rituals urges the seasonal cycles of nature to advance a bit more. Cumulatively, the nine *works* reflect the responsibility the Tewa people bear for the earth and its inhabitants. Deeply embedded in traditional Tewa society is the certainty that Homo sapiens have a sacred, ongoing obligation to give generously to the world, periodically and without fail, spiritual and material riches and energies.

So every winter, in the last days of February, Made People gather again in community plazas and other sacred places to devote their precious time and thoughts, songs and movements, to Bringing the Buds to Life *everywhere* in the world one more time.

Knowing this, those of us not personally blessed with Tewa blood, who are perhaps living urban lives of unparalleled prosperity, seemingly far removed from the annual birth cries of a writhing and animate earth, should pause to utter a few words of gratitude to the natural world and to the Made People of San Juan Pueblo, who once again are *reawakening all of nature for the new year.*

10

The Fate of the Earth

Voices of the Elders

It is the story of all life that is holy and is good to tell, and of us two-leggeds sharing in it with the four-leggeds and the wings of the air and all green things; for these are children of one mother and their father is one Spirit.

—Black Elk, Sioux elder[1]

A single protein molecule or a single finger print, a single syllable on the radio or a single idea of yours, implies the whole historical reach of stellar and organic evolution. It is enough to make you tingle all the time.

—John Platt, biophysicist[2]

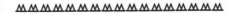

Native and scientific modes of thinking about the natural world are often complementary and mutually enriching not only in their perceptions of the workings of nature but also in their prescriptions for a viable future. This resonance is particularly apparent in their dire warnings of the possible long-term consequences of destructive global ecological practices and their prescriptions for protecting planetary ecosystems—in short, in their shared concern for the earth's fate.

As we approach the end of the twentieth century, it is abundantly clear that we have not achieved a technological utopia. Instead, the planet is beset with a staggering array of problems that have been created or exacerbated by modern science and technology—from overpopulation and the mass extinction of species to prospective global climatic change, to soil loss and pollution, to the proliferation of deadly weapons of mass destruction.

Not all scientists, of course, are blind to this paradox. A number of vocal scientists have openly questioned some of our current assumptions about the limits of scientific knowledge and its role in modern society. These are largely *older* scientists who have firmly established their place in science through their impeccable academic credentials and exceptional professional achievements, then have turned to more philosophical questions about nature, science, and society, often relatively late in their careers.

The Role of Elders

Throughout human history, *elders* have occupied a special position in society. They have painstakingly accumulated reservoirs of personal experience, knowledge, and *wisdom*—or compassionate insight and a sense of the enduring qualities and relationships around them. They freely offer this wisdom to living generations of their people in an effort to help them connect harmoniously with their past, present, and future.

Perhaps out of a sense of their own mortality, or concern for the uncertain future of their children and grandchildren, or a burning curiosity to fit their life's work into the broader scheme of things, some scientists begin to ask profound questions about society's direction and have much to contribute to their fellow scientists and to society as a whole.

Not all elder scientists are equally worthy of our attention; nor are all of their writings about the wider world steeped in wisdom. Distinguishing between an ordinary elderly scientist and a true scientific "elder" will always present a challenge to the general public.

According to Pam Colorado, a Wisconsin Oneida of the Iroquois Confederacy who teaches at the University of Calgary, Native cultures fully recognize that all elderly people have lessons to offer based on their life experiences. But they also realize that only a few have the specialized knowledge of the cosmos that uniquely equips them to provide wise counsel to the community and the world. *These master scientists,** says Colorado, *are characterized by a deep, abiding humility, a reverence of life and the natural world.* Traditionally, they have served as facilitators, or guides, rather than simply as instructors. *One of the tenets of American Indian science,* she says, as she actively promotes a new synthesis of Native and scientific knowledge, *is that the search for truth and learning is a spiritual relationship between the individual and the Creator.* The role of elder has traditionally been to point people toward the rituals and

---

* In her writings, Colorado deliberately refers to Native shamans, medicine people, and other traditional elders as "scientists." She also refers to traditional Native knowledge about the natural world as "Native science." She adopts this convention for good reason—to counter the "intellectual imperialism" of the West in aggressively denigrating indigenous knowledge, and to place Native nature-wisdom on par with Western science. Throughout this book, we have deliberately chosen to restrict the use of the term "science" to conventional, reductive Western approaches to understanding nature, without in any way intending to impugn the value of Native thought.

growth processes that might help them become more aware of themselves as well as of the natural world and their place within it. *The guidance of Elders, the teaching of the natural world and its catalysts,* she says, using another Western analogy, *comprise the Native literature search.*[3]

In science and in Native societies, genuine wisdom is attributed to those with the capacity to *feel,* to exhibit *compassion* and *generosity* toward others, and to develop intimate, insightful, and empathetic *relationships* not just with fellow human beings but, in some sense, with the entire membership of the natural world.

As we decide which scientific "elders" are most worthy of our attention, we need to look for these crucial qualities. Unfortunately, our cultural biases often devalue these very qualities, perhaps because, as pioneering Swiss psychiatrist Alice Miller has suggested, emotionally suffocating childrearing practices in our society tend to instill in us the notion that wisdom is inevitably the exclusive province of chronologically older, more experienced individuals, regardless of their capacity to feel, to empathize, and to develop deep, meaningful connections with their surroundings.

As a result, in science as elsewhere many of us embrace too eagerly the perilous illusion that age, gender, and continuity of experience are always reliable indices of wisdom. *Naturally, older craftsmen have more experience in their trades, and older scientists have more facts in their heads, but in both cases their knowledge* [may have] *precious little to do with wisdom,* warns Miller. *Of what use are instructions and moral sermons if one's capacity for feeling and compassion has been lost?*[4]

The Nature-Wisdom of Western Elders

Over the years, a host of prominent life scientists, ranging from ecologists like Paul Ehrlich and brain biologists like Roger Sperry to anthropologists like Gregory Bateson, biologists like George Wald, and molecular geneticists like François Jacob, have taken passionate public stands that seem in some way heretical to the "conventional wisdom" of the mainstream scientific community. As their brief quotations throughout this book suggest, however, their philosophical views on how human beings *ought* to relate to the natural world often imply that certain aspects of nature *ought* to be treated as "sacred" or as worthy of profound veneration, for the well-being of all life on earth. Some openly concede that scientific thought has its limits and that certain aspects of the universe may forever remain mysterious to scientists. Some of them publicly grieve for the ecological destruction they have witnessed during their lifetimes and question whether we possess the will and stamina to alter the environmental deterioration that the march of Western civilization has wrought.

The views of these highly articulate and academically re-spected scientific elders are often strikingly compatible with those of Native elders. In fact, some of these scientific elders imply that Western society has much to learn from indigenous and other ancient traditions of nature-wisdom. Howard T. Odum, one of the pioneers of modern ecosystems science, for example, openly ponders the extraordinary resonance be-tween Native and scientific thought about the intricate ecolog-ical networks that he has spent his life trying to comprehend and mathematically model. In *Environment, Power, and Society,* a still timely personal exploration of the underlying order of ecological systems written nearly two decades ago, he writes:

When man was a tiny part of the stable complex forest, his faith was in an umbrella-like energy system with God identified as the intel-ligence within the mechanisms of forest control, the system. Primi-tive [sic] forest peoples . . . had religious faith in the forest as a network of gods operating with intelligence. A stable forest <u>actually</u> <u>is</u> a system of compartments with networks, flows, and logic circuits that do constitute a form of intelligence beyond that of its individual humans[5] [our emphasis].

226

Other scientific elders speak out on what they suspect may be inherently sacred, or spiritual, dimensions of nature. One remarkable public statement, titled "Preserving and Cherishing the Earth: An Appeal for Joint Commitment in Science and Religion," was issued at a recent international conference on the environment and economic development in Moscow, attended by religious, political, and scientific leaders from eighty-three nations.* Importantly, it was signed by a number of the most respected and articulate Western scientists of our time, including astronomers Carl Sagan and Freeman Dyson, physicist Hans Bethe, atmospheric scientist Stephen Schneider, and biologists Peter Raven, Roger Revelle, and Stephen Jay Gould. One of its most scientifically daring passages states:

As scientists, many of us have had profound experiences of awe and reverence before the universe. We understand that what is regarded as sacred is more likely to be treated with care and respect. Our planetary home should be so regarded. Efforts to safeguard and cherish the environment need to be infused with a vision of the sacred.

In his thoughtful philosophical essays, Roger Sperry, the Nobel Prize–winning brain biologist, has discussed society's desperate need to reconcile the electrifying insights of modern science with compatible value systems that honor and protect the natural world. He suggests that to facilitate this search for a new global ethos by which we can navigate the ecologically turbulent seas of our times, each of us should engage in an intriguing thought experiment. Our challenge is, by a leap of the imagination, to divine what environmental values the wisest spiritual elders of the world's great religious traditions might be publicly proposing today if they were alive and were scientifically well informed. *The task,* muses Sperry, *can be*

* Interestingly (if anyone really needed proof that many Native thinkers have long been aware of the precious resonance between their own and scientific perspectives on nature), the person who first brought this statement to our attention was the well-known Native American elder Thomas Banyacya, who has served as a spokesman for certain traditional Hopi communities for several decades.

The statement represents an urgent appeal for a joint alliance between the world's religious and scientific leaders to forge a new, scientifically compatible ethos that might "preserve and cherish the Earth."

likened in some respects to that of trying to deduce what form of religion
the teachings of Christ, Mohammed, Buddha, Confucius, and other
founders [and, we would add, unsung prescientific Native spiritual figures] might have taken if Copernicus, Darwin, Einstein, and
all the rest had come before their time instead of after.[6]

We might weigh the words of wisdom offered by another
well-known scientific maverick, anthropologist Gregory
Bateson, on the perils of relying too heavily upon the vaunted
value-free truths of modern science. Scientific truths, suggests
Bateson, are by their very nature incomplete. To rely too
exclusively upon such dispassionate thought, he suggests, is to
court a numbing spiritual dissociation. *It is the attempt to separate intellect from emotion that is monstrous,* warns Bateson, *and I
suggest that it is equally monstrous—and dangerous—to attempt to
separate the external mind from the internal. Or to separate mind
from body.*[7] In a similar vein, science historian Morris Berman,
in his book *The Reenchantment of the World,* has described the
progressive despiritualization of nature as *intrinsic to the scientific world view* and referred to ongoing efforts to render science
more holistic and perceptually complete as nothing less than
the great project, and the great drama, of the twentieth century.[8]

These and other contemporary scientists and science observers are implicitly expressing a yearning for the same sort of
integration of knowledge and human values that takes place in
the undivided Native Mind. Where will we find the wisdom to
make our way through the maze of global overpopulation,
industrial toxins, loss of biodiversity, ozone depletion, and
countless other unfolding environmental crises that cast a
long, uncertain shadow over the earth's fate?

We may find it, suggests well-known population ecologist
Paul Ehrlich, in popular movements that offer a timely blend of
the sometimes spiritually numbing truths of modern science
and a complementary spiritual quality capable of altering our
collective behavior. Ehrlich's comments were originally directed at the emerging international, nature-centered Deep
Ecology movement, which tends to envision a more biocentric
and egalitarian world—one dominated more by interspecies

228

empathy than by scientific rationality. But they would apply equally well to a host of other nature-embracing disciplines, including traditional Native nature-wisdom, that increasingly represent an integral part of Deep Ecological thought.

I am convinced that such a quasi-religious *movement, one concerned with the need to change the values that now govern much of human activity, is essential to the persistence of our civilization,* says Ehrlich. *But agreeing that science, even the science of ecology, cannot answer all questions—that there are* "other ways of knowing"*— does not diminish the absolutely critical role that good science must play if our over-extended civilization is to save itself*[9] [our emphasis].

This sense that Western society urgently needs to begin to seek a uniquely twentieth-century blend of mutually enriching scientific and spiritual truths is echoed in a succinct statement by systems ecologist Howard Odum:

The key program of a surviving pattern of nature and man is a subsystem of religious teaching *which follows the laws of the energy ethic. . . . We can teach the energy truths through general science in the schools and teach the* love of system *and its requirements of us in the changing churches*[10] [our emphasis].

The Nature-Wisdom of Native Elders

The search for science-compatible spiritualities that can somehow infuse human beings with a "love of ecological system" will always be fraught with difficulty. Even if Native and scientific ecological perspectives sometimes seem to offer luminously complementary truths about the natural world, they will always remain, as anthropologist Lévi-Strauss and other thinkers have meticulously shown, fundamentally separate, if parallel, categories of knowledge. In the end, Western scientific thought does not *need* the Native Mind (as many indignant scientists would probably be only too eager to remind us). Nor does it *need* the Native Mind's ancient, painstakingly accumulated, and spiritually charged knowledge about nature—or even its promise, however faint, of a more harmonious relationship between human beings and nature. Science can only remain, by its very nature, forever *devoid of mind and soul, of joy and sadness, of desire and hope,* in the wistful words of Francois Jacob, the French molecular biologist and Nobel laureate.

But if Western science does not need the Native Mind, the *human* mind and, in particular, the Western mind and society *do*. We will always need the Native Mind's vibrant images of a living natural world that can penetrate to the deepest and most heartfelt (what science calls "irrational" or "intuitive") realms of human understanding. We need the Native Mind's bold assurance that while much of the universe is accessible to human sensibilities, it possesses dimensions that may remain forever beyond human logic and reason, and that the cosmic forces of mystery, chaos, and uncertainty are eternal. Perhaps more than anything else, we need the glimmer of hope for the kind of future that indigenous nature-wisdom foreshadows— by its historic precedent of sustaining a long-term ecological equilibrium with the natural world, despite occasional lapses.

The most fruitful dialogue between Native and Western modes of thought will take place not under the scorching light of scholarly Western intellectual analysis but within and among individuals. *Within* individual human minds, it occurs through mental and emotional processes of personal transformation that take place as culturally different ideas and values collide. It will occur *without* the need for any final "proof," mutual exclusion, or conclusive "conquest" of one tradition's vision over the other.

In his recent book *In Defense of the Land Ethic,* environmental philosopher J. Baird Callicott shares this hope. He suggests that traditional Native American nature-wisdom might become living, cultural "role models" for all the world to witness and emulate. The idea that Native worldviews are steeped in genuine environmental wisdom is not, he insists, some sort of "neoromantic invention" or a return to guilt-ridden, Western notions of "noble savages." On the contrary, it arises from a clear-eyed recognition of indigenous societies' sense of *relationship* with the natural world, from which flow very different environmental values and responsibilities. *If we are to suppose,* he writes, *that some American Indian peoples portrayed their relationship with nature as essentially social and thus, by implication, as essentially _moral_, then their rich narrative heritage could provide, _ready-made_, the myths and parables missing from abstract articulations of biosocial environmental ethics like* [ecologist] *Aldo Leopold's*[11] [emphasis ours].

Even as some Westerners begin to bask in such optimism, we emphasize again that ancient traditions of indigenous knowledge, in North America and around the world, have intrinsic value and an inalienable right to exist. They do not need the nodding approval of Western societies or of well-intentioned Western scientists somehow finally to "confirm" their truth and relevance. Nor can their worth be measured in terms of injections of hope or possible rainforest cures for cancer or AIDS that traditional indigenous knowledge might one day offer the bloated and voraciously expanding modern industrial societies of the West.

By openly acknowledging the inherent intelligence, coherence, and relevance of traditional Native knowledge about the natural world, the West can, if not to its satisfaction finally "prove" or "disprove" them, affirm their right to flourish by honoring the dignity of all First Peoples and by honorably settling their legitimate claims to the sacred lands that are so vital to their worldviews and survival.

Beyond this, we can also quietly admire Native knowledge and value systems from afar as they continue to evolve to meet the needs of aboriginal peoples in an ever-changing world. For as Lévi-Strauss suggested, simply by according Native worldviews the basic respect they have always deserved, Western civilization and its cherished *scientific spirit in its most modern form will have contributed to legitimize the principles of savage* [or Native] *thought and to re-establish it in its rightful place.*[12]

Even in the wake of five centuries of monumental European "discovery" and expansion—mirrored, in Native memory, by

five centuries of extraordinary suffering and resistance—we
might permit ourselves a measure of optimism. We might
hope, for example, that in the years ahead a global science-
compatible Native ecological consciousness might emerge and
help inspire non-Natives to adopt similar environmental
values. And we might hope that, in the process, a host of the
calmer, more compassionate, and more far-sighted voices of
society's wisest elders—Native and scientific—might be
heard more clearly above the din.

Native voices are rooted in an ever-present Distant Time
that binds together all forms of life in a "sacred ecology" that
unabashedly embraces and sanctifies nature. Yet they remain
informed by the most subtle and compelling truths of modern
science. These voices can convey to ordinary people a vision of
the natural world that has embedded within it an enduring
environmental ethic and that is imbued with a visceral feeling
for the horrific consequences of human folly, ignorance, and
denial of the biosphere's fate.

It's not too late to turn around the ecological catastrophe, insists
Alfonso Ortiz. *I'd despair if I thought it was too late.* But genuine
change on a global scale, he suggests, can only come about by
collectively drawing upon the wisest and most adaptive features of our respective cultural heritages. Even then, meaningful change will require radically different ways of thinking
about and relating to the natural world. *You don't use technology
alone to clean up the mess technology created,* says Ortiz. *We [are]
talking about new ways of perceiving relationships among human
beings—a troublesome species—and the earth. Those ways are already there in Indian teachings.*[13]

One can sense those ways of perceiving human relationships with nature in the following brief selection of Native
commentaries on what might be called the "state of the natural world." They include contemporary personal testimonies
of Native leaders, public proclamations of Native groups, and
ancient—yet timeless—Native nature prophecies that do not
naively *predict* that the past will repeat but that offer a vision of

the possible *reassertion* of the recurring patterns of human nature and the natural world upon the earth's unfolding fate.

∧∧∧∧∧∧∧∧∧∧∧∧∧∧∧∧∧∧∧∧∧∧

Communicating a Sense of the Sacred [14]

SOUTHWESTERN BRITISH COLUMBIA:
Lil'wat

> The truth is that we never conquered the world, never understood it; we only think we have control. We do not even know why we respond a certain way to other organisms, and need them in diverse ways, so deeply.
> —E. O. Wilson, entomologist and
> evolutionary biologist[15]

I feel pain and anger that the ancestors—the grandmothers and the grandfathers—were so neglected when they offered up the best of their collective wisdom—their sacred rituals and ceremonies and songs for you [non-Natives] to better understand the laws of the world you thought you had civilized. I feel pain and anger that in your rush toward development, the fabric of this globe has been rent, and what you call the biosphere or ecosphere—but which my people more simply call Mother—has been so neglected and so hurt. . . .

All over the world, indigenous peoples have been and are being systematically destroyed in the name of development. Languages are being eradicated, family relationships are being stretched and broken, traditional values are belittled, and, as a last resort, genocide is being practiced. What is by now the well-oiled and finely tuned machine of the elimination of the indigenous people and thoughts has been practiced at least since the dawn of that day called Industrial Development.

Why?

Because the perspectives and philosophies of indigenous peoples—our traditional rules and laws—would never allow this stripping of resources from our traditional homelands on this planet at a net cost to future generations and to life itself. The very thinking of indigenous peoples runs counter to the course of rampant, unsustainable development, so we, as indigenous peoples, have been removed from the picture. And removed we have been—mercilessly and efficiently, around the globe. . . .

The global environment crisis has more than adequately demonstrated that business as usual will not and cannot ensure global survival. What is needed is a fundamental shift in consciousness, and this means that the views of indigenous peoples—our laws and rules and relationships to the natural world—have to be brought back into the picture. In fact, these natural laws and rules have to become the focus of humanity.

This is the first role of the indigenous peoples in the survival of the planet, the Earth. Our continuing primary commitment has been to communicate the indigenous perspective to all who will listen. . . . Our elders tell us we have to do more than save what is left of our traditional homelands. We need to contribute to an overall change of mind . . . so that human-kind can begin to initiate strategies which will preserve and sustain the environment all cultures and nations share. . . .

As indigenous peoples we have always tried to convey [a] sense of the sacred[ness of all life] to the newcomers to our traditional territories and homelands. With generosity and compassion we have attempted to share our ceremonies and our songs with the newcomers to our homelands because these rituals convey our successful relationship with the lands and seas around us and our necessary knowledge for those who would share our lands with us. But the forces of development have refused to recognize the fact that indigenous peoples around the globe have in place complex systems of obviously sustainable resource management which have been successfully practiced for millennia.

*Our people's authority in and responsibility for our traditional
homeland has been handed us by our ancestors and cannot be lightly
dismissed. Let's get it straight. Our homelands, as indigenous peoples around the globe, have either been stolen or are threatened to be
stolen at the present time and when these homelands pass from our
control they are mismanaged beyond repair. . . .*

*The second role of indigenous peoples is to protect what is left of
the natural world within their traditional homeland with every ounce
of their strength and every resource at their disposal. We have declared the Stein Valley a park—the Stein Valley Tribal Heritage
Park, a living museum of natural and cultural history—and any
government or corporation that does not extend this park the recognition and respect it should have does so at its own peril. . . .*

*We know similar necessary actions in protection of what is left of
the natural world are occurring all over the world, and I want to
salute the strength and tenacity of indigenous peoples.*

—Ruby Dunstan, Lytton Indian Band

MWWWWWWWWWWWWWWWWWW

Indigenous People—Caretakers
of All Life [16]

HOTEVILLA, ARIZONA:
Hopi

Four Laws of Ecology:

Everything is connected to everything else.

Everything must go somewhere.

Nature knows best.

There is no such thing as a free lunch.

—Barry Commoner, ecologist[17]

*The things that were created and given to us are all very precious. We
are to protect and use all these precious things wisely, and to share
them in order to keep harmony among all people. But we are forget-*

235

ting these things, making the search for peace extremely difficult. We fear that mankind has gone too far and forgotten too much to find this peace.

During the ages of life the ancient Hopi have seen and experienced many things, such as changing of an old world order to a new order because of some dreadful disaster [caused] by [the] mindless action of man forgetting the Creator's divine laws. This kind of mindless action has happened in three previous world orders which have then been destroyed. It is very sad indeed that mankind will never learn from our past history. Once again, mankind has failed to live by the divine laws which we promised with our Creator to live by, and so, gradually, the land and nature are getting out-of-balance. Technology is rapidly eroding our ancient culture and tradition. The wildlife and forest are diminishing rapidly, the precious water and air are becoming unhealthy to drink and breathe. Changing climate also is important to consider seriously for it symbolizes a grave warning to man.

How can we correct the faults? Would retracing our steps back to divine laws be a solution? This will be a difficult step because we are tempted on all sides into material values. The moral values we once followed have now become make-believe living like playthings we use. If we correct our ways we could turn the course of the future. Our prophecy foretold that the time might come that a man with a very clever mind will seek out the secret of Nature and defy its laws. Much of what is discovered will benefit man in good ways, but most of it also has a dangerous side. Because Nature has its own mysterious protection, man will eventually harvest misfortune. It has become clear now that the products of modern science and technology such as medicine, drugs and weapons are what was prophesied.

While this is going on, the Hopi who turn against their original vows will unbalance the earthly cycles that control the seasons. This will be done in Hopi land because that is a spiritual center of the earth. This change will affect the entire earth. Hopi land will be the first to feel the effect. We will know the imbalance is coming about when our planting month is delayed by cold weather or when frost comes before our crops are mature for harvest. This happened this very year so our harvest will be less. *With trained eyes, we see some wild life begin to disappear. Most summer insects did not return in accordance with seasonal cycles. Perhaps they have gone in search of their natural environment. We look at all these events as signs of some great change or new turn of events coming soon but only the Great Spirit knows exactly when. Perhaps this is fulfilling Hopi prophecy of a great purification of the present world order. No one knows what form this will take. It can come in peaceful ways or in the form of terrible catastrophe because we are not above the laws of Creation. We Hopi are ready for the outcome. Whatever it may be we all deserve what will be given. . . .*

The way one nation treats another serves either to strengthen or destroy the spiritual basis of peace in the world. Serious wars are bound to result throughout the world, as long as America continues to oppose the spiritual way of life we call the Hopi way. Contrary to the opinion of many, the greater the military force of a nation, the greater the danger to that nation. Peace can come to the world only through an honest, non-violent relationship with the indigenous people, who are the caretakers of life.

—Carolyn Tawangyowma, Sovereign Hopi
Independent Nation

ᗰᗰᗰᗰᗰᗰᗰᗰᗰᗰᗰᗰᗰᗰ

Our Mother the Earth Is Growing Old Now [18]

NORTHEASTERN NORTH AMERICA:
Iroquois Confederacy

Science has a useful set of insights and they depend on the rigorous adherence to fact and inferential reasoning. It has a certain power. It also has a certain narrowness because it cannot illuminate the larger question of beginning, end, and purpose.

—Robert Jastrow, physicist[19]

The Haudenosaunee, or Six Nations Iroquois Confederacy, is among the most ancient continuously operating governments in the world. Long before the arrival of the European peoples in North America, our people met in council to enact the principles of peaceful coexistence among nations and the recognition of the right of peoples to a continued and uninterrupted existence. European people left our council fires and journeyed forth into the world to spread principles of justice and democracy which they learned from us and which have had profound effects upon the evolution of the Modern World. . . .

Brothers and Sisters: When the Europeans first invaded our lands, they found a world filled with the bountiful gifts of creation. . . . Everywhere the game was plentiful, and sometimes the birds darkened the sky like great clouds, so great were their numbers. Our country teemed with elk and deer, bear and moose, and we were a happy and prosperous people in those times.

Brothers and Sisters: Our Mother the Earth is growing old now. No longer does she support upon her breast the teeming herds of wildlife who once shared this place with us, and most of the great forest which is our home is gone today. The forest was butchered a century ago to make charcoal for the forges of the Industrial Revolution, most of the game was destroyed by sport hunters and farmers, most of the bird life has been destroyed by hunters and pesticides which are common this century. Many of the rivers flow thick with the effluence of great population centers throughout the country. We see the "scorched earth" policy has not ended.

Brothers and Sisters: We are alarmed at the evidence that is before us. The smoke from industrial centers in the Midwest around the Great Lakes rises in a deadly cloud and returns to earth in the form of acid rains over the Adirondack Mountains, and the fish life cannot reproduce in the acid waters. In the high country of the Adirondack Mountains, the lakes are still, the fish are no more.

The people who plant the lands that we have occupied for thousands of years display no love for the life of this place. Each year they plant the same crops on the same land and they must then spray those crops with poisons to kill the insects which naturally infest their fields because they do not rotate crops or allow the land to rest. *Their pesticides kill the bird life, and the runoff poisons the surface waters.*

They must spray also the other plant life with herbicides, and each year the runoff from the fields carries these poisons into the watersheds of our country and into the waters of the world.

Brothers and Sisters: Our ancient homeland is spotted today with an array of chemical dumps. Along the Niagara River dioxin, a particularly deadly substance, threatens the remaining life there and in the waters which flow from there. Forestry departments spray the surviving forests with powerful insecticides to encourage tourism by people seeking a few days or weeks away from the cities where the air hangs heavy with sulphur and carbon oxides. The insecticides kill the black flies, but also destroy much of the food chain for the bird, fish and animal life which also inhabit those regions.

The fish of the Great Lakes are laced with mercury from industrial plants, and fluoride from aluminum plants poisons the land and the people. Sewage from the population centers is mixed with PCBs and PBS in the watershed of the Great Lakes and the Finger Lakes, and the water is virtually nowhere safe for any living creature.

Brothers and Sisters: We are alarmed that a string of nuclear power plants is being built around our country and that at Three Mile Island in the southern portion of our ancient territories an "accident" has occurred which is of a type of accident which could hasten the end of life in this place. We are dismayed that a nuclear waste dump at West Valley (N.Y.) upstream from one of our communities is releasing radioactive substances through our lands and into the watershed of Lake Erie. We are offended that the information about the nature of these plants is known only to the highest officials of the United States, leaving the people unarmed to defend themselves from such development and the development of nuclear power is encouraged to continue.

We are concerned for the well-being and continued survival of our brothers and sisters in the Southwest and Northwest who are exposed to uranium mining and its inherent dangers. The mining end is the dirtiest portion of the nuclear fuel cycle and has progressed beyond questions of whether or not the machinery is dependable. Already vast amounts of low-level radioactive uranium tailings have been dumped in cities and used in building materials of dwellings and public buildings over a wide area of the Southwest. People have died, and many more can be expected to die.

Proponents of the Nuclear Fuel Cycle issue statement after statement to the people, urging that the nuclear reactors are fitted with safety devices so sophisticated that a meltdown is only the most remote of possibilities. Yet we observe that no machinery or other invention made by human hands was a permanent thing. Nothing humans ever built, not even the pyramids of Egypt, maintained their purpose indefinitely. The only universal truth applicable to human-made devices is that all of them fail in their turn. Nuclear reactors must also fall victim to that truth.

Brothers and Sisters: We cannot adequately express our feelings of horror and repulsion as we view the policies of industry and government in North America which threaten to destroy all life. Our fore-fathers predicted that the European Way of Life would bring a Spiritual imbalance to the world, that the Earth would grow old as a result of that imbalance. Now it is before all the world to see—that the life-producing forces are being reversed, and that the life-potential is leaving this land. Only a people whose minds are twisted beyond an ability to perceive truth could act in ways which will threaten the future generations of humanity.

Brothers and Sisters: We point out to you the Spiritual Path of Righteousness and Reason. We bring to your thought and minds that right-minded human beings seek to promote above all else the life of all things. We direct to your minds that peace is not merely the absence of war, but the constant effort to maintain harmonious existence between all peoples, from individual to individual and between humans and the other beings of this planet. We point out to you that a Spiritual Consciousness is the Path to Survival of Humankind. We who walk about on Mother Earth occupy this place for only a short time. It is our duty as human beings to preserve the life that is here for the benefit of the generations yet unborn.

Brothers and Sisters: The Haudenosaunee are determined to take whatever actions we can to halt the destruction of Mother Earth. In our territories, we continue to carry out our function as spiritual caretakers of the land. In this role as caretakers we cannot, and will not, stand idly by while the future of the coming generations is being systematically destroyed. We recognize that the fight is a long one and that we cannot hope to win it alone. To win, to secure the future, we must join hands with like-minded people and create a strength through unity. We commemorate two hundred years of injustice and the destruction of the world with these words.

—The Haudenosaunee Declaration of the Iroquois

∿∿∿∿∿∿∿∿∿∿∿∿∿∿∿∿∿∿∿∿∿

The Gourd of Ashes [20]

ORAIBI, ARIZONA:
Hopi

A disenchanted world is, at the same time, a world liable to control and manipulation. Any science that conceives of the world as being governed according to a universal theoretical plan that reduces its various riches to the drab applications of general laws thereby becomes an instrument of domination. And man, a stranger to the world, sets himself up as its master.

—Ilya Prigogine, physicist, and
Isabelle Stengers, chemist [21]

Our prophecies foretold of the day when young people from this country would move from a western direction seeking to stop the elements aimed at destroying all living things. Today people from this country, and from countries all around the world, are coming together for peace bringing further realization of the Hopi prophecies.

When the Hopi found out about the nuclear bombing of Nagasaki and Hiroshima they recalled the Hopi Prophecy that spoke of a small but devastating gourd of ashes. It was said that this gourd, if allowed to fall to the ground, would bring devastating destruction, burning everything around it. Living things under the water would also be

241

destroyed from the heat. Many sicknesses would arise which our medicines would not be able to cure. We were told never to go beyond this step, never to allow the manufacture of other such destructive things. We now know that these foreseen destructive forces were nuclear weapons. We were told that if we were to continue on this path even greater destruction would follow. Wars can no longer be conducted as a way to reach peace. Peace can only be brought about through spiritual ways, through kindness, understanding, gentleness and love. Only through these spiritual ways can we put aside the wrong action of the past and repair the damage done to our Mother Earth and the peoples of the Earth. It is time for all people to join, actively working to stop the development of war and the use of nuclear forces. . . .

Through religion we are going to find those who are searching for the right way of living the truth and the peaceful way of harmony with each other and with nature all around, the clouds, the rain, the animals and the plant life. We are all a part of Mother Earth. We cannot break away from that. We are going to have to understand this so that we can look at each other. We are just like the trees out there—all different people with different languages, different colors and ways of expression. We are just like any other part of nature that is around us. This, we must understand.

—Thomas Banyacya, spokesman for Hopi religious leaders

ΛΛΛΛΛΛΛΛΛΛΛΛΛΛΛΛΛΛΛΛΛΛΛΛΛ

The Destruction of the
Wooden People 22

MESOAMERICA:
Maya

In seeking the ultimate answer to the meaning of
existence, that is, reading God's mind, as early
scientists considered their work, modern man has
foreclosed the possibility of experiencing life in

favor of explaining it. Even in explaining the
world, however, Western man has misunder-
stood it.

—Vine Deloria[23]

The
Destruction
of the Wooden
People

Today, after nearly five centuries of suffering and resistance in the wake of Christopher Columbus's fateful arrival on the edge of the world of their ancestors, many millions of Maya Indians survive, still speaking their myriad Native tongues. Despite continuing racist oppression—especially in Guatemala, where a succession of military-dominated regimes continues to manipulate a Mayan majority estimated at between 60 and 80 percent (that is, between five and seven million people) of the total population—many Maya still look upon vast tracts of traditional lands spanning Guatemala, as well as portions of Mexico, Honduras, El Salvador, and Belize, as their sacred trust.

The great Mayan text known as the *Popol Vuh* is probably the best known example of their civilization's extraordinary legacy of written literature; to many Maya, it is no mere book. The Quiché-speaking Maya of highland Guatemala, the living descendants of its authors, view this ancient collection of Mayan creation stories, chronicles, astronomical calculations, and prophecies as an *ilbal,* a precious "seeing instrument" or lens, with which to perceive the true relationships within the universe. This sacred Book of Council, is, they suggest, a sort of corrective lens. If used wisely, it can help myopic human beings, so prone to seeing events in the short term of their own mortal lives, to gaze out to the very limits of space and time, just as their primordial, all-knowing ancestors once routinely did.

To the world's collective shame, only four Mayan hieroglyphic books out of perhaps many hundreds are known to have escaped the bonfires of overzealous Christian missionaries, who, in the bloody wake of invading Spanish conquistadores, deliberately set out to destroy every expression of traditional Mayan belief. In response to this tragic burning of books, knowledgeable Mayan scribes, often tutored lin-

guistically by unsuspecting Spanish clerics, quietly encoded
aspects of traditional Mayan knowledge in the alphabetic
symbols of their European oppressors. According to Dennis
Tedlock, upon whose meticulous translation of the *Popol Vuh*
our discussion is based, today the two most important "alphabetic substitutes" for the ancient hieroglyphic texts are the
Popol Vuh, from highland Guatemala, and the *Chilam Balam*
books, from the Yucatan Peninsula of Mexico.

These well-known works are among the most eloquent,
evocative, and accessible examples of the written literature of
First Peoples in the world. Is it possible that in the often elusive
and multilayered meanings of these rich accounts of the
Mayan cosmos, we might discover faint clues to modern society's current environmental woes? Might they not serve as a
modern "seeing instrument"—a sacred Native vision of
nature—that complements the emerging Western ecological
wisdom and can help us all in our collective passage through
the decades ahead?

Perhaps a few such clues can be found in the *Popol Vuh*'s
fragmentary tale of the gods' first failed attempts to create
healthy, wise, and emotionally complete human beings. In the
first epoch of human creation, we are told, people were made
of mud. In the second—our focus here—they were fashioned
from wood. In the third, the Maya themselves were molded
from the flour of maize, or corn, a sacred botanical element of
the Maya world, as well as a precious food resource. And
world transformations continue to take place, they say, to the
rhythm of ancient Maya calendars of the sacred circular patterns of time.

In the beginning, according to the *Popol Vuh,* the world was
nothing more than a vast serenity of empty skies and primordial waters. Then Heart of Sky, Heart of Earth, Newborn
Thunderbolt, Raw Thunderbolt, and Hurricane descended
from the sterile heavens. Maker, Modeler, Bearer, Begetter,
Heart of the Lake, Heart of the Sea, and Sovereign Plumed
Serpent surfaced in the sterile seas. And after some discussion,

this momentous gathering of divine beings—of *great knowers, great thinkers*—decided to bring the earth into being. They did this by simply saying its name.

In their first life-generating act, they populated the earth with an abundance of animal and plant life—with cypresses and pines, deer and birds, jaguars and serpents—simply by conceiving of these things in their minds. But sadly, these new creatures, for all their wondrous gifts of diverse color and form, could not speak. They could do no more than squawk, chatter, or howl.

The gods desired to include in their magnificent design a people who, unlike the flora and fauna, might offer articulate prayers to the sacred primordial forces of creation and painstakingly chronicle the sacred passage of time. So they fashioned the first rudimentary human beings. And they molded them from mud.

But these crude Mud People proved unequal to the task. They were ugly and misshapen. They mumbled incoherently. They could not walk, and in the solitude of their paralysis, they could not even reproduce. In the end, their earthen bodies grew soft and dissolved away into nothingness.

In their next attempt to fashion a people who might function as an articulate *giver of praise, giver of respect, provider, nurturer,* the gods boldly conceived of human beings made not of mud but of wood. They carved a man's body from the wood of a coral tree, and a woman's from the pith of reeds. Unlike their soft predecessors, these hardy wood carvings prospered. They quickly populated the world and cleverly harnessed the plants, animals, and other elements of the universe to meet their own needs. *They became the first numerous people here on the face of the earth.*

But the Wooden People too possessed fatal flaws. For all their technological ingenuity—their ability to cultivate maize, to grind flour and fry tortillas, to manufacture kitchen pots and utensils, to domesticate dogs and turkeys—they were utterly devoid of compassion, of empathy, of spirituality honoring the sacred shared origins of all life. *There was nothing in their hearts and nothing in their minds, no memory of their mason and builder.* In short, they *just went and walked wherever they wanted.*

So that in time, despite their extraordinary dexterity in fashioning material things and manipulating the elements of the natural world, the Wooden People were perhaps an even greater disappointment to the gods than the Mud People. Like their unworthy earthen predecessors, they seemed bent, however unknowingly, on engineering their own demise.

In despair, the gods observed the arrogance, greed, and spiritual numbness with which the wooden manikins lived out their materialistic lives. Finally, overcome with remorse at what they had created, they decided to end this unsuccessful thought experiment. They chose not merely to punish the Wooden People but to utterly extirpate them from the surface of the earth.

To carry out this plan, Heart of Sky unleashed a catastrophic flood. This great deluge was followed by a succession of other disasters. Day and night, rains of black resin pelted down upon the Wooden People from the skies. Monstrous beings gouged their eyes from their sockets, smashed their faces, flayed their bodies, devoured their flesh. Perhaps most telling, all the organisms of the natural world and all the manikins' clever inventions were instantly endowed with the power of speech. Screaming fierce oaths, they viciously turned upon their former masters.

In retrospect, it was as if the gods were trying to impress indelibly upon the Wooden People—and upon future *designs* of human beings—precisely *why* they were being so decimated. By granting each element of the universe that had ever been wronged—each indignant object, tool, or life-form— a chance to voice its grief, the Mayan gods empowered nature to retaliate against humankind. In the process, the gods reawakened in the manikins' surroundings the very spiritual quality that the Wooden People had forgotten and that, unacknowledged, had precipitated their downfall.

As this angry elemental throng hurled first invectives, then themselves, at the frozen wooden faces of their former masters, even the bloodless manikins must have had some faint inkling of the terrible damage that they had wrought to the earth by their persistently self-centered ways.

"You caused us pain, you ate us, but now it's you whom we shall eat," shouted the turkeys, as the cornered Wooden People tried desperately to fend off their attacks.

"Pain! That's all you've done for us," screamed the cooking pots and tortilla griddles, remembering the manikins' daily displays of indifference to the divine interconnectedness of all things and their searing kitchen flames. *"Since we felt no pain, you try it."*

Even their pet dogs, incensed by memories of their recurrent physical beatings, their missed meals, and the countless petty humiliations they had silently endured at their cruel masters' hands, rose up in a fury. Articulate now, they seemed to speak for every abused element of the Wooden People's world that was finally directly confronting them for their misdeeds.

"We don't talk, so we've received nothing from you," howled the hounds, in an anger tinged with sadness. *"How could you not have known?"*

Snarling, the dogs sank their foam-flecked fangs into the faces of fleeing manikins, eventually crushing them and the legacy of their heartless, human-centered ways. By the end of this didactic episode, the only visible sign of the failed wooden human beings was the monkeys of the forest. They are said to be a *sign of previous human work.* In this sense, they may be seen as living reminders of a previous time when the whole natural world revealed its divine interconnections with humankind by openly challenging unchecked human hubris, technologies, and appetites, lamenting, as if with one voice, *How could you not have known?*

This version of the *Popol Vuh* reflects ancient elements of traditional Mayan knowledge and greatly predates the earnest, ongoing scientific debate over global atmospheric changes, toxic pollutants, soil loss, commercial forestry and fishery practices, and possible postnuclear environmental cataclysms. Nonetheless, it may still have something profound to teach modern Western society about the long-term consequences of human greed, waste, and despiritualization of nature.

Among its multilayered insights, it may encode a coherent, perhaps painfully learned sense of the innate capacity of natural systems to respond in a self-regulatory manner to chronic excesses by one of their components—in this case, humans—by seeking new, more appropriate ecological equilibriums. It may also envision a natural world that is, in some sense, capable of eventually "retaliating" against humankind—paralleling the dire warnings by modern ecologists of possible dark decades ahead, involving crashing human populations, fickle regional climatic regimes, relentlessly rising seas, or lethal rays from a sun no longer veiled by atmospheric ozone.

One hears echoes of similar ecological themes in this solemn, darkly apocalyptic passage from the revered Mayan *Chilam Balam*. It seems to herald a number of destructive social and environmental transformations, among them a time when "the tender leaf shall be destroyed":

> *Eat, eat, while there is bread,*
> *Drink, drink, while there is water;*
> *A day comes when dust shall darken the air,*
> *When a blight shall wither the land,*
> *When a cloud shall arise,*
> *When a mountain shall be lifted up,*
> *When a strong man shall seize the city,*
> *When ruin shall fall upon all things,*
> *When the tender leaf shall be destroyed;*
> *When there shall be three signs on a tree,*
> *Father, son, and grandson hanging dead on the same tree;*
> *When the battle flag shall be raised,*
> *And the people scattered abroad in the forests.*

248

Here, as in the *Popol Vuh*'s poignant tale of the extinction of Wooden People, readers can recognize threads of ecological wisdom without being accused of the scientific "heresy" of looking upon them as mystical Native "nature prophecies" (even if many living Maya might choose to see them in precisely that prophetic light). Even the most skeptical Western minds can admire the timeless human insights of the Native Mind into the recurring patterns of human nature and our need for healthier relationships with the natural world.

Appendix

Excerpt from the United Nations Draft "Universal Declaration on the Rights of Indigenous Peoples," Reflecting an Emerging International Consensus on the Rights of First Peoples Around the World

(United Nations Working Group on Indigenous Populations—August 15, 1991)

Operative Paragraphs to the Draft Declaration as Submitted by the Members of the Working Group At First Reading

PART I

Operative paragraph 1

❖ Indigenous peoples have the right to self-determination, in accordance with international law. By virtue of this right, they freely determine their relationship with the States in which they live, in a spirit of co-existence with other citizens, and freely pursue their economic, social, cultural and spiritual development in conditions of freedom and dignity.

Operative paragraph 2

✦ Indigenous peoples have the right to the full and effective enjoyment of all of the human rights and fundamental freedoms which are recognized in the Charter of the United Nations and other international human rights instruments.

Operative paragraph 3

✦ Indigenous peoples have the right to be free and equal to all other human beings and peoples in dignity and rights, and to be free from adverse distinction or discrimination of any kind based on their indigenous identity.

PART II

Operative paragraph 4

✦ Indigenous peoples have the collective right to exist in peace and security as distinct peoples and to be protected against genocide, as well as the individual rights to life, physical and mental integrity, liberty and security of person.

Operative paragraph 5

✦ Indigenous peoples have the collective and individual right to maintain and develop their distinct ethnic and cultural characteristics and identities, including the right to self-identification.

Operative paragraph 6

✦ Indigenous peoples have the collective and individual right to be protected from cultural genocide, including the prevention of and redress for:
  - (a) any act which has the aim or effect of depriving them of their integrity as distinct societies, or of their cultural or ethnic characteristics or identities;
  - (b) any form of forced assimilation or integration;
  - (c) dispossession of their lands, territories or resources;
  - (d) imposition of other cultures or ways of life; and
  - (e) any propaganda directed against them.

Operative paragraph 7

✦ Indigenous peoples have the right to revive and practise their cultural identity and traditions, including the right to maintain, develop and protect the past, present and future manifestations of their cultures, such as archaeological and historical sites and structures, artifacts, designs, ceremonies, technology and works of art, as well as the right to the restitution of cultural, religious and spiritual property taken from them without their free and informed consent or in violation of their own laws.

Operative paragraph 8

✦ Indigenous peoples have the right to manifest, practise and teach their own spiritual and religious traditions, customs and ceremonies; the right to maintain, protect, and have access in privacy to religious and cultural sites; the right to the use and control of ceremonial objects; and the right to the repatriation of human remains.

Operative paragraph 9

✦ Indigenous peoples have the right to revive, use, develop, promote and transmit to future generations their own languages, writing systems and literature, and to designate and maintain the original names of communities, places and persons. States shall take measures to ensure that indigenous peoples can understand and be understood in political, legal and administrative proceedings, where necessary, through the provision of interpretation or by other effective means.

Operative paragraph 10

✦ Indigenous peoples have the right to all forms of education, including access to education in their own languages, and the right to establish and control their own educational systems and institutions. Resources shall be provided by the State for these purposes.

Operative paragraph 11

✦ Indigenous peoples have the right to have the dignity and diversity of their cultures, histories, traditions and aspirations reflected in all forms of education and public information. States shall take effective measures to eliminate prejudices and to foster tolerance, understanding and good relations.

Operative paragraph 12

✦ Indigenous peoples have the right to the use of and access to all forms of mass media in their own languages. States shall take effective measures to this end.

Operative paragraph 13

◆ Indigenous peoples have the right to adequate financial and technical assistance, from States and through international co-operation, to pursue freely their own economic, social and cultural development, and for the enjoyment of the rights contained in this Declaration.

Operative paragraph (to be numbered)

◆ Nothing in this Declaration may be interpreted as implying for any State, group or individual any right to engage in any activity or to perform any act contrary to the Charter of the United Nations or to the Declaration of Principles of International Law on Friendly Relations and Co-operation among States in Accordance with the Charter of the United Nations.

PART III

Operative paragraph 14

◆ Indigenous peoples have the right to maintain their distinctive and profound relationship with their lands, territories and resources, which include the total environment of the land, waters, air and sea, which they have traditionally occupied or otherwise used.

Operative paragraph 15

◆ Indigenous peoples have the collective and individual right to own, control and use the lands and territories they have traditionally occupied or otherwise used. This includes the right to the full recognition of their own laws and customs, land-tenure systems and institutions for the management of resources, and the right to effective State measures to prevent any interference with or encroachment upon these rights.

Operative paragraph 16

◆ Indigenous peoples have the right to the restitution or, to the extent this is not possible, to just and fair compensation for lands and territories which have been confiscated, occupied, used or damaged without their free and informed consent. Unless otherwise freely agreed upon by the peoples concerned, compensation shall preferably take the form of lands and territories of quality, quantity and legal status at least equal to those which were lost.

Operative paragraph 17

❖ Indigenous peoples have the right to the protection of their environment and productivity of their lands and territories, and the right to adequate assistance including international cooperation to this end. Unless otherwise freely agreed upon by the peoples concerned, military activities and the storage or disposal of hazardous materials shall not take place in their lands and territories.

Operative paragraph 18

❖ Indigenous peoples have the right to special measures for protection, as intellectual property, of their traditional cultural manifestations, such as literature, designs, visual and performing arts, cultigens, medicines and knowledge of the useful properties of fauna and flora.

Operative paragraph (to be numbered)

❖ In no case may any of the indigenous peoples be deprived of their means of subsistence.

Operative Paragraphs as Revised by the Chairperson / Rapporteur Pursuant to Sub-Commission Resolution 1990/26

PART IV

Draft operative paragraph 18

❖ "The right to maintain and develop within their areas of lands and other territories their traditional economic structures, institutions and ways of life, to be secure in the traditional economic structures and ways of life, to be secure in the enjoyment of their own traditional means of subsistence, and to engage freely in their traditional and other economic activities, including hunting, fresh- and salt-water fishing, herding, gathering, lumbering and cultivation, without adverse discrimination. In no case may an indigenous people be deprived of its means of subsistence. The right to just and fair compensation if they have been so deprived;"

Draft operative paragraph 19

❖ "The right to special State measures for the immediate, effective and continuing improvement of their social and economic conditions, with their consent, that reflect their own priorities;"

Draft operative paragraph 20

❖ "The right to determine, plan and implement all health, housing and other social and economic programmes affecting them, and as far as possible to develop, plan and implement such programmes through their own institutions;"

PART V

Draft operative paragraph 21

❖ "The right to participate on an equal footing with all the other citizens and without adverse discrimination in the political, economic, social and cultural life of the State and to have their specific character duly reflected in the legal system and in political and socioeconomic and cultural institutions, including in particular proper regard to and recognition of indigenous laws and customs;"

Draft operative paragraph 22

❖ "The right to participate fully at the State level, through representatives chosen by themselves, in decision-making about and implementation of all national and international matters which may affect their rights, life and destiny;"

❖ "The right of indigenous peoples to be involved, through appropriate procedures, determined in conjunction with them, in devising any laws or administrative measures that may affect them directly, and to obtain their free and informed consent through implementing such measures. States have the duty to guarantee the full exercise of these rights;"

Draft operative paragraph 23

❖ "The collective right to autonomy in matters relating to their own internal and local affairs, including education, information, mass media, culture, religion, health, housing, social welfare, traditional and other economic and management activities, land and resources administration and the environment, as well as internal taxation for financing these autonomous functions;"

Draft operative paragraph 24

✦ "The right to decide upon the structures of their autonomous institutions, to select the membership of such institutions according to their own procedures, and to determine the membership of the indigenous people concerned for these purposes; States have the duty, where the peoples concerned so desire, to recognize such institutions and their memberships through the legal systems and political institutions of the State;"

Draft operative paragraph 25

✦ "The right to determine the responsibilities of individuals to their own community, consistent with universally recognized human rights and fundamental freedoms;"

Draft operative paragraph 26

✦ "The right to maintain and develop traditional contacts, relations and cooperation, including cultural and social exchanges and trade, with their own kith and kin across State boundaries and the obligation of the State to adopt measures to facilitate such contacts;"

Draft operative paragraph 27

✦ "The right to claim that States honour treaties and other agreements concluded with indigenous peoples, and to submit any disputes that may arise in this matter to competent national or international bodies;"

PART VI

Draft operative paragraph 28

✦ "The individual and collective right to access to and prompt decision by mutually acceptable and fair procedures for resolving conflicts or disputes and any infringement, public or private, between States and indigenous peoples, groups or individuals. These procedures should include, as appropriate, negotiations, mediation, arbitration, national courts and international and regional human rights review and complaints mechanisms;"

PART VII

Draft operative paragraph 29

❖ "These rights constitute the minimum standards for the survival and the well-being of the indigenous peoples of the world;"

Draft operative paragraph 30

❖ "Nothing in this Declaration may be interpreted as implying for any State, group or individual any right to engage in any activity or to perform any act aimed at the destruction of any of the rights and freedoms set forth herein."

Notes

Authors' Note

1. Quoted in Roger Moody, *Indigenous Voices: Visions and Realities.* International Work Group for Indigenous Affairs, Copenhagen, (London, New Jersey: Zed Books, 1988), pp. 40–50.

2. Rudolf Kaiser, "A Whole Religious Concept: Chief Seattle's Speech(es): American Origins and European Reception" (Nortrf, Germany: Vökerkundiche Arbeitsgemeinschaft, 1985). (To be published in Christian F. Feest, ed., *Indians and Europe,* Gottingen: Edition Herodot.)

Chapter 1 Visions of the Natural World

1. Claude Lévi-Strauss, "The Concept of Primitiveness," in *Man the Hunter,* edited by Richard B. Lee and Irven de Vore (New York: Aldine Publishing Co., 1968), p. 351.

2. Gladys A. Reichard, *Navaho Religion: A Study of Symbolism,* Bollingen Series (Princeton: Princeton University Press, 1970), pp. 21, 28, 77.

3. Steve Wall and Harvey Arden, *Wisdomkeepers: Meetings with Native American Spiritual Elders* (Hillsborg Oregon: Beyond Words Publishing, 1990), p. 81.

4. Quoted in Ferdinand Anton, *Art of the Maya* (London: Thames and Hudson, 1978), p. 74. A Mayan friend, Alejandro Ruiz, singled out this text as a particularly eloquent example of a prayer to the natural world in his culture.

5. Signe Howell, *Chewong Myths and Legends,* The Malaysian Branch of the Royal Asiatic Society, Monograph no. 11 (Kuala Lumpur: M.B.R.A.S., 1982), p. 6.

6. Claude Lévi-Strauss, *The Savage Mind* (Chicago: University of Chicago Press, 1966), p. 14.

7. Ibid., p. 269.

8. Ibid., p. 268.

9. Åke Hultkrantz, *Native Religions of North America* (San Francisco: Harper and Row, 1987), p. 24.

10. Alfonso Oritz, "Why Nature Hates the White Man," interview by Jane Bosveld, *Omni* (March 1990), p. 77.

11. World Commission on Environment and Development, *Our Common Future* (Oxford and New York: Oxford University Press), pp. 114–15.

Chapter 2 Distant Times

1. Ernst May, "Darwinian Flights" (interview by Carol A. Johnmann), in *The Omni Interviews* (New York: Ticknor & Fields, 1984), p. 50.

2. James D. Watson, Nancy H. Hopkins, Jeffrey W. Roberts, Joan A. Steitz, and Alan M. Weiner, *Molecular Biology of the Gene,* 4th ed. (Menlo Park, CA: Benjamin/Cummings, 1987).

3. Gerardo Reichel-Dolmatoff, *Amazonian Cosmos: The Sexual and Religious Symbolism of the Tukano Indians* (Chicago: University of Chicago Press, 1971); pp. 142, 145.

4. Lynn Margulis, *Early Life* (Boston: Science Books International, 1982), p. 138.

5. Hamilton Tyler, *Pueblo Gods and Myths* (Norman: University of Oklahoma Press, 1964), pp. 86, 104–108.

6. Roger Sperry, "Changed Concepts of Brain and Consciousness: Some Value Implications," *Zygon: Journal of Religion and Science* 20:1 (1985), p. 26.

7. Joseph Campbell, *The Masks of God: Primitive Mythology* (New York: Penguin Books, 1976), p. 274; Richard K. Nelson, *Make Prayers to the Raven* (Chicago and London: University of Chicago Press, 1983), pp. 14, 16, 17, 53–54, 56.

8. John R. Platt, *The Steps to Man* (New York: John Wiley and Sons, 1966), p. 185.

9. Robin Ridington, *Trail to Heaven: Knowledge and Narrative in a Northern Native Community* (Vancouver/Toronto: Douglas & McIntyre, 1988).

10. Aldo Leopold, *A Sand County Almanac* (New York: Oxford University Press, 1968), p. 109.

11. Signe Howell, *Society and Cosmos: Chewong of Peninsular Malaysia* (Chicago: University of Chicago Press, 1989), pp. 63, 80, 85, 181, 182.

12. Stephen Jay Gould, *The Mismeasure of Man* (New York: W.W. Norton, 1981), p. 324.

13. Deborah Bird Rose, *Dingo Makes Us Human: Life and Land in an*

Aboriginal Culture (Cambridge: Cambridge University Press), pp. 64, 357–58, 378.

14. Platt, *Steps to Man,* p. 185.

15. Knud Rasmussen, "Intellectual Culture of the Caribou Eskimos," *Report of the Fifth Thule Expedition 1921–24,* vol. 7, no. 2
(Copenhagen, 1930), p. 79; Knud Rasmussen, "Iglulik and Caribou
Eskimo Texts," *Report of the Fifth Thule Expedition 1921–24,* vol. 7, no.
3 (Copenhagen, 1930), pp. 59–60.

16. George Wald, "The Search for Common Ground," *Zygon: Journal of Religion and Science* 11 (1966), p. 46.

Chapter 3 Mother Earth

1. Howard T. Odum, *Environment, Power, and Society* (New York: John Wiley and Sons, 1971), p. 8.

2. James Lovelock, *The Ages of Gaia* (Oxford: Oxford University Press, 1988).

3. Gerardo Reichel-Dolmatoff, *Amazonian Cosmos: The Sexual and Religious Symbolism of the Tukano Indians* (Chicago: University of Chicago Press, 1971).

4. René Dubos, *The World of René Dubos: A Collection of Historical Writings,* edited by Gerard Piel and Osborn Segerberg, Jr. (New York: Henry Holt, 1990), pp. 386–87.

5. John P. Harrington, *Ethnography of the Tewa,* 29th Annual Report, Bureau of American Ethnology (Washington, DC, 1916), pp. 46–47; Alfonso Ortiz, *The Tewa World: Space, Time, Being and Becoming in Pueblo Society* (Chicago: University of Chicago Press, 1969), pp. 13, 102, 103.

6. Lovelock, *The Ages of Gaia,* p. 22.

7. Darryl A. Posey, "Indigenous Ecological Knowledge and Development of the Amazon," in *The Dilemma of Amazonian Development,* edited by Emilio F. Moran (Boulder, CO: Westview Press, 1983), pp. 234–35. We have transposed the original Kayapó red ant tale recorded by Posey into verse format.

8. Edward O. Wilson, *Biophilia* (Cambridge, MA: Harvard University Press, 1984), p. 8.

9. Harvey A. Feit, "The Ethno-Ecology of the Waswanipi Cree; or How Hunters can Manage Their Resources," in *Cultural Ecology,* edited by Bruce Cox (Toronto: McClelland and Stewart, 1973), pp. 115–25.

10. Charles Birch and John B. Cobb, Jr., *The Liberation of Life: From the Cell to the Community* (Cambridge and New York: Cambridge University Press, 1981), p. 83.

11. Reichel-Dolmatoff, *Amazonian Cosmos,* p. 42.

12. Odum, *Environment,* p. 244.

Chapter 4 Ways of Seeing

1. Alan Guth quoted in A.J.S. Rayl and K.T. McKinney, "The Mind of God," *Omni* 13:11 (August 1991), p. 48.

2. Albert Einstein quoted in Ronald W. Clark, *Einstein: The Life and Times* (New York: Avon Books, 1971), p. 243.

3. Marguerite Anne Biesele, *Folklore and Ritual of !Kung Hunter-Gatherers,* thesis presented to Harvard University (Cambridge, MA, 1975), pp. 160–61, 168; Joseph Campbell, *Historical Atlas of World Mythology,* vol. 1: The Way of Animal Powers, part 1: *Mythologies of the Primitive Hunters and Gatherers* (New York: Harper and Row, 1988), pp. 90–101; Hans J. Heinz, "The Bushmen's Store of Scientific Knowledge," in *The Bushmen: San Hunters and Herders of Southern Africa,* edited by Phillip V. Tobias (Cape Town and Pretoria: Human and Rousseau, 1978); Richard B. Lee, "What Hunters Do for a Living, or How to Make Out on Scarce Resources," in *Man the Hunter,* edited by Richard B. Lee and Irven de Vore (New York: Aldine Publishing Co., 1968), pp. 3, 30–48; and Lorna Marshall, "!Kung Bushman Religious Beliefs," *Africa* 32:3 (1962), p. 242.

4. Clark, Einstein: *The Life and Times,* p. 755.

5. Gerardo Reichel-Dolmatoff, "Brain and Mind in Desana Shamanism," *Journal of Latin American Lore* 7:1 (1981), pp. 73–98; Peter Knudtson, "Portraits of Neurons: The Artistry of Neuronatomist Santiago Ramón y Cajal," *Science 85,* May, 1985.

6. Lewis Thomas, *The Medusa and the Snail* (New York: Bantam, 1980), p. 128.

7. Wilder Penfield quoted in George Wald, "The Cosmology of Life and Mind," in *Synthesis of Science and Religion: Critical Essays and Dialogues,* edited by T.D. Singh and Ravi Gomatam (San Francisco and Bombay: Bhaktivedanta Institute, 1988), p. 128.

8. Darryl A. Posey, "Indigenous Ecological Knowledge and Development," in *The Dilemma of Amazonian Development,* edited by Emilio Moran (Boulder, CO: Westview Press, 1983), pp. 225–57.

9. Paul Ehrlich, *The Machinery of Nature* (New York: Simon and Schuster, 1986), p. 13.

10. Signe Howell, *Society and Cosmos: Chewong of Peninsular Malaysia* (Chicago: University of Chicago Press, 1989), pp. 44, 54, 66–67.

11. Ehrlich, *Machinery of Nature,* p. 291.

Chapter 5 Animal Powers

1. Santiago Ramón y Cajal, *Recollections of My Life,* trans. by E. Horne Craigie (Cambridge, MA: Harvard University Press), 1969.

2. Knud Rasmussen, "Intellectual Culture of the Caribou Eskimos," *Report of the Fifth Thule Expedition 1921–24,* vol. 7, no. 2 (Copenhagen, 1930). Story told by Kibkaruk.

3. Loren Eiseley, *The Invisible Pyramid* (New York: Charles Scribner's Sons, 1970), p. 144.

4. Harvey A. Feit, "The Ethno-Ecology of the Waswanipi Cree; or How Hunters Can Manage Their Resources," in *Cultural Ecology,* edited by Bruce Cox (Toronto: McClelland and Stewart, 1973), pp. 115–25.

5. Aldo Leopold, *A Sand County Almanac* (New York: Oxford University Press, 1968), p. 161.

6. Richard J. Preston, *Cree Narrative: Expressing the Personal Meaning of Events,* National Museum of Man Mercury Series, Canadian Ethnology Service, no. 30 (Ottawa, 1975), p. 208. Song by George Head.

7. Signe Howell, *Chewong Myths and Legends,* Malaysian Branch of the Royal Asiatic Society, Monograph no. 11 (Kuala Lumpur: M.B.R.A.S., 1982), pp. xxiii–xxv, 72–73; Signe Howell, *Society and Cosmos: Chewong of Peninsular Malaysia* (Chicago: University of Chicago Press, 1989), pp. 143–44, 164–66.

8. Niko Tinbergen, *The Study of Instinct* (Oxford: Clarendon Press, 1951), p. 16.

9. Hans J. Heinz, "The Bushmen's Store of Scientific Knowledge," in *The Bushmen: San Hunters and Herders of Southern Africa,* edited by Phillip V. Tobias (Cape Town and Pretoria: Human and Rousseau, 1978).

10. Donald R. Griffen, *Animal Thinking* (Cambridge: Harvard University Press, 1984), p. 47.

11. Gerardo Reichel-Dolmatoff, *Amazonian Cosmos: The Sexual and Religious Symbolism of the Tukano Indians* (Chicago: University of Chicago Press, 1971), pp. 80–86, 218–225, 274–75; Gerardo Reichel-Dolmatoff, *The Shaman and the Jaguar: A Study of Narcotic Drugs Among the Indians of Colombia* (Philadelphia: Temple University Press, 1975), p. 92.

12. Edward O. Wilson, *Biophilia* (Cambridge: Harvard University Press, 1984), p. 324.

13. Peter Knudtson, *The Wintun Indians of California* (Healdsburg, CA: Naturegraph Publishers, 1988); Dorothy Lee, "Linguistic Reflection of Wintu Thought," in *Freedom and Culture* (Englewood Cliffs, NJ: Prentice-Hall, 1979), pp. 121, 128, 129; Cora Du Bois, *Wintu Ethnography,* University of California Publications in American Archaeology and Ethnology, vol. 36 (Berkeley: University of California Press, 1940), p. 73.

14. George Wald, "Life and Mind in the Universe," *International Journal of Quantum Chemistry,* Quantum Biology Symposium no. 11 (1984), p. 8.

15. Francisco J. Varela, "Laying Down a Path in Walking: A Biologist's Look at a New Biology and Its Ethics," in *Human Survival and Consciousness Evolution,* edited by Stanislav Grof (Albany: State University of New York Press, 1988), p. 209.

Chapter 6 Plant Powers

1. Howard T. Odum, *Environment, Power, and Society* (New York: John Wiley and Sons, 1971), p. 13.

2. Barbara McClintock quoted in Evelyn Fox Keller, *A Feeling for the Organism: The Life and Work of Barbara McClintock* (San Francisco: W.H. Freeman, 1983), pp. 198–99.

3. Richard K. Nelson, *Make Prayers to the Raven* (Chicago: University of Chicago Press, 1983), pp. 17, 31, 47–57.

4. Edward O. Wilson, *Biophilia* (Cambridge, MA: Harvard University Press, 1984), pp. 84–85.

5. Burger, *Gaia Atlas,* p. 36; Jason W. Clay, *Indigenous People and Tropical Forests: Models of Land Use and Management from Latin America,* Cultural Survival Report no. 27 (Cambridge, MA: Cultural Survival, 1988), p. 55; Darryl A. Posey, "Keepers of the Campo," *Garden* (Nov.–Dec. 1984), pp. 8–32; Darryl A. Posey, "Indigenous Ecological Knowledge and Development of the Amazon," in *The Dilemma of Amazonian Development,* edited by Emilio F. Moran (Boulder, CO: Westview Press, 1983), pp. 225–56.

6. Paiakan, quoted in Julian Burger, *The Gaia Atlas of First Peoples* (London: Anchor Books, Doubleday, 1990), p. 32.

7. Chris Maser, *The Redesigned Forest* (San Pedro, CA: R. & E. Miles, 1988), pp. 173–74.

8. Signe Howell, *Society and Cosmos: Chewong of Peninsular Malaysia* (Chicago: University of Chicago Press, 1989), pp. 18, 21, 24, 89, 92–94, 104, 159, 163.

9. Arne Naess, *Ecology, Community, and Lifestyle: Outline of an Ecosophy* (New York: Bantam Books, 1988), pp. 164–65.

10. Carol Rubenstein, *The Honey Tree Song: Poems and Chants of Sarawak Dayaks* (Athens, OH: Ohio University Press, 1985).

11. Paul Ehrlich, *The Machinery of Nature* (New York: Simon and Schuster, 1986), p. 164.

Chapter 7 Sacred Space

1. Aldo Leopold, *A Sand County Almanac* (New York: Oxford University Press, 1949), pp. 230–31.

2. J. Donald Hughes, "How Much of the Earth Is Sacred Space?" *Environmental Review* 10:4 (Winter 1986), pp. 247–60.

3. Sam D. Gill, *Sacred Words: A Study of Navajo Religion and Prayer* (Westport, CT: Greenwood Press, 1981), pp. 62–64; Susan Kent, "Hogans, Sacred Circles and Symbols: The Navajo Use of Space," in *Navajo Religion and Culture: Selected Views,* edited by David M. Brugge and Charlotte J. Frisbie (Santa Fe: Museum of New Mexico Press, 1975), pp. 128–137; Ray B. Lois, *Child of the Hogan* (Provo, UT: Brigham Young University Press, 1978), p. 3; Frank Mitchell, *Navajo Blessingway Singer* (Tucson: University of Arizona Press, 1978), pp.

171–75; Rik Pinxten, Ingrid van Dooren, and Frank Harvey, *Anthropology of Space: Explorations in the Natural Philosphy and Semantics of the Navajo* (Philadelphia: University of Pennsylvania Press, 1983), pp. 9–11.

4. Loren Eiseley, *The Invisible Pyramid* (New York: Scribner's, 1970), p. 70.

5. Gisday Wa and Delgam Uukw, *The Spirit of the Land: The Opening Statement of the Gitksan and Wetśuwetén Hereditary Chiefs in the Supreme Court of British Columbia* (Gabriola, B.C.: Reflections, 1987), pp. 7, 26.

6. Roger Sperry, "Changed Concepts of Brain and Consciousness: Some Value Implications," *Zygon: Journal of Religion and Science* 20:1 (Summer 1983), p. 29.

7. A.E. Newsome, "The Eco-Mythology of the Red Kangaroo in Central Australia," *Mankind* 12:4 (Dec. 1980), pp. 327–33; W.E.H. Stanner, *White Man Got No Dreaming* (Canberra: Australian National University Press, 1974); and T.G.H. Strehlow, *Aranda Traditions* (Melbourne: Melbourne University Press, 1947), pp. 17, 26, 31, 36–37, 140. Bruce Chatwin, *The Songlines* (New York: Penguin Books, 1987), p. 13.

8. Leopold, *A Sand County Almanac,* p. 236.

9. Lomayaktewa, Starlie, Mina Lansa, Ned Nayatewa, Claude Kewanyama, Jack Pongayesvia, Thomas Banyacya, Sr., David Monogye, and Carlotta Shattuck, "Statement of Hopi Religious Leaders" (mimeographed statement given to Knudtson by Banyacya in Kykotsomovie, AZ, March 1990; quoted with permission of Banyacya).

10. Nicolas Peterson, "Totemism Yesterday: Sentiment and Local Organisation among the Australian Aborigines," *Man* 7:1 (Mar. 1972), pp. 13–32.

11. Leopold, *A Sand County Almanac,* p. 176.

Chapter 8 Time as a Circle

1. Stephen Hawking, *A Brief History of Time* (Toronto and New York: Cambridge University Press, 1988), p. 145.

2. Knud Rasmussen, "Iglulik and Caribou Eskimo Texts," *Report of the Fifth Thule Expedition 1921–24,* vol. 7, no. 3 (Copenhagen, 1930), pp. 125–26. Moon names provided by Igyugaryuk. Spelling of Inuit words has been reduced to simplified phonetic English spellings.

3. James Lovelock, *The Ages of Gaia* (Oxford: Oxford University Press, 1988), p. 65.

4. Robin Ridington, *Trail to Heaven: Knowledge and Narrative in a Northern Native Community* (Vancouver/Toronto: Douglas & McIntyre, 1988), pp. 70, 78, 99, 104.

5. Aldo Leopold, *A Sand County Almanac* (New York: Oxford University Press, 1966), pp. 96–97.

6. Berard Haile, *The Upward Moving and Emergence Way* (Lincoln: University of Nebraska Press, 1981), p. 129; Rik Pinxten, Ingrid van Dooren, and Frank Harvey, "The Natural Philosophy of Navajo Language and World View," in *Anthropology of Space* (Philadelphia: University of Pennsylvania Press, 1983); Gladys A. Reichard, *Navaho Religion: A Study of Symbolism,* Bollingen Series (Princeton: Princeton University Press, 1963), pp. 159–60.

7. Hawking, *Brief History,* p. 145.

8. Gisday Wa and Delgam Uukw, *The Spirit of the Land: The Opening Statement of the Gitksan and Wetśuwetén Hereditary Chiefs in the Supreme Court of British Columbia* (Gabriola, BC: Reflections, 1987), p. 23.

9. Prigogine and Stengers, *Order Out of Chaos,* pp. 22–23.

10. Georges, Condominas, *We Have Eaten the Forest: The Story of a Montagnard Village in the Central Highlands of Vietnam,* translated from the French by Adrienne Foulke (New York: Hill and Wang, 1957), p. xvii, 4–5, 231–32, 254.

11. Northrop Frye, *The Great Code: The Bible and Literature* (Toronto: Penguin Books, 1990), p. 124.

Chapter 9 World Renewal

1. Victor B. Scheffer, *Spire of Form: Glimpses of Evolution* (University of Washington Press, 1983), p. 28.

2. Ilya Prigogine and Isabelle Stengers, *Order Out of Chaos: Man's New Dialogue with Nature* (New York: Bantam, 1984), p. 312.

3. Edward O. Wilson, *Biophilia* (Cambridge: Harvard University Press, 1984), p. 140.

4. Cora Du Bois, *Wintu Ethnography,* University of California Press Publications in American Archaeology and Ethnology, no. 35 (1935), pp. 75–76; Peter Knudtson, "Flora, Shaman of the Wintu," *Natural History,* May, 1975, p. 6.

5. Aldo Leopold, *A Sand County Almanac* (New York: Oxford University Press, 1949), p. 183.

6. Sam D. Gill, *Sacred Words: A Study of Navajo Religion and Prayer,* Contributions in Intercultural and Comparative Studies, no. 4 (Westport, CT, and London: Greenwood Press), p. 67; Sam D. Gill, "The Trees Stood Deep Rooted," in *I Become Part of It* (New York: Parabola Books, 1989), pp. 23–31.

7. Leopold, *A Sand County Almanac,* p. 96.

8. Darryl A. Posey, "Time, Space, and the Interface of Divergent Cultures: The Kayapó Indians of the Amazon Face the Future," *Revista de Antropologia* 25 (1982), pp. 89–104.

9. Loren Eiseley, *The Invisible Pyramid* (New York: Scribner's, 1970), p. 115.

10. Peter Raven, "What the Fate of the Rain Forests Means to Us," in *The Cassandra Conferences,* edited by Paul Ehrlich and John Holdren, (College Station: Texas A & M University Press), 1988, p. 121.

11. Gerardo Reichel-Dolmatoff, *Amazonian Cosmos: The Sexual and Religious Symbolism of the Tukano Indians* (Chicago: University of Chicago Press, 1971), p. 219.

12. Gregory Bateson, *Steps to an Ecology of Mind* (New York: Ballantine Books, 1985), p. 492.

13. Dorothy Lee, "Responsibility Among the Dakota," in *Freedom and Culture* (Englewood Cliffs, NJ: Prentice-Hall, 1959), pp. 61–67.

14. Alice Miller, *The Untouched Key: Tracing Childhood Trauma in Creativity and Destructiveness* (New York: Doubleday, 1990), p. 167.

15. Signe Howell, *Society and Cosmos: Chewong of Peninsular Malaysia* (Chicago: University of Chicago Press, 1989), pp. 132, 133.

16. Paul Davies quoted in A.J.S. Rayl and K. T. McKinney, "The Mind of God," *Omni* 13:11 (August 1991), p. 46.

17. Alfonso Ortiz, *The Tewa World: Space, Time, Being and Becoming in Pueblo Society* (Chicago: University of Chicago Press, 1969), p. 21.

18. Henry David Thoreau, *Walden* (Princeton: Princeton University Press, 1971).

Chapter 10 The Fate of the Earth

1. John G. Neihardt, *Black Elk Speaks* (New York: Washington Square Press, 1959), p. 1. As in the case of Chief Seattle, there has been some recent debate over the extent to which this book faithfully reflects the spoken words of the late Black Elk.

2. John R. Platt, *The Steps to Man* (New York: John Wiley and Sons, 1966), p. 185.

3. Pam Colorado, "Bridging Native and Western Science," *Convergence* 21: 2–3 (1988), p. 57.

4. Alice Miller, *The Untouched Key: Tracing Childhood Trauma in Creativity and Destructiveness* (New York: Doubleday, 1990), pp. 155, 158.

5. Howard T. Odum, *Environment, Power, and Society* (New York: John Wiley and Sons, 1971), p. 245.

6. Roger Sperry, "Changed Concepts of Brain and Consciousness: Some Value Implications," *Zygon: Journal of Religion and Science* 20:1 (1985), p. 28.

7. Gregory Bateson, *Steps to an Ecology of Mind* (New York: Ballantine Books, 1972), p. 464.

8. Morris Berman, *The Reenchantment of the World* (New York: Bantam, 1989), pp. 10, 186.

9. Paul Ehrlich, *The Machinery of Nature* (New York: Simon and Schuster, 1986), pp. 17–18.

10. Howard T. Odum, *Environment, Power, and Society*, p. 253.

11. J. Baird Callicott, "Traditional American Indian and Western European Attitudes Towards Nature: An Overview," in *In Defense of the Land Ethic: Essays in Environmental Philosophy* (Albany: State University New York, 1989), p. 219.

12. Claude Lévi-Strauss, *The Savage Mind* (Chicago: University of Chicago Press, 1966), p. 269.

13. Alfonso Ortiz, "Why Nature Hates the White Man," *Omni* (March 1990), p. 97.

14. Ruby Dunstan, former administrative chief of the Lytton Indian Band, British Columbia, speech presented at Globe 90 Conference on Business and the Environment, Vancouver, March 1990, quoted with permission of Ruby Dunstan.

15. Edward O. Wilson, *Biophilia* (Cambridge: Harvard University Press, 1984), pp. 139–40.

16. Carolyn Tawangyowma, spokesperson, from press release issued by the Sovereign Hopi Independent Nation, Hotevilla, AZ., October 1983; reprinted in *The Indigenous Voice: Visions and Realities,* edited by Roger Moody, International Work Group for Indigenous Affairs, Copenhagen (London and NJ: Zed Books, 1988), pp. 189–90.

17. Barry Commoner, *The Closing Circle: Nature, Man, and Technology* (New York: Knopf, 1971), pp. 33–48.

18. Six Nations Iroquois Confederacy, "The Haudenosaunee [People-of-the-Longhouse] Declaration of the Iroquois," passed on April 17, 1979; published in *Akwesasne Notes* (Spring 1979). The council has requested that their declaration to the world be given "the widest circulation possible." (Quoted with permission of *Akwesasne Notes.*)

19. Robert Jastrow quoted in A.J.S. Rayl and K.T. McKinney, "The Mind of God," *Omni* 13:11 (August 1991), p. 48.

20. Thomas Banyacya, spokesperson for Hopi religious leaders, "A Message to the United Nations from the Hopi to the World Leaders" (mimeographed statement, given to Knudtson by Banyacya in Kykotsomovie, AZ., March 1990), quoted with permission of Banyacya.

21. Ilya Prigogine and Isabelle Stengers, *Order Out of Chaos: Man's New Dialogue with Nature* (New York: Bantam, 1984), p. 32.

22. *Popol Vuh,* translated by Dennis Tedlock (New York: Simon and Schuster, 1985); D.G. Brinton, *The Books of Chilam Balam,* quoted in *The Indigenous Voice,* edited by Roger Moody, pp. 15–16; Michael D. Coe, *The Maya,* 4th ed. (New York: Thames and Hudson, 1987); Regoberta Menchu, *I Rigoberta Menchu—An Indian Woman in Guatemala,* edited by Elisabeth Burgos-Debray (London: Verso Editions, 1984); Jean-Maire Simon, *Guatemala: Eternal Spring—Eternal Tyranny* (New York and London: W.W. Norton, 1987).

23. Vine Deloria, *God Is Red* (New York: Grosset, 1973), p. 298.

Index

About the Authors

David Suzuki, Ph.D., is a professor of zoology at the University of British Columbia in Vancouver. A distinguished environmentalist and broadcaster, he is the host of CBC's *The Nature of Things* and *A Planet for the Taking,* for which he received the Governor General's Award for Conservation. Dr. Suzuki is a recipient of the United Nations Environmental Program medal and UNESCO'S Kalinga Prize for Science, which has previously been awarded to Bertrand Russell, Julian Huxley, and Margaret Mead. A steadfast advocate of Native people's rights, he lives with his wife, Tara, and two children in Vancouver and Toronto.

Peter Knudtson is a Vancouver-based writer whose articles have appeared in numerous American and Canadian publications, including *Natural History, Science 85, Equinox,* and *Oceans.* He has a master's degree in biology, with a specialty in ecology and animal behavior, from California State University, Arcata, a B.A. in premedical zoology from the University of California, Riverside, and has studied at U.C. Berkeley's Graduate School of Journalism. He is currently writing a post-conquest history of the Maya Indians of Guatemala.